Leadership Lessons

from

Comprehensive School Reforms

To: Linda C. Holste
&
Jonathan Jaffee

Leadership Lessons

from

Comprehensive School Reforms

Joseph Murphy Amanda Datnow

CORWIN PRESS, INC.
A Sage Publications Company
Thousand Oaks, California

For information:

Corwin Press, Inc.
A Sage Publications Company
2455 Teller Road
Thousand Oaks, California 91320
www.corwinpress.com

Sage Publications Ltd.
6 Bonhill Street
London EC2A 4PU
United Kingdom

Sage Publications India Pvt. Ltd.
M-32 Market
Greater Kailash I
New Delhi 110 048 India

Printed in the United States of America

Library of Congress Cataloging-in-Publication Data

Leadership lessons from comprehensive school reforms / [edited by] Joseph Murphy, Amanda Datnow.
   p. cm.
Includes bibliographical references and index.
  ISBN 0-7619-7845-3 (cloth) — ISBN 0-7619-7846-1 (pbk.)
  1. School improvement programs—United States. 2. Educational leadership—United States. I. Murphy, Joseph, 1949- II. Datnow, Amanda.

  LB2822.82 .L424 2003
  370.15′23—dc21   2002006451

02   03   04   05   06   07   6   5   4   3   2   1

This book is printed on acid-free paper.

Acquisitions Editor: Rachel Livsey
Editorial Assistant: Phyllis Cappello
Copy Editor: Jon Preimesberger
Production Editor: Diane S. Foster
Typesetter: C&M Digitals (P), Ltd.
Proofreader: Sally M. Scott
Indexer: Teri Greenberg
Cover Designer: Michael Dubowe
Production Artist: Michelle Lee

Contents

About the Editors

Joseph Murphy is Professor of Public Policy and Education at Vanderbilt University. He also chairs the Interstate School Leaders Licensure Consortium. Earlier he served as an Associate Professor at the University of Illinois and the William Ray Flesher Professor in the College of Education at The Ohio State University and President of the Ohio Principals Leadership Academy. He is a former Vice President of the American Educational Research Association (Division A, Administration). Earlier in his career, he served as a School Administrator at the school, district, and state levels. His work is in the area of school improvement with particular emphasis on leadership and policy. His most recent books are *Understanding and Assessing Charter Schools* (2002), *The Productive High School* (2001), and *The Quest for a Center: Notes on the State of the Profession of Educational Leadership* (1999).

Amanda Datnow is an Assistant Professor in the Department of Theory and Policy Studies in Education at the Ontario Institute for Studies in Education of the University of Toronto. She teaches in the graduate program in educational administration and in teacher education. Her research focuses on school reform policy and politics, particularly with regard to the professional lives of educators and issues of equity. Current projects include a longitudinal study of whole school improvement through the Comprehensive Educational Reform Demonstration Program. Recent publications include *Extending Educational Reform: From One School to Many* (2002), "Power and Politics in the Adoption of School Reform Models" (2000, *Educational Evaluation and Policy Analysis*), and "Teachers' Responses to Success for All: How Beliefs, Experiences, and Adaptations Shape Implementation" (2000, *American Educational Research Journal*).

About the Contributors

Mark Berends is Associate Professor of Education and Policy at Vanderbilt University. He was formerly a Senior Social Scientist at RAND. He has expertise in the sociology of education, stratification, organizations, and school reform. With experience with both quantitative and qualitative methodologies, much of his current research involves quantitative analyses of national databases to assess the effects of families, schools, and communities on student outcomes. His published work includes studies of Title I and standards-based reform, comprehensive school reform, the effects of schools as organizations on teachers and students, and the effects of secondary school tracking on students' cognitive and social development.

Susan Bodilly is a Senior Policy Researcher at RAND, where she has worked for 20 years. Her primary research interests and expertise lie in comprehensive school reform at the K-12 level, resource allocation and its impact on reforms, formative evaluation, and implementation analysis. She is currently coleading RAND's evaluation of the New American Schools Initiative; leading an effort to assess the Ford Foundation's Collaborating for Educational Reform Initiative; editing a book with Thomas Glennan on scale-up issues in education; and analyzing the impact of Perkins legislation on vocational programs for the National Assessment of Vocational Education.

Marisa Castellano is an Associate Research Scientist at the Center for Social Organization of Schools at Johns Hopkins University. Her research interests span the entire K-12 spectrum. She has conducted qualitative research on elementary and middle school reform designs, as well as on remedial and adult literacy programs in community colleges. Currently she is carrying out a longitudinal study examining the effects of whole school reform on career and technical education at the high school and community college levels. Common to all of this research is an interest in improving education and life chances for underserved populations.

Michael Aaron Copland is an Assistant Professor of Educational Leadership and School Renewal at the University of Washington. His research interests include leadership in the context of school reform, the principalship, research and development of problem-based instructional materials, and study of outcomes associated with the use of problem-based learning in preparing students for educational leadership. He teaches courses in educational leadership for masters and doctoral students, and for students preparing for administrative credentials. He was formerly a teacher and school administrator in the Bellingham, Washington, public schools.

John B. Diamond is a sociologist of education who studies the relationship between family background and children's educational experiences and leadership and organizational change. He is currently Research Assistant Professor at the School of Education and Social Policy at Northwestern University and Research Director for the Minority Student Achievement Network, a national consortium of school districts working to reduce racial achievement gaps through research and evidence-based interventions.

Greg Farrell is President of Expeditionary Learning Outward Bound. He has been a high-school English teacher, an Assistant Dean of Admissions at Princeton, a reporter for the *Trenton Times*, head of the antipoverty organization in Trenton, New Jersey, and an Assistant Commissioner of the New Jersey Department of Community Affairs. Before coming to Outward Bound, in 1990, he was President of the Fund for the City of New York, a private foundation established by the Ford Foundation to help improve the quality of life and government in New York City.

Carol R. Fendt is a Field Researcher and Qualitative Data Analyst with the Chicago Annenberg Research Project at the Consortium on Chicago School Research and a doctoral student in educational policy studies at the University of Illinois at Chicago. She received her M.A. in educational leadership from Dominican University and her B.S. from the University of Wisconsin at Milwaukee. Fendt has worked as a high school English teacher and principal in schools of the Archdiocese of Chicago.

Christine Finnan is the Director of the South Carolina Accelerated Schools Project and an Assistant Professor in the Elementary and Early Childhood Department at the College of Charleston. She applies her training in anthropology and education to understanding the change process in schools and classrooms.

Bruce Goldberg is the Founder and Chief Education Officer of Co-nect. He has been a Division Scientist at BBN Corporation, Director of the Center for Restructuring Schools at the American Federation of Teachers, and President of the Colorado Federation of Teachers. He has taught philosophy at the college and university levels and holds a Ph.D. in philosophy from the University of Colorado.

Peter M. Hall is a Professor Emeritus of Sociology and Educational Leadership and Policy Analysis at the University of Missouri-Columbia. Hall has written on power, politics, organizations, inequality, and educational policy. His research has been supported by the National Institute of Education, the Spencer Foundation, and the National Science Foundation. He has been active in the Missouri state educational policy community and with the Coalition of Essential Schools.

James D. Jones is Professor of Sociology at Mississippi State University. His areas of specialization are the sociology of education, complex organizations, and social stratification. His research has focused on the internal structure of schools, most especially the structure of high school tracking and how this relates to the stratification systems of communities and society. Currently he is exploring how the structure of tracking has changed during the last half of the twentieth century, how this change has been influenced by larger social events, and the consequences of the change for the achievement levels of students that vary by gender, ethnicity, and class.

Sally B. Kilgore is the President of the Modern Red SchoolHouse Institute in Nashville, Tennessee, and has been with the design effort since its inception. Her previous research focuses on how the organization of schools affects student learning. She is currently working to integrate research on learning from cognitive psychologists into a framework for school organization. Her work has appeared in leading scholarly journals, including the *American Sociological Review, Harvard Education Review*, and *Sociology of Education*. In the early 1980s, she coauthored *High School Achievement* with Thomas Hoffer and noted scholar James S. Coleman. She has also served on the editorial boards of the *American Education Research Journal* and *Sociology of Education*.

Sheila Nataraj Kirby is a Senior Economist at RAND and the Associate Director of the organization's Washington, D.C., office. Her primary research interests are in the areas of economics of education and military manpower. Her current research focuses on teacher preparation programs, teachers of at-risk children, and evaluations of comprehensive school reform. She is an Adjunct Professor of Economics and Public Policy at George Washington University, where she has taught both economics and public policy courses for 17 years.

James Meza, Jr. is the Dean of the College of Education at the University of New Orleans and is Director of the University of New Orleans Accelerated Schools Center. He led the team working with the Accelerated Schools Project in Memphis, Tennessee. He is interested in reform at the state, district, school, and classroom levels.

Chip Morrison has served in various capacities with Co-nect since 1992. He is currently Senior Director, Operations Research. He holds an Ed.D. in Human Development from the Harvard Graduate School of Education.

Charles M. Payne is the Sally Dalton Robinson Professor of African American studies, history, and sociology at Duke University, where he also directs the African and African American Studies Program. His areas of research interest include urban education and social change. With the support of the Joyce and Spencer Foundations, he is currently writing a book titled *Fragile Victories: The Dynamics of Successful Schooling in Urban America*.

Peggy L. Placier is an Associate Professor in Educational Leadership and Policy Analysis at the University of Missouri-Columbia. She has worked as an educator and community activist with programs for low-income children and adults. Her research concerns teacher education and educational policy processes at state and local levels, and her teaching focuses on developing critical understandings of education policy and research among preservice teachers and graduate students.

Mark A. Smylie is Professor of Education at the University of Illinois at Chicago. His research interests include urban school improvement, leadership, teacher learning and development, and the relationship of school organization to classroom teaching and learning. Smylie received his Ph.D. in educational leadership from Peabody College at Vanderbilt University and his M.Ed. and B.A. from Duke University. He is a former high school social studies teacher.

Stacy A. Wenzel directs the fieldwork research portion of the Chicago Annenberg Research Project at the Consortium on Chicago School Research and the evaluation of the University of Illinois at Chicago–Community College Collaborative for Excellence in Teacher Preparation. She received her Ph.D. in higher education from the University of Michigan and her B.S. from the University of Notre Dame. Her research interests include issues of educational change, teacher professional learning and development, math and science education, and gender equity.

**CORWIN
PRESS**

The Corwin Press logo—a raven striding across an open book—represents the happy union of courage and learning. We are a professional-level publisher of books and journals for K-12 educators, and we are committed to creating and providing resources that embody these qualities. Corwin's motto is "Success for All Learners."

Preface

The purpose of this volume is to explore the role of leadership in comprehensive school reform (CSR). The movement has grown substantially over the last 10 years, as evidenced by the thousands of schools that are engaged in such efforts, and it is seen as one of the most promising avenues for improving student achievement in U.S. schools. While the movement is continuing to gain ground, there are still unanswered questions as to what can help to make CSR more successful.

We were drawn to this project by the belief that leadership was one issue that deserved considerable attention and yet has not received much notice to date. As we engaged in conversations with leaders of reform design teams, conducted our own studies of CSR, and reviewed research on CSR implementation and effects, we found that leadership was frequently acknowledged as a prime factor in the successful implementation of CSR. However, apart from knowing that leadership was important, there seemed to be little information about what type of leadership was important, which individuals' roles in leadership were most critical and why, and whether different reform models had different leadership requirements. Hence, we decided to develop this volume that aims to explore leadership in the context of a variety of CSR designs. We were guided by the belief that a focus on studying leadership within these models would tell us about the nexus of leadership and CSR, as well as about leadership and reform more generally.

The volume includes chapters on a number of different types of CSR designs. Following an introductory section in which we place CSR in historical context, the volume spotlights chapters on several of the New American Schools designs, including Expeditionary Learning, Co-nect, Modern Red SchoolHouse, and Accelerated Schools, as well as a chapter by RAND researchers that discusses leadership implications from the scale-up of New American Schools in several districts. The next section of the volume features chapters on the Annenberg Challenge Initiatives in Chicago and in the San Francisco Bay area. The fourth section of the volume explores other nationally recognized CSR designs, including Success for All the Coalition of Essential Schools, and the Comer School Development Program, which operate mostly as independent entities (e.g., as nonprofit organizations or out of universities). We conclude the book with a chapter that discusses the themes, insights, and implications that can be drawn about leadership from the chapters in the volume. Here we show how the chapters deepen our understanding of principal and superintendent leadership and enrich the emerging narrative on distributed leadership.

The chapters in this volume are written from a variety of different perspectives. On the one hand are authors who write from the "insider" perspective as leaders of reform design teams, including Farrell who writes about Expeditionary Learning and Goldberg and Morrison who write about the Co-nect model. On the other hand, the chapters on Annenberg by Smylie et al. and Copland, on the Comer School Development Program by Payne and Diamond, and on Success for All by Datnow and Castellano are all written by "outsiders"—university academics who are not associated with the reform initiatives under study. The Modern Red SchoolHouse chapter is a collaborative effort between an insider and an outsider, as Kilgore is the president of Modern Red SchoolHouse and Jones is an academic who has conducted research on the model.

Representing yet another type of insider-outsider perspective, the chapters on Accelerated Schools by Finnan and Meza and on the Coalition of Essential Schools by Hall and Placier are written from the perspective of individuals who are based in universities but who also have or have had formal associations with the reform design teams as well. We believe that the diversity of perspectives offered by these authors adds to the complexity and richness of the findings about leadership and school reform and makes the volume appealing to a broad audience of practitioners, policy makers, and researchers in education.

PART I

Setting the Stage

CHAPTER ONE

The Development of Comprehensive School Reform

JOSEPH MURPHY AND AMANDA DATNOW

Comprehensive School Reform (CSR) is a powerful strategy schools can use to redesign themselves and increase the academic achievement of their students. The CSR concept involves an integrated, rather than fragmented, approach to change. (National Clearinghouse for Comprehensive School Reform, n.d.).

If we could do only one thing to build school capacity, we would develop a cadre of leaders who understand the challenges of school improvement, relish academic achievement, and rally all stakeholders to higher standards of learning. (Consortium on Renewing Education, 1998, p. 35)

The purpose of this volume is to explore the role of leadership in comprehensive school reform (CSR). The comprehensive school reform movement has grown substantially over the past 10 years, as evidenced by the thousands of schools that are engaged in such efforts, and it is seen as one of the most promising avenues for improving student achievement in U.S. schools. While the movement is continuing to gain ground, there are still some unanswered questions as to what can help to make comprehensive school reform more successful.

We were drawn to this project by the belief that leadership was one issue that deserved considerable attention and yet had not received much to date. As we engaged in conversations with leaders of reform design teams, conducted our own studies of comprehensive school reform, and reviewed research on CSR implementation and effects (e.g., Bodilly, 1998), we found that leadership was frequently acknowledged as a prime factor in the successful implementation of comprehensive school reform. However, apart from knowing that leadership was important, there seemed to be little knowledge about what type of leadership was important, which individuals' roles in leadership were most critical and why, and whether different reform models had different leadership requirements. Hence, we decided to develop this volume that would aim explore leadership in the context of a variety of CSR designs. We were guided by the belief that a focus on studying leadership within these models would tell us about the nexus of leadership and comprehensive school reform, as well as about leadership and reform more generally.

The volume includes chapters on a number of different types of comprehensive school reform designs. Following this introductory section, the second section of the volume includes chapters on several of the New American Schools designs, including Expeditionary Learning, Co-nect, Modern Red SchoolHouse, and Success for All, as well as a chapter that discusses leadership implications from the scale up of New American Schools in several districts. The third section of the volume includes chapters on the Annenberg Challenge Initiatives in Chicago and in the San Francisco Bay Area. The Annenberg reform initiative involves many schools across the country and shares the focus on the systemic nature of reform that is common to the other CSR designs discussed here. However, the major difference is that funding for implementation comes from the Annenberg Foundation, rather than local or federal sources as is often the case with the other models (and which is explained below).

The fourth part of the volume includes chapters on other nationally recognized comprehensive school reform designs, including Accelerated Schools, the Coalition of Essential Schools, and the Comer School Development Program, which operate mostly as independent entities (e.g., as nonprofit organizations or out of universities).[1] We conclude the volume with a chapter that discusses the themes, insights, and implications that can be drawn about leadership from the chapters in the volume.

The chapters in this volume are written from a variety of different perspectives. On the one hand, there are authors who write from the "insider" perspective as leaders of reform design teams, including Farrell who writes about Expeditionary Learning and Goldberg and Morrison who write about the Co-nect model. On the other hand, the chapters on Annenberg by Smylie et al. and Copland, on the Comer School Development Program by Payne and Diamond, and on Success for All by Datnow and Castellano are all written by "outsiders"—university academics who are not associated with the reform initiatives under study. The Modern Red SchoolHouse chapter is a collaborative effort between an insider and an outsider, as

Kilgore is the president of Modern Red SchoolHouse and Jones is an academic who has been conducting research on the model.

Representing yet another type of insider-outsider perspective, the chapters on Accelerated Schools by Finnan and Meza and on the Coalition of Essential Schools by Hall and Placier are written from the perspective of individuals who are based in universities but who also have or have had formal associations with the reform design teams as well. We believe that the diversity of perspectives offered by these authors adds to the complexity and richness of the findings about leadership and school reform and makes the volume more appealing to a broad audience of practitioners, policy makers, and researchers in education.

As with most large-scale initiatives (e.g., charter schools), the CSR portrait was painted from a palette containing a number of elements from earlier reform eras. In this section, we create the CSR picture as follows. We provide a snapshot of school reform from 1980 to today. We then connect CSR to key ideology from the three eras of reform unfolding over that time. We close by outlining the history of CSR.

SCHOOL REFORM 1980–2002

It is possible to conceptualize reform analysis in a myriad of ways. We find three methods to be especially helpful: by time or phase of reform, especially the broad sweeps of change; by level of the system affected, that is, core technology, management, or institution; and by the dominant mechanism or governance system emphasized: government, profession, citizens, or market (see Murphy, 1990, 1991; Murphy & Adams, 1998). For purposes here, our brief history attends primarily to eras and mechanisms of reform.

Intensification Era (1980–1987)

Early school reform action was almost entirely located in the government sector. There was a widespread feeling that, while seriously impaired, the educational system could be repaired by strong medicine. Because the government was the dominant player in the educational enterprise, reformers expected the state to develop and administer appropriate remedies. The philosophical infrastructure of early suggestions to repair schooling was highly mechanistic, composed mainly of centralized controls and standards. This approach assumed that conditions of schooling contributing to poor student outcomes were attributable to low expectations and effort and inadequate tools. Reformers viewed these conditions as subject to revision through top-down initiatives, especially those from the state. In those early reform efforts, using a government model to institute improvement proposals led to an emphasis on policy mechanisms such as prescriptions, tightly specified resource allocations, and performance components that focused on repairing parts of the system (such as writing better textbooks; raising the quality of the workforce by telling employees how to work—for example, specifying instructional models; and mandating higher expectations by increasing graduation requirements).

Of special importance here is the fact that the frameworks for this intensification strategy were constructed from the growing body of research on teachers' effectiveness and school effects. As we will see below, the focus was on specific content strands, content strands that were to be hard wired into the CSR movement.

The Restructuring Era (1986–1995)

The reform platform from the intensification era came under attack on philosophical and practical grounds. On the first front, analysts were critical of what they saw as an excessive reliance on government as the reform engine, to the near exclusion of professionals, markets, and citizens as catalysts for improvement. The top-down architecture of intensification was found to be particularly troubling. There was a sense that the process of change was seriously undervalued. On practical grounds, critics made two points: that reforms did not seem to be producing desired outcomes, and that reforms were never likely to do so because they were not designed to get to the heart of the problem. Judging the intensification movement as inadequate at best and wrongheaded at worst, reformers clamored for fundamental revisions in the ways schools were organized and governed (Carnegie Forum on Education and the Economy, 1986; Elmore, 1987).

A central tenet of the restructuring movement is that educational improvement is contingent on empowering teachers to work more effectively with students. A less well-ingrained, but still persistent, theme is that real change also depends on empowering parents. The major policy mechanism employed in those reforms was "power distribution." Unlike the strategy employed in the intensification era, reformers designed the restructuring model to capitalize on the energy and creativity of individuals at the school-site level.

Underlying almost all restructuring proposals was the assumption that problems in education could be ascribed to the structure of schooling. The bureaucratic infrastructure of education was subjected to close scrutiny and found to be failing. It is not surprising that the focus of improvement in this era of reform was on the professionals who populated schools and the conditions they required to work effectively, including basic changes in the organizational arrangements of schooling. Restructuring would require a shift from mechanistic, structure-reinforcing strategies to a professional approach to reform, and from "regulation and compliance monitoring to mobilization of institutional capacity" (Timar & Kirp, 1988, p. 75). Nor is it surprising that reformers who considered the basic structure of schools as the root of education's problems should also propose more far-reaching and radical solutions than their predecessors who believed that the current system could be repaired.

Two broad content areas dominated the portfolio of reformers in the restructuring movement: decentralization/site-based management (SBM) and initial forays into school choice. On the decentralization front, there were concentrated efforts to download decision-making authority to the school level, to teachers within schools, and to parents who sent their children to these institutions (Murphy & Beck, 1995). At the same time that administrative, professional, and community decentralization initiatives were sweeping over the educational landscape, the restructuring era witnessed efforts to introduce the underpinnings of the market philosophy into schools, especially market-sensitive measures of accountability. Controlled choice plans appeared, which permitted parents to select among traditionally defined public schools. While limited in scope, these early choice initiatives brought "the market" into the reform equation in a systematic fashion for the first time and with it new ways of thinking about educational improvement, ones built on sensitivity and responsiveness to customer needs and interests.

Reformation Era (1992–Present)

While the dividing line between the intensification and restructuring reform eras is fairly clear, the demarcation between the reforms of the restructuring era (roughly 1986–1995) and the subsequent reformation era is much less obvious. Still, enough information is available to indicate that in the early 1990s the United States entered a stage of reform that is distinct from the improvement efforts of the restructuring period.

In some ways, the reform infrastructure of the reformation era parallels that found in earlier eras, especially the feeling that prior change efforts did not produce the improvements for which advocates had hoped. In important ways, however, the reformation period is different. To begin, for the first time in the history of American educational reform, all four reform mechanisms fully share center stage.

Reform initiatives of this era indicate that the government reform portfolio is dominated by efforts to develop standards and accountability mechanisms and very recently capacity building strategies. Standards development falls into three groups: content, performance, and opportunity-to-learn standards. Moreover, accountability systems are employing more rigorous assessments of student performance and a host of approaches (for example, school-based incentive programs, school reconstitution, district bankruptcy) to hold schools and the professionals that work in them responsible for student outcomes.

In the reformation era, reforms that privilege the profession look both to nurturing shared governance and professional community at the school site and to strengthening the teaching profession. Key initiatives include the creation of professional standards for individual educators and for the institutions that prepare them. These standards support more effective systems of licensure and, through the National Board for Professional Teaching Standards, bring advanced certification to bear for the first time.

Citizen-based reforms of the reformation era are designed to build on gains made in the restructuring era in enhancing parental voice. While this picture remains somewhat cloudy, reforms in this domain might best be grouped together under the heading of "parents' rights." Such initiatives often blend with the market-grounded reforms discussed below.

In the restructuring era, market influences began to work their way into reform designs. In the reformation era, marketization has become a central reform ideology in its own right, one that is used at times to jar public schools from their perceived complacency and at other times to provide alternatives to public provision of educational services. The central strategies here are best captured under the concept of privatization. The most important of these broad strategies are deregulation, contracting out, vouchers, and home schooling, all of which were barely on the radar screen in the late 1980s and all of which are gaining considerable momentum as the nation moves into the new millennium (see Murphy, 1996; Murphy, Gilmer, Weise, & Page, 1998).

ROOTS OF THE COMPREHENSIVE SCHOOL REFORM MOVEMENT

A thoughtful unfolding of CSR reveals that much of its architecture was constructed from ideology from each of the three eras of reform discussed above, especially reform concepts that took shape between 1980 and 1995, by which time the blueprints for this movement had been largely developed.

Ideology from the Intensification Era

Key pieces of the CSR scaffolding can be located in the effectiveness studies that fueled intensification era reform designs. The four key ideas developed during this era that have been riveted deeply into CSR include: the educability of learners, a focus on outcomes, taking responsibility for students, and attention to consistency and coordination throughout the school community.

The Educability of Learners. Central to the intensification era was a broad attack on the prevailing conception of student learning, one that has been eloquently captured in the dominant aphorism of effective schools advocates: All students can learn. The broadside from the intensification era was directed against schools that throughout most of the 20th century had been organized to provide results consistent with the normal curve, to sort youth into those who would work with their heads and those who would toil with their hands. While the attention to the importance of policy-manipulable variables and the concern for academic success of all students was not always well-crafted in terms of policy and practice, deep-rooted reform advocates believe in the educability of students along with the expectation that schools would reshape themselves to ensure this end was infused deep into the heart of CSR.

A Focus on Outcomes. For a wide variety of reasons, before the intensification era, educators in the United States avoided serious inspection of the educational process. Even less attention was devoted to examining educational outcomes. The quality of education had historically been defined in terms of two interrelated inputs—the wealth (and the extra resources wealth allows schools to secure, such as better facilities, more equipment, additional staff, and so forth) and socioeconomic status (SES) of students. Given the chance, parents would move into high-income, high-SES school districts and out of low-income, low-SES ones. The inescapable conclusion, even to the most casual observer, is that the good schools are to be found in the former group and the bad schools in the latter one.

Intensification reforms, powered by the effectiveness studies, provided the first systemic challenge to extant systems of accountability in education. In Finn's (1990) terms, effective schools proponents realized that the input and output end of the oar "were not firmly joined at all. Indeed they were more like two separate oars, capable of moving independently. To pull the one labeled 'inputs,' however energetically, did not necessarily have an effect on the one labeled 'outcomes'" (p. 586). They also saw quite clearly the pernicious effects of the operant definition of effectiveness on large groups of students. Intensification era reformers developed the following platform of ideas, all of which have become tightly woven in CSR: (a) rigorous assessments of schooling are needed and one can judge the quality of education only by examining student outcomes, especially indices of learning; (b) success should not be defined in absolute terms but in terms of the value added to what students bring to the educational process; and (c) effectiveness depends on the equitable distribution of learning outcomes across the entire population of youngsters.

Taking Responsibility for Students. When quality education is defined primarily in terms of resources and student SES, when failure is an inherent characteristic of the learning model employed, and when the function of schooling is to sort children into "heads" and "hands," it is not difficult to discern responsibility for what happens to students—accountability lies elsewhere than with school personnel. Indeed, the prevailing explanations for student failures before the intensification era focused on deficiencies in the students themselves and in the home/community environments in which they were nurtured: "in short, since the beginning of public education, poor academic performance and deviant behavior have been defined as problems of individual children or their families" (Cuban, 1989, p. 781).

As Cuban (1989, p. 784) correctly notes, "the effective schools movement shifted the focus of efforts to deal with poor academic performance among low income minorities from the child to the school." The attack on the practice of blaming the victim for the shortcomings of the school itself has been enjoined by the CSR movement. So too has the demand that the school community take a fair share of responsibility for what happens to the youth in its care.

Attention to Consistency Throughout the School Community. One pundit has described a school as a collection of individual entrepreneurs (teachers) surrounded by a common parking lot. Another says a school is a group of classrooms held together by a common heating and cooling system. While we acknowledge the hyperbole in these definitions, we also realize that it is the accuracy of the statements that brings a smile to our faces when we hear them for the first time. The picture they convey captures an essential condition of schools in the United States: They are very loosely linked organizations. What unfolds in one classroom may be quite different from what happens in another. Activity in the principal's (or superintendent's) office is likely to have little impact on classrooms. A unified sense of mission is generally conspicuous by its absence. Curriculum is not well-integrated across grade levels or among various program areas. We claim to teach one thing (objectives), while we generally teach something quite different (textbooks), and almost invariably test students using assessment instruments (norm referenced achievement tests) based on neither.

One of the most powerful and enduring lessons from all the research in the intensification era is that the better schools are more tightly linked— structurally, symbolically, and culturally—than the less effective ones. They operate more as an organic whole and less as a loose collection of disparate subsystems. There is a great deal of consistency within and across the major components of the organization, especially those of the production function—the teaching-learning process. Staff, parents, and students share a sense of direction. Components of the curriculum—objectives, materials, assessment strategies—are tightly aligned. Staff share a common instructional language. Expectations for performance are similar throughout the school community, and rewards and consequences are consistently distributed to students. This overarching sense of consistency and coordination has become a central plank in CSR. As we see below, CSR advocates carried the coordination ideology well beyond prevalent conceptions of the intensification era.

Ideology From the School Restructuring Era

The CSR movement has also incorporated significant material from the restructuring era of school reform. One such idea is the understanding that change is a process, a quest for improvement rather than the search for a final resting place (Fullan, 1991), or what Sirotnik (1989) labels as the acknowledgement that "the prospect is for a continuous process of reconstruction" (p. 104).

A second restructuring era idea (with roots in the notion of the school as an organic whole from the intensification era) that is woven in CSR is perhaps best captured by the phrase "systemic work." At one level, this means that reform cannot be compartmentalized. Improvement efforts must unfold so that changes become welded into the basic structure of the organization. According to Prestine (1993), this requires attending to all the important parts of the organization simultaneously as well as recognizing "the integrated (and) interactive . . . nature of the restructuring process." At a second level, working systemically means keeping one eye focused on the process issues of restructuring and the other on content matters. At still another level, it necessitates working to ensure greater coherence across all levels of the educational system from the statehouse to the classroom, especially often overlooked layers such as the district office. It means having the key participants using the same scorecard, communicating fewer messages about what is important throughout the system, and then focusing activity on those important issues. It requires a rational (not bureaucratic) approach to improvement work that recognizes the importance of local context and mutual adaptation as well as the importance of each individual voice. Finally, working systemically means bringing frames of analysis in line with belief structures. In particular, it means redefining policymaking to recognize the centrality of stakeholders at the local school level.

The CSR movement has also borrowed heavily from the empowerment ideology that anchored school restructuring. Key aspects of the subtext here include an emphasis on organic, decentralized, and professionally controlled systems, in lieu of a focus on hierarchical, bureaucratic structures—a shift from what Sergiovanni (1991) calls "a power over approach . . . to a power to approach" (p. 105); a privileging of values such as participation, community, and reflection; and basic changes in the roles and responsibilities of actors in the school, including alternations in traditional notions of authority and extant conceptions of roles.

CSR has also adapted another central plank of school restructuring reforms, the notion that all change efforts are contexualized, or as Siskin (1994) and Portin, Beck, Knapp, and Murphy (in press) inform us: "context matters." In short, even when schools use a common framework (or CSR design), the reform agenda must be tailored to the needs of a specific school and must be co-constructed at the site level—it must focus on what is important for that particular school community. As Prestine (1993) reminds us, this means that "the paths taken . . . will be richly varied— reflective of the individual characteristics and unique contextual settings of the schools attempting such change" (p. 33–34). What works at one school may not work at another—or at the same school at a different time or with a cast of players with different values and interests. Variations across schools do not so much represent deviations from a norm as they "reflect the realities of implementing . . . grass-roots innovation" (Hallinger & Hausman, 1993, p. 115). However, it is important to note that the ideology that comprehensive school reform efforts must be heavily contextualized is more apparent in some school reform designs, such as Accelerated Schools, than others, such as Success for All.

Ideas From the Reformation Era

The draftspersons for CSR had done a fair amount of work by the time the reformation era broke over the reform landscape. Nonetheless, important ideas from this third period of reform—especially those foreshadowed in early eras—have found a home in CSR. The most important of these is the infusion of market forces into the change process, although somewhat soft market dynamics. The key notion here is the idea of developing innovative new products that will, through the market, both (a) spread to other consumers (e.g. schools and school districts) and (b) "encourage" nonadaptors to strengthen their own educational offerings. And as is the case with other market influenced reforms, such as charters, there is a sense that this type of supply side work will be influential in overhauling the education system writ large (Murphy & Shiffman, 2002).

Already we hear of reform design teams, also referred to as "vendors," "peddling" their reforms and of schools as "shoppers" choosing among the growing menu of reforms. "Name-branding" of schools has also become apparent, as some schools have not only taken on reforms, they have incorporated the name of the reform into their school name such as the "Pine Core Knowledge School" or the "Sunnyside Comer School." This trend has been particularly apparent among charter schools that have adopted CSR models. Much like the way familiar food franchises and brand names attract customers more so than unknown entities, brand name reforms have helped educators garner resources for their efforts, attract public attention, and serve as a signal of quality.

GROWTH OF THE COMPREHENSIVE SCHOOL REFORM MOVEMENT

The CSR movement marks a shift away from the notion that school improvement should proceed organically, one school at a time. Instead, what we now see is the extension of a particular reform model from one school or a handful of schools to many schools in diverse locales. Single schools located in a variety of places adopt particular reform models and are joined together in a network of hundreds or thousands of schools undertaking a particular reform. What is distinctive among these efforts is the use of an external model or an external provider to assist with school reform efforts. CSR effectively means that schools and districts are now "outsourcing" school improvement services. This represents a shift from the traditional arrangement where services were provided by district offices or state departments of education (Sunderman & Nardini, 1998).

As the chapters in this volume make clear, the reform models that are available to schools are a varied group. Reform models array along a continuum of those that are highly specified and provide curriculum, lesson plans, school organizational models, implementation plans, and professional development, to those that are process-oriented, asking schools to commit to a guiding set of principles and engage in an inquiry-guided, locally driven process of self-renewal. In this regard, some reform designs are more nearly "prepackaged," whereas others are much looser and presume local development of the change effort. Reform designs also have different foci, with some focusing more directly on pedagogical practices, and others attempting to change the school culture or structure. Accordingly, the design teams have different theories of school change and theories of action.

At the less specified end of the continuum, the Coalition of Essential Schools, Accelerated Schools, and the Comer School Development Program provide frameworks for reform and leave particulars to each school. These designs point to the primacy of local development efforts, as long as the process is guided by a set of overarching principles (and school management structures, in the case of the Comer program) and democratic processes for achieving goals. A bit further along the continuum, Expeditionary Learning Outward Bound, Co-nect, and Modern Red SchoolHouse, offer some materials and provide technical assistance with these reforms but leave quite a few of the details to local educators, such as developing lesson plans. At the most "highly specified" end of the continuum is Success for All, a design that provides detailed descriptions of how to organize both schools and classrooms with respect to reading. However, Success for All is only prescriptive in the area of reading, not in all school subjects.

One might argue that the roots of the waves of reform we have seen in the past two decades manifest themselves differently in the various reform models, with more prescribed, prepackaged models finding their roots in the intensification era and models aimed at empowering educators to come up with their own reform plans finding their roots in the ideologies of the restructuring era. Some models, of course, find their roots in multiple eras. Nevertheless, though the reforms differ in their approaches to change, common to them are an interest in whole-school change, strong commitments to improving student achievement, new conceptions about what students should be expected to learn, and an emphasis on prevention rather than remediation (Oakes, 1993).

Most comprehensive school reform models arrived on the educational landscape beginning in the 1980s, with the exception of the Comer School Development Program that originated in the late 1960s. More than half of the reform models listed in the *Catalog of School Reform Models* (Northwest

Regional Educational Laboratory, 1998) have been created since 1983 (Hatch, 2000a). The Coalition of Essential Schools dates to the early 1980s, Success for All dates back to 1984, and the Accelerated Schools movement began in the late 1980s. Although the number of schools implementing these and other models has grown steadily over the years, rapid growth in the adoption of CSR models did not occur until the mid-to-late 1990s.

The growth in recent years is in part due to two key federal policy changes. Changes in federal Title I regulations in 1988 and 1994 through the Improving America's Schools Act (IASA) have meant that schools serving large number of students in poverty can use Title I funds for school-wide programs (Desimone, 2000). In previous years, Title I funds had to be used for targeted programs. The change in Title I regulations is supported by research findings documenting the advantages of schoolwide improvement efforts rather than pull out programs in improving the achievement of at-risk students (see Borman, D'Agostino, Wong, & Hedges, 1998; Stringfield et al., 1997). Consequently, in the past decade, many schools have used Title I funds to pay for the costs associated with comprehensive school reform models.

However, most significant for its impact on the growth of CSR was the passage of the Comprehensive School Reform Demonstration Program (CSRD) in the U.S. Congress in 1997. CSRD, also known as the Obey-Porter initiative, allocated $145 million dollars initially (and additional funds in subsequent years, e.g., $260 million in 2001) to schools for the adoption of "research-based" school reform models. The legislation lists 17 CSR models as examples. However, schools are not limited to these particular models and, in fact, can choose others or propose their own whole-school reform program, providing they have evidence of effectiveness to support it. Typically, schools apply to their state departments of education for CSRD funds, which are at least $50,000 annually for three years. Most CSRD funding is allocated for Title I schools. An estimated 4,000 schools or more have received CSRD funding since 1998.

The scale-up of CSR models was also bolstered early on by the founding of the New American Schools (NAS) Corporation, as explained in detail in the chapter six by Berends, Bodilly, and Kirby. Created in 1991 as part of Goals 2000, NAS was charged with securing financial support from foundations and corporations to fund new designs for "break-the-mold" schools (Kearns & Anderson, 1996). In 1995, after supporting the development and piloting of nine designs, NAS formally launched its "scale-up" operation by inviting school districts and states to participate as jurisdictions that would implement the designs in individual schools over a five-year period (Kearns & Anderson, 1996). NAS continues to exist as a business-led, nonprofit organization and it plays a key role in the reform movement. In addition to currently partnering with nine reform model providers, NAS serves as a source of consulting for educational organizations, a source of capital for reform design teams, and as a policy advocate in the comprehensive reform movement (New American Schools, n.d.).

As Hatch (2000b) points out, "the creation of the CSRD Program sent a strong message that the time is right to scale up comprehensive designs around country." Not only has CSRD let to an increase in the number of schools adopting CSR models, it has also contributed to the emergence of many new CSR model providers since 1997 (New American Schools, 2002). The options of CSR models have increased, as has the competition among model providers. Several design teams are making changes to their models or service delivery in order to be more competitive, often enhancing the services they offer schools. In several cases, the design teams have further specified their reform models, or at least what is required to implement their models, in order to make them more marketable in the CSRD landscape (Datnow, Hubbard, & Mehan, 2002). The market for CSR models it quite an active one; it has been estimated that more than $1 billion was spent by local school systems on school improvement services by the year 2001 (New American Schools, n.d.).

Overall, we now find that the scaling up of CSR models is occurring at an unprecedented rate, affecting thousands of schools in the United States and elsewhere. To give an example of the type of growth some of the models have experienced in recent years, Success for All, one of the most popular reforms, has expanded by about 60% per year over a 10-year period (Slavin, 1998). Most of the schools implementing CSR models are public schools, including many charter schools among the group as well. Considering that the number of schools implementing CSR models is estimated at 6,000 (Education Quality Institute, n.d.), these schools comprise 6.5% of the approximately 92,000 public schools in the United States. But this estimate may be conservative, as there are already more than 4,000 schools with CSRD funding, and many schools fund CSR efforts with other funding sources, such at Title I. We also know that there are currently more than 1,300 Accelerated Schools, more than 1,000 schools in the Coalition of Essential Schools, more than 700 schools implementing the Comer School Development Program, more than 800 Core Knowledge schools, and more than 1,800 Success for All schools.

There is considerable evidence to suggest that the CSR movement will continue to grow and thrive in the next few years. Congress has continued to support CSRD, an increasing amount of research is being conducted on the implementation and effects of CSR (and hence our knowledge base has increased), and the reform models are maturing and design teams are becoming more adept at working with schools. There is still much to be learned from the CSR movement and its implications for school improvement and for leadership.

We now turn our attention to the chapters on the New American Schools designs, beginning with a chapter on leadership in Expeditionary Learning schools by Greg Farrell.

REFERENCES

Bodilly, S. (1998). *Lessons from New American Schools' scale-up phase: Prospects for bringing designs to multiple schools.* Santa Monica, CA: RAND.

Borman, G. D., D'Agostino, J. V., Wong, K. K., & Hedges, L. V. (1998). The longitudinal achievement of Chapter 1 students: Preliminary evidence from the Prospects study. *Journal of Education for Students Placed at Risk, 3*(4), 363–399.

Carnegie Forum on Education and the Economy. (1986). *A nation prepared: Teachers for the 21st century.* Washington, DC: Carnegie Forum on Education and the Economy.

Consortium on Renewing Education. (1998). *20/20 vision: A strategy for doubling America's academic achievement by the year 2020.* Nashville, TN: Peabody Center for Education Policy, Vanderbilt University.

Cuban, L. (1989, June). The "at-risk" label and the problem of urban school reform. *Phi Delta Kappan, 70*(10), 780–784,799.

Datnow, A., Hubbard, L., & Mehan, H. (2002). *Extending educational reform: From one school to many.* London and New York: Routledge Falmer Press.

Desimone, L. (2000). *Making comprehensive school reform work.* New York: ERIC Clearinghouse on Urban Education.

Education Quality Institute. (n.d.). Frequently asked questions. Retrieved June 21, 2002, from www.eqireports.org/About%20EQI/frequently_asked_questions.htm Why was EQI created?

Elmore, R. F. (1987, November). Reform and the outline of authority in schools: *Educational Administration Quarterly, 23*(4), 60–78.

Finn, C. E. (1990, April). The biggest reform of all. *Phi Delta Kappan, 71*(8), 583–592.

Fullan, M. G. (1991). *The new meaning of educational change* (2nd ed.). New York: Teachers College Press.

Hallinger, P., & Hausman, C. (1993). In J. Murphy & P. Hallinger (Eds.), *Restructuring schools: Learning from ongoing efforts* (pp. 114–142). Thousand Oaks, CA: Corwin Press.

Hatch, T. (2000a). *Incoherence in the system: Three perspectives on the implementation of multiple initiatives in one district.* Menlo Park, CA: Carnegie Foundation for the Advancement of Teaching.

Hatch, T. (2000b). What does it take to "go to scale"? Reflections on the promise and the perils of comprehensive school reform. *Journal of Education for Students Placed At Risk, (5)*4, 339–354.

Kearns, D. T., & Anderson, J. L. (1996). Sharing the vision: Creating new American schools. In S. Stringfield, S. M. Ross, and L. Smith (Eds.), *Bold plans for school restructuring: The New American Schools designs.* Mahwah, NJ: Erlbaum.

Murphy, J. (1990). The educational reform movement of the 1980s: A comprehensive analysis. In J. Murphy (Ed.), *The reform of American public education in the 1980s: Perspectives and cases* (pp. 3–55). Berkeley, CA: McCutchan.

Murphy, J. (1991). *Restructuring schools: Capturing and assessing the phenomena.* New York: Teachers College Press.

Murphy, J. (1996). *The privatization of schooling: Problems and possibilities.* Thousand Oaks, CA: Corwin Press.

Murphy, J., & Adams, J. E. (1998). Educational reform in the United States 1980–2000. *Journal of Educational Administration. 36*(5), 426–444.

Murphy, J., & Beck, L. G. (1995). *School-based management as school reform: Taking stock.* Newbury Park, CA: Corwin Press.

Murphy, J., Gilmer, S., Weise, R., & Page, A. (1998). *Pathways to privatization in education.* Norwood, NJ: Ablex.

Murphy, J., & Shiffman, C. D. (2002). *Understanding and assessing the charter school movement.* New York: Teachers College Press.

National Clearinghouse for Comprehensive School Reform (n. d.). Retrieved June 21, 2002, from www.goodschools.gwu.edu/about_csr/index.html.

New American Schools. (n.d.). Retrieved June 21, 2002, from www.naschools. org/contentViewer.asp?highlightID=7

New American Schools. (2002). *New American Schools: Driven by results.* Arlington, VA: Author. Retrieved June 21, 2002, from www.naschools.org/uploaded-files/policy.pdf.

Northwest Regional Educational Laboratory. (1998). *Catalog of school reform models.* Portland, OR: Northwest Regional Educational Laboratory.

Oakes, J. (1993). *New standards and disadvantaged schools. Background paper prepared for research forum on Effects of New Standards and Assessments on High Risk Students and Disadvantaged Schools.* Cambridge, MA: Harvard University.

Portin, B., Beck, L., Knapp, M., & Murphy, J. (In Press.). The school and self-reflective renewal: Taking stock and moving on In B. Portin, L. Beck, M. Knapp, & J. Murphy (Eds.), *Self-reflective renewal in schools: Lessons from a national initiative:* Westport, CT: Greenwood.

Prestine, N. (1993). Feeling the ripples, riding the waves: Making an Essential school. In J. Murphy & P. Hallinger (Eds.), *Restructuring schools: Learning from changing efforts* (pp. 32–62). Thousand Oaks, CA: Corwin Press.

Sergiovanni, T. (1991). *The principalship: A reflective practice perspective* (2nd ed.). Boston: Allyn & Bacon.

Sirotnik, K. A. (1989). The schools as the center of change. In T. J. Sergiovanni & J. H. Moore (Eds.), *Schooling for tomorrow: Directing reforms to issues that count* (pp. 89–113). Boston: Allyn & Bacon.

Siskin, L. S. (1994). *Realms of knowledge: Academic departments in secondary schools.* Bristol, PA: Falmer Press.

Slavin, R. (1998, Fall). Far and wide: Developing and disseminating research-based programs. *American Educator, 8*(11), 45.

Stringfield, S., Millsap, M. A., Herman, R., Yoder, N., Brigham, N., Nesselrodt, P., Schaffer, E., Karweit, N., Levin, M., & Stevens, R. (with Gamse, B., Puma, M., Rosenblum, S., Beaumont, J., Randall, B., & Smith, L.). (1997). *Urban and suburban/rural special strategies for educating disadvantaged children. Final report.* Washington, DC: U.S. Department of Education.

Sunderman, G., & Nardini, G. (1998). *Constraints on institutionalizing school reform: Lessons from Chicago.* Oak Brook, IL: North Central Regional Educational Laboratory.

Timar, T. B., & Kirp, D. L. (1988, Summer). State efforts to reform schools: Treading between regulatory swamp and an English garden. *Educational Evaluation and Policy Analysis*, 10(2), 75–88.

NOTE

1. We know that Accelerated Schools has since become one of the reforms in the New American Schools portfolio. However, as it existed independently for most its history, we decided to keep it separate in this volume.

PART II

New American Schools Designs

CHAPTER TWO

Expeditionary Learning Schools

Tenacity, Leadership, and School Reform

GREG FARRELL

Tenacity is a kind of intelligence. Those who care the most, for the longest, win.

—Herb Sturz[1]

I consider it the foremost task of education to ensure the survival of these qualities: an enterprising curiosity; an undefeatable spirit; tenacity in pursuit, sensible self-denial, and above all, compassion.

—Kurt Hahn

OUTWARD BOUND AND EXPEDITIONARY LEARNING

As Outward Bound aims at personal transformation, Expeditionary Learning aims at the transformation of whole schools. Both work at challenging and helping people to do more and learn more than they would have thought possible. Both view learning as an act of discovery, and experience as the most potent teacher. They are based on the same ideas about what it is important for a person to learn and practice: curiosity and enterprise; resilience; tenacity; doing without; teamwork; and compassion.

My perspective on leadership and school reform is shaped by the particular experience, during the past 10 years, of applying Outward Bound's insights about personal development, learning, leadership, teamwork, and "bringing out the best in people" to the day-to-day business of improving entire schools. Expeditionary Learning, our design for whole-school reform, is demanding in its expectations of teachers and school leaders in ways that others perhaps are not. We may be somewhat more mission-driven than other organizations active in the educational marketplace. So it may help to understand my views if I first explain where we are coming from, why and how Outward Bound came to enter the world of school reform, and what we are trying to do.

Kurt Hahn founded the Salem Shule in Germany, Gordonstoun School in Scotland, the Atlantic Colleges (and through them the International Baccalaureate), the Duke of Edinburgh Award Scheme, and Outward Bound. A common set of educational ideas motivated all these schools and programs, which were established in the 1930s, 1940s, and 1950s, and continue to be active and influential today. At Salem and at Gordonstoun, in the Duke of Edinburgh Awards, and in the first Outward Bound courses, all students were required to pursue an individual project of some complexity. "The chief thing was that it require a sustained effort," recalled Josh Miner, in his book *Outward Bound USA* (2001).

Some people are surprised to learn that Outward Bound, the organization that takes people into the wilderness for transformational experiences, is in the field of school reform. In fact, Outward Bound first took shape in Great Britain in 1941 as an educational innovation arising from a secondary school that was itself an effort at school reform. Outward Bound was the "short course," a month of compressed experience of the kind that students at Salem (Kurt Hahn's first school, in Germany) and Gordonstoun (his second school, in Scotland) had on a year-round basis.

Expeditionary Learning is an application of Kurt Hahn's educational ideas and insights, Outward Bound's 60-year history and craft wisdom, and the thinking of other educational scholars and leaders such as Eleanor Duckworth[2] and Paul Ylvisaker[3] to institutional change and the business of "doing school." We are trying to see how far it is useful to go in teaching academic subjects through active, hands-on experience. We are trying to develop schools that have high expectations and a lot of support for teacher learning and growth as well as for student learning and growth, where all children are known, and where, in Ylvisaker's phrase, "values are clear, and the value of values is clearly demonstrated" (2000).

Private school leaders brought Outward Bound to the United States in 1962.[4] Outward Bound did a great deal of outreach to public and private schools throughout the 1960s and 1970s and helped to create and support dozens of other organizations and programs that use adventure, service, and other forms of direct and engaging experience to teach and motivate people. Project Adventure, which builds ropes courses in gyms and helps improve public and private school physical education and counseling programs, is one example. The Outward Bound-like courses that many colleges and universities run for incoming freshmen to provide them with a bonding and motivating experience are another.

Outward Bound established urban centers in New York, Boston, Atlanta, and Baltimore in the 1980s. The first idea was to provide better recruiting and follow-up with minority students from low-income areas of big cities. Then these urban centers began to develop programs in public schools, bringing the teaching technology of Outward Bound, as well as the spirit of adventure and service, to schools and other urban institutions. In the late 1980s, Outward Bound developed a joint project with the Harvard Graduate School of Education to add experiential dimensions to the Harvard Education School curriculum and to bring more academic rigor into Outward Bound's work with schools. In the 1990s Outward Bound began a national urban/education initiative to build on all of this work, and to identify, develop, and replicate its most effective models of urban and school-based programming.

In 1992, Outward Bound's Expeditionary Learning proposal was selected by the New American Schools Development Corporation (NASDC) for potential five-year support. A forest ranger gave me the news just as I was about to start on an Outward Bound course on the Green River in Utah with a wonderful group of educators, many of whom had helped us think through our proposal. I was elated; but I had a sinking feeling, too. Writing a proposal had been only a few weeks' work. What we had proposed was going to take a long time to do.

We started with 10 demonstration schools in the 1993–1994 school year, 9 of which are still active partner schools in our national network. In 2001–2002 this network comprised 117 schools, and almost 50,000 students and 3,000 teachers, in 31 states, the District of Columbia, and Puerto Rico. Roughly half the schools we are working with are elementary schools. The other half are almost equally divided between middle schools and high schools. About one-fourth are charter schools. Three-quarters have high proportions of minority and low-income students. They are grouped in eight geographic regions. We plan to grow at a modest rate, commensurate with our ability to deliver a high-quality program, and we expect to have about 200 active school partners, with roughly 100,000 students and 6,000 teachers, in the Expeditionary Learning school network by 2005–2006. We are trying to cluster growth as much as possible to serve schools more effectively and to permit more robust regional networks of Expeditionary Learning schools that can more easily support and encourage each other over time.

The ideas and ideals behind Outward Bound have attracted and sustained good people for many years, both in this country and abroad. I believe that is the main reason Outward Bound has been able to develop and grow around the world over the past 60 years and at the same time help to spawn a movement of hundreds of similar but separate organizations. Expeditionary Learning's ability to grow also—and to attract and develop leaders within our own organization and among the schools in our network over the past 10 years—has been greater because of the appeal of the ideas, principles, and practices shared by Outward Bound and Expeditionary Learning. If the ideas are compelling to people, and they see something that matters, they are more likely to commit themselves and work hard. Leaders emerge and improve. Attracting and keeping new leaders is less difficult when there are shared ideals, a common language, and the will to get better. Any truly comprehensive school reform design asks its partner schools to make a leap of faith, to hold hands and plunge into the new work together; with us, making the leap is an integral part of the program. We ask and expect principals and other leaders to model the qualities we want to bring to schools, to lead by example, to be present at the professional development sessions we schedule with their faculties, to be prepared to make a more than ordinary commitment to the work. As Roland Barth (2001) writes, "you can't lead where you won't go. But you can lead where you will go."

LEARN TO GROW TREES

School reform, by its very nature, requires a sustained effort. It takes more time to improve schools than is generally discussed or acknowledged in the press and in political debate, and it takes longer than our political structures support. Ideas are important, but they come in a moment. Doing is what counts, and doing takes years. "If you want to change schools," one superintendent-reformer told me—in 1964—"learn to grow trees."

Leaders have to provide a focus: Choose a direction and stick to it. They have to be reliable and persistent. For school reform to succeed, we, and especially the leaders, have to keep tending the trees. With respect to the work of improving schools and student achievement, leaders do not accomplish much if they are not there for the long haul. Trust and time are the fundamental requirements for growing good schools. Trust is built through constancy. Constancy is demonstrated over time.

What the majority of the schools we work with need most is focus: a clear idea of what the school is trying to become, and time to work on it. Peter Buttenweiser, who works with individual schools for the Ewing & Marion Kaufman Foundation, says that he does not care what programs or design the school has chosen. He just asks, "What things are you doing that contribute or support your mission?" and "What are you doing that doesn't?" And then he tries to help them do more of the first and less of the second.

When our partner schools choose Expeditionary Learning they are choosing a direction, and our work with them is first to help them pick a few key targets, such as better instructional practices for reading and writing, or more and better use of common planning time for teachers, and to help them pursue them. Angela Jolliffe, Expeditionary Learning's field director for the Southeast, says it all boils down to paying attention. "You pay attention to it; you work on it; it gets better." As the president of Expeditionary Learning, a design and organization I believe in with all my heart, I have to say my impression is that it does not matter nearly so much which design a school chooses as it does how well it implements and follows through on what it has chosen. All the reform designs in the New American Schools group are well thought through and well supported with design-based assistance. I believe any of them, well implemented, would produce very positive results in most schools.

This in mind, it appears to me that the culture of engagement and support that has grown up around comprehensive school reform concerns itself too much with the wedding and not enough with the marriage. There is a lot of state and district-level activity around making the best matches between schools and designs. There is much less effort focused on seeing that the matches work once they have been made.

Good implementation is not easy, and it is not the norm. The political environment of public education in this country makes it very difficult for schools and districts to stay with a direction once chosen. The districts seem to be the least reliable partners of all. School boards have elections every two years, often changing superintendents (and directions) in the process, thus ensuring that no strategy will work because no strategy is actually tried long enough to work. The average big-city superintendent now stays in the job less than two and a half years, an all-time low. Smaller districts keep their superintendents longer, I believe, though it is rare to find a district where the superintendent has been in the job a decade. As someone said, "the trouble with being a leader today is that you don't know whether the people are following you or chasing you." "Over the long term, you can't rely on the authority of anyone over the level of principal," says Bob Slavin, head of Success for All/Roots and Wings, perhaps the largest and one of the most successful reform organizations. It is true. In our experience, school-level leadership is much more constant and consistent than leadership at the district level.

Why is it that we as a society are unwilling or unable to give our leaders the time it takes to do what they need to do? The literature on school reform says—and our experience confirms—that it takes at least five years of steady effort to bring schools to a place where they show consistent gains in student learning. The political rhetoric promises or suggests or demands big improvements in a year or two. Even Comprehensive School Reform grants are available to schools for only three years, with no requirement in most states that recipient schools show how they are going to finance and continue ongoing work in years four, five, six, and beyond. This reinforces the idea that reform is a three-year project that will be complete or go away when the grant funds do. Comprehensive School Reform funding provides a great boost to the very idea of whole-school reform. It provides a large part of the means for many schools to begin to pursue it. But one of the serious obstacles to the long-term success and sustainability of school transformation is the idea that reform is done mainly with outside grants and takes just three years.

THE POWER AND NECESSITY OF DOGGED PERSISTENCE

Marshall Smith, the former dean of the Stanford Graduate School of Education and former Assistant Secretary of Education in the Clinton administration, took an Outward Bound course a number of years ago at Hurricane Island, in Maine, with a number of education school deans and big-city superintendents. Afterwards he wrote that, looking at his companions struggle with the unaccustomed demands of the course, he was especially struck with how powerful a force dogged persistence could be in solving problems and overcoming difficulties.

In the system we have it takes uncommon amounts of dogged persistence to keep on doing what needs to be done long enough for it to make a difference. Not all countries are organized this way. In Scotland, Denmark, and Japan, for example, whose students regularly score well above the United States in international tests, public school leaders at all levels are encouraged to stay at the task, and do, for 15 to 20 years or more. These countries, and others, apparently, retain a sense of urgency about improving things now without sacrificing constancy in leadership and the pursuit of a long-term plan. They invest more in teachers and less in central office administration. In these countries 60 to 80% of education employees are classroom teachers, as compared to 43% in the United States. These foreign schools are much more focused and organized around teachers and the craft of teaching. Their curricula emphasize fewer topics studied in greater depth than ours do, allowing for more focused and better supported teaching. We should be studying and importing more tree-tending practices from abroad.

SCHOOLS AT THE CENTER

I am more and more certain that improving individual schools, school-by-school, should be the central strategy that all other strategies support. If school reform does not happen at the individual school level, it does not happen. This is what an old friend of mine calls "a blinding glimpse of the obvious." Students go to schools, not to districts or state departments of education. In schools, people work in close enough proximity to develop familial relations, a special culture, trust, love, and loyalty. Developing a school, as Tom James[5] has said, is like building a family.

The idea of the school as the center of reform was encouraged and supported by developments in education policy when the New American Schools group of design teams got going 10 years ago. Site-based decision-making, charter schools, and grants from the federal and state government to individual schools are all policies and programs that encourage a more decentralized, school-by-school approach. But actual practice in the over-whelming majority of districts has not mirrored the policy changes: The relationship between districts and schools has not changed much. Very few principals know the amount of their school's annual budget, much less control or manage it. There is still a pervasive passivity in most schools, a belief that the real power is in the district office, and that even-tually the district will tell the school what to do, or perhaps shut the school down, or decide to turn it from a neighborhood elementary to a K-8 magnet school.

The tasks at the federal, state, and district level should be to create the conditions and provide the means for building and sustaining good schools. In the past 10 years, all these levels of government have found and combined and distributed resources to support comprehensive reform, put the very idea of whole-school reform on the agenda, promoted stock-taking and planning at the school level, and shepherded matches between schools and organizations like Expeditionary Learning. These governmen-tal actors have gotten the attention of schools and systems regarding the importance of standards. They have hardened the environment and made states and in turn districts and schools more accountable through more explicit standards and standardized tests. They are making efforts to improve the tests and align them better with standards. They have been critical to getting things going. They have been much less effective at help-ing schools stay the course. With a few exceptions, most of the schools in our network that have continued to grow and improve seem to have done so in spite of rather than because of district activity.

It is clearly much harder to develop a good school district or a good state department of education, and to keep it good, than it is to do the same with a school. There are many excellent schools in poor districts. There are few if any districts "of any size or complexity," as David Kearns[6] has said, where excellence is the norm.

If the objective is to encourage and support the maximum feasible growth in quality in the greatest number of schools, most districts have barely begun to emerge from an approach to professional development that is wrong, an organizational structure that is wrong, and an approach to curriculum that is wrong. They are wrong because they assume these things should be designed and planned and organized by the district and then promulgated to and required of the schools. Even districts that have gone to great pains to promote partnerships between design and professional development providers such as Expeditionary Learning and their schools, will, without apology or notice, grab days in the school's calendar that are scheduled for work with us for "required" workshops downtown. "Even when we're the only game in town," one of our design-team colleagues said, talking about a district where they were working with all the schools, "they plan without us." Teachers are put off by the clumsy way in which they are invited to participate, and by the poor quality of the offerings, which together have given "professional development" a bad name.

There are districts that require all their middle schools to choose the same comprehensive design, though some of them want to work with one design, and some with another. The district's rationale is that with high student mobility in the district, no matter where the students go in the district they will encounter the same approach. That is an understandable rationale, but it is based on two misconceptions: that it is the district rather than the school that is the effective vehicle for bringing teaching and learning to students; and that nothing can be done about high student mobility. A school-centered strategy would have each school choose the design they think is best for that school, and help all the schools work to reduce student mobility. In our experience, student mobility goes down when schools get better. We have one excellent K-8 school partner in the heart of a large urban ghetto where there is such a strong connection between the school and the community that there is no student mobility out of the school at all. There is another, a very good middle school in the urban Northeast with the highest portion of free and reduced lunch-eligible students of any middle school in its district, that used to have the highest mobility rate and lowest levels of student learning. As the quality of student work and test scores went up over a five-year period, the mobility rate declined to the lowest among the city's middle schools. Families had moved their children out of the school to place them in private schools at the beginning of the five-year period. Five years later, there were no transfers out, but there were more transfers in from private schools than there had been transfers out before.

I get the sense in the field that the push to decentralize decision-making to the school level has lost steam. Here is a federal-state initiative that could use a second-stage rocket to give it a boost. Diane Ravitch has written that we do not need a school system, but a system of schools. It is important for the federal and state departments of education and local school districts to persist in their efforts to make individual schools the center of the reform enterprise, and to continue to take opportunities to move in the direction of support of schools and away from control of schools. As Diana Lam, the reform-minded superintendent of the Providence, Rhode Island schools says, "a central office should, first and foremost, have an orientation toward service. And if that orientation doesn't exist, then really, why is there a central office?"

BUILDING THE TEAM AND THE SCHOOL CULTURE

School leaders need the time and opportunity to build faculties that create and support the school's vision for change. Nothing is more important to the quality of a school than the quality and behavior of the people working and teaching there. "As we know," writes Roland Barth, "more than anything else it is the culture of the school that determines the achievement of teacher and student alike." All the leadership literature suggests that the first and most essential attribute of leadership is the ability to attract and retain good people and to get them working well together. In our network, the schools that have done best at this are the ones who have worked hardest on it, and who thought they *could* have some effect.

The states and districts vary in how much formal authority they allow individual schools in hiring teachers or letting them go. But whatever the formal constraints, successful school leadership teams manage to recruit and hire teachers they think will help improve the school and weed out those they think will not. In most districts, despite the hard work they entail, Expeditionary Learning schools tend to attract a fair number of applicants for every open position. It sounds different. The ideas attract. Many teachers are interested because they want to be in an environment where they will be allowed, encouraged, and prepared to teach in different and hopefully better ways. We attract principals and teachers who are prepared to make a dedicated effort to improve their teaching and the culture of their schools. I have noticed most good schools, and improving schools, Expeditionary Learning or not, attract such people.

When a school chooses a design such as Expeditionary Learning, teachers who do not want to make the effort needed, or to change their instructional practice, should be encouraged and helped to find situations elsewhere. We do not work with schools unless at least 80% of the faculty vote in favor of the partnership. But voting and doing are different things. There are almost always people who did not understand what they were voting for, did not understand how much work would be involved, did not understand they would be expected to make some changes themselves. How many people in the building are "on board" with the direction the school is taking is a constant concern and a regular topic of conversation between our field staff, who work directly with schools, and the building leadership. "There are three kinds of teachers," says one of our principals, "winners, whiners, and won'ts. The winners will go for it right away, push things forward. The whiners will complain, but you can bring them around. The won'ts you have to get to go someplace else."

"It's amazing how much you can get done when you get rid of the right people," another principal wrote. In her case, this involved making instructional expectations very clear, "calling it hard, early," doing the documentation, and following through. "No amount of informal hallway conversation would have gotten the job done," she said. Another principal neutralized the negative influence of an obstructive senior faculty member by changing his assignment to one that preserved his dignity and used his strengths but removed him from the team he was making dysfunctional. Developing and shaping the school team, the various school teams, putting the right people together, keeping certain people apart, is one of leadership's central and continuing tasks. Was it Casey Stengel who defined leadership as keeping those who hate you away from those who still have not made up their minds?

THE IMPORTANCE OF AUTONOMY

The more autonomous the school, in our experience, the more likely it is to implement and practice our design successfully and improve. The more the school has developed its own vision and culture, the more of its budget it is in charge of, the more it controls its schedule and its program of professional development, the better the prospects for its using our assistance well.

Autonomy comes naturally to charter schools; it is harder to achieve for regular public schools. In our network there are some regular public schools that have arrived at relative autonomy because of indifference or a laissez-faire approach to management at the district level, but they are few. Most often the school's freedom to develop according to its own lights has been bought with high or improving test scores and other indicators of effectiveness and progress. In general, the better the test scores, the more autonomy the school is allowed to have.

One urban middle school principal in our network is able, he says, to get the district to support "anything I want to do" as long as the vital signs for the school—attendance, disciplinary action, parent participation, test scores, the overall quality of student work—are good. Another says he uses the Expeditionary Learning framework as leverage in negotiating with the district concerning which of the district's "requirements" the school should and should not be responsible for. "We shouldn't have to meet this district requirement in the way you propose because we are dealing with the same issues through Expeditionary Learning," is his argument.

At least one district, on the other hand, has taken the position that it will not support an Expeditionary Learning partnership with one or more of their schools because they fear it would make them "too different" from the other schools in the district.

THE PRINCIPAL

"You rarely see a school get out very far ahead of its principal," says John Bennion, a school reform leader in Utah and a New American Schools adviser. He is right. The single best predictor of success Expeditionary

Learning has found in working with and helping a school improve is a good principal who understands and wants to use Expeditionary Learning, and stays at it for five years or more. In our experience, principals are the single most important group of leaders in the world of schooling. As someone said recently, "if in real estate the three main considerations are location, location, location, in school reform they are leadership, leadership, leadership."

Good principals are a precious resource. It is clear they are not always, or even usually, treated as though they were. Many of the principals and teachers who lead the change effort in our schools feel "jerked around" by the system. Sometimes they *are* jerked around. At least two of the best principals we have worked with, both making great progress implementing Expeditionary Learning and raising student achievement in their schools, were moved by their districts to other schools without consultation, one of them in the middle of the year. Another good principal in a very low-income school with very high rates of student mobility commented recently that she was "made to feel like a pariah" by her district when her school failed to show enough progress on the state standardized test two years in a row. These things would not happen in districts where schools were at the center and good principals were considered to be key.

The social architecture of the school has to be built by the people in the school, led usually by the principal. It takes time. Fortunately, principals tend to stay in their jobs two to three times longer than superintendents do. "No wonder superintendents don't last very long." one principal told me, "They have to be with adults all the time. We don't."

In Outward Bound the idea is to bring out the leader in everyone. Good Outward Bound instructors structure things so everyone in the group takes responsibility for moving the expedition forward and looking after the group's needs. "We are crew, not passengers." They rotate formal leadership assignments, and gradually turn over expedition responsibility to the students. In the leadership literature I have read, this is called "transformational" leadership, meaning that it motivates, engages, and changes people, and it helps them bridge the commitment gap. We expect principals and other formal school leaders in Expeditionary Learning schools to do the same thing with their faculties. As part of the professional development program we offer our partner schools, we take principals and teachers on Outward Bound courses in the wilderness and in the city to give them first-hand, put-your-body-on-the-line experiences with leadership transfer they do not easily forget. One of the chief lessons of such courses is "that you don't have to be or become a principal or a superintendent in order to influence the course of a vessel—or a school."[7]

These courses are always rich in metaphors relating the qualities and details of the physical, outdoor expedition to the world of schooling back home. This past winter I was on such a course, conducted by the Colorado Outward Bound School for Expeditionary Learning principals. We were camping and sea-kayaking in the Sea of Cortez, in Mexico. The weather was colder and the wind stronger and more persistent than we had bargained for. After the first cold night on a rocky beach, several in our group were uncomfortable and unhappy enough to want to go home. "My superintendent thinks I'm down here sipping Margaritas by the side of some pool. I wish he could see me now. I wish he were here and I was back where he is!" At the end of our week paddling and camping and working together, we were tired but glowing; we were all still together; we had persisted and helped each other through some hard and scary things and surprised ourselves with what we had done. We had started as strangers to one another and had become friends. We were a team. One of our number, Steven Levy, a fourth grade teacher from Lexington, Massachusetts, who had been working with us as a school designer, distilled some "Lessons From the Sea" for school leaders. They included:

1. Never be complacent: a lapse of attention, even for a moment, can have dire, or at least unpleasant consequences.

2. You have absolutely no control over the circumstances around you: all you can control is how you react. Plan carefully, read the signs, and adjust your course.

3. There is no such thing as standing still. If you are not active, you will drift off course.

4. To find your way, line up your short term plans with your long range goals.

5. Use your big muscles. Go with your strength.

6. But finesse over strength, whenever you can.

7. Some effort on the right turns you right. Some effort on the right turns you left. Know when to use your hands and when to use your feet.

The principal's job is demanding and complicated. It is time-intense and can be overwhelming. It requires an understanding of good instructional practice and the ability to manage money and people. It calls for diplomacy, negotiating skills, and resilience. We focus on improving instructional practice more than anything else in our work with schools. Many of the principals we work with are interested in instruction, but do not feel they can afford to put much time into it because of the other, often random demands on their time. "I relaxed a little when I realized the interruptions were the job," one principal told me. Another said, "This business of the principal as the instructional leader is just a lot of baloney unless you've got somebody there to take care of the things that'll trump instruction."

One way is to get someone else in there to take care of some of these things: discipline; relations with parents; purchasing; fundraising; the schedule. Another is to have an assistant principal for instruction. I have been conducting a personal, informal poll of principals and assistant principals, and I am surprised at how often there appears to be little explicit division of responsibility between them. "We both do everything" is the leading answer so far. This seems to be workable when the principal and assistant principal or assistant principals communicate regularly and trust each other. Some of the most thoughtful principals seem to be adjusting the distribution of responsibilities every year, seeking to find the right matches of talent and task. One principal of a four-year-old charter school said, when asked, that in the first couple of years he did everything. Then in the third year the school doubled in size, and the arrangements that had worked well in years one and two were now dysfunctional. His organizational response was, in hindsight, a disaster. "I had one person in charge of families and student discipline and another in charge of instruction. And that left me with all the little decisions I hate making and am not any good at." By the fourth year, though, he had found a configuration that allowed him to exercise his strengths as an instructional leader and to bring other teacher-leaders into that role with him.

The particular skills and the kind of leadership it takes to shape instructional practice while managing the other aspects of the work, according to our principals and other school leaders, is learned almost entirely though experience, on the job. "It's having a wide range of experiences, wearing a lot of different hats, that prepared me for this job," one principal told me, echoing the testimony of many others. "Mentors are very important; both positive and negative ones. And you need the opportunity to make mistakes." There are some good principal preparation and certification programs, and more of them now include some internships and fieldwork. But it is rare to hear preparatory coursework cited by any of our school leaders as a significant contributor to their understanding of their job or their capacity to carry it out.

There seem to be a fair number of leadership development programs, but almost all of them focus on new leaders. I think there is a greater need and opportunity for leadership development among those who are on the job *now*. Developing leaders internally is a job individual schools and districts ought to take on, as companies in the private sector do. I do not believe they have done so in any systematic way. We started our work with schools 10 years ago without specific components for leadership development, but soon learned we needed them. Today our own leadership development program for principals, assistant principals, and other teacher-leaders includes:

1. The above-mentioned Outward Bound courses

2. Week-long summer leadership institutes attended by 40 to 50 principals and instructional leaders each year from all over the country,

during which they each focus on one or two things they want to accomplish in the coming year and develop concrete action plans to fulfill them

3. Local school-level leadership institutes preceding the week-long all-faculty institutes we do with each school each summer

4. Regional meetings and other programming for Expeditionary Learning principals and building leaders

5. A national leadership institute for principals and other Expeditionary Learning school leaders that annually draws about 200 participants

6. Summits, or learning expeditions for teachers, in which teachers and principals spend a week as students immersed in experience with and study of geology, architecture, the human body, the physics of bicycles, poetry, children's books, and other subjects

7. Lots of on-site coaching

We have been working on improving and our expanding this dimension of our services to schools. We have become more explicit about the skills and competencies required of Expeditionary Learning principals and other school leaders. We are beginning to engage successful veteran Expeditionary Learning principals to mentor and coach new principals and principals new to Expeditionary Learning; we are doing more cluster programming for groups of principals and leadership teams in the same regions to build on existing support groups. We are also helping schools and districts recruit principals, gathering and analyzing data on our principals and instructional leaders, asking the more veteran Expeditionary Learning principals to play a part in advising and guiding Expeditionary Learning in its development; and in general paying more attention to them. I think most of our sister organizations are doing something similar. My friends from Success for All tell me that the best addition they have made to their program in the last year is a Leadership Academy for principals and assistant principals that focuses on data management and takes 10 full days the first year and 5 the second.

The 10-year history of our work with schools is to a large degree a story of accommodating ideals to realities. New American Schools' request for proposals 10 years ago invited us to imagine the best possible schools we could conceive. The Comprehensive School Reform movement today is concerned primarily with intervention in very low performing schools. When we began, the testing and accountability culture was not nearly so preeminent as it has become. We have had to adjust and tailor our offerings to the situations we have found ourselves in, and to the needs of our particular school-partners. Though it all, we have had a surprising amount of success. It has been due, I believe, to the strength and appeal of our ideals and an ability and willingness to be flexible in practice. And to tenacity. I keep coming back to my friend Herb Sturz's remark, "Tenacity is a kind of intelligence. Those who care the most, for the longest, win."

REFERENCES

Barth, R. (2001). *Learning by heart.* San Francisco: Jossey-Bass.

Bennis, W., & Nanus, B. (1985). *Leaders: The strategies for taking charge.* New York: HarperCollins.

Blanchard, K., & Bowles, S. (1998). *Gung ho!: Turn on the people in any organization.* New York: Morrow.

Hoachlander, G., Alt, M., & Beltranena, R. (2001). *Leading school improvement: What research says.* Berkeley: MPR Associates, Southern Regional Education Board.

Miner, J. L., & Boldt, J. (1981). *Outward Bound USA.* New York: Morrow.

Ylvisaker, P. (2000). The missing dimension. In E. Cousins (Ed.), *Roots: From Outward Bound to Expeditionary Learning.* Dubuque, IA: Kendall-Hunt.

NOTES

1. Herb Sturz is for me a guiding light in the work of school reform. Except in after-school education, his name is not much known in the world of education. He was the Founder and Director of the Vera Institute of Justice, Deputy Mayor and Chairman of the New York City Planning Commission, head of the Trotwood Corporation, an editorial writer for the *New York Times.* He is now a Trustee of the Open Society Institute and Chairman of the After School Corporation. Herb has been responsible for more significant and lasting improvements in public systems in New York, the United States, and abroad—criminal justice, welfare, housing, employment, and training, and now after-school education—than anyone I know.

2. Eleanor Duckworth is a Professor at the Harvard Graduate School of Education. One of Expeditonary Learning's design principles, "the having of wonderful ideas," is taken from her work.

3. Paul Ylvisaker was Dean of the Harvard Graduate School of Education from 1972 to 1982. When head of National Affairs at the Ford Foundation in 1965, he made a grant to United Progress, Inc, the nonprofit community action agency in Trenton, NJ, to develop an early prototype of Outward Bound as a school-within-a-school at Trenton's Central High School. In 1986, he invited Outward Bound into a partnership with the Harvard Graduate School of Education, which in turn gave inspiration and intellectual support to the development of Expeditionary Learning as a model for whole-school reform.

4. They were Joshua Miner, a science and math teacher and for many years Director of Admissions at Phillips Andover Academy, and Charles Froelicher, headmaster of Colorado Academy. Miner became the first President of Outward Bound USA and Froelicher was instrumental in starting the Colorado Outward Bound School, the first Outward Bound organization in the United States, in 1962.

5. Tom Jams is Vice-Dean of the New York University School of Education, and one of the main contributors to the conceptual base of Expeditionary Learning.

6. David Kearns, former CEO of Xerox and former Assistant Secretary of Education, is one of the founders of the New American Schools Development Corporation.

7. Roland Barth, in *Learning by Heart*. Barth is a former Principal and Founder of the Principal's Center at the Harvard Graduate School of Education.

CHAPTER THREE

The Modern Red SchoolHouse

Leadership in Comprehensive School Reform Initiatives

SALLY B. KILGORE AND JAMES D. JONES

The Modern Red SchoolHouse (MRSH) is a comprehensive design for school reform that helps teachers and building administrators establish classroom and school practices to improve student mastery of high academic standards. It purports to be "modern" in its pedagogy—relying on recent developments in cognitive science to inform best practices, yet traditional in its commitment to student mastery of traditional academic subjects. The design sets expectations for parent and community support that hark back to the legends of the little red schoolhouse, yet the design encourages schools to rely upon modern technology to foster that support.

Development of the Modern Red design began in 1992 when the Hudson Institute was awarded a contract from the New American Schools Development Corporation (now New American Schools) to design and pilot a comprehensive design for 21st century schools. Practitioners from six school districts in Arizona, Indiana, New York, and North Carolina collaborated with Hudson Institute researchers to develop a design for schools that would enable all, rather than some, students to master high academic standards. The original design rested on the fundamental premise that realizing high academic standards for all students required school and classroom practices that allow students different paths (in time

Figure 3.1   Distribution of Implementation Training Days by Module

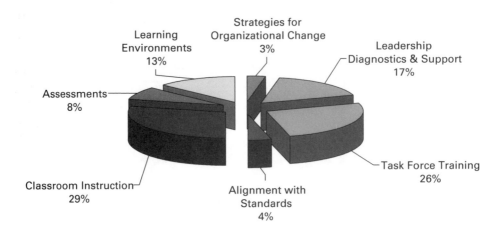

and instructional experiences) to reach the same standards (Kilgore & Pendleton, 1993).

Implementing the Modern Red design generally requires three to five years of intense technical support. As do the students they serve, schools are understood to have different needs when they begin implementing the Modern Red design—not only in terms of leadership and organization, but also in terms of technology, instruction, and community and family partnerships. Technical support for implementing the design, then, is customized to meet those needs. The more general objective, that is, inclusive of all those components of the design, is to help schools develop and continually adapt an effective instructional program that supports student mastery of high academic standards. For the leadership component, the ultimate objective is to build a school staff's capacity to reflect upon the effectiveness of its instructional programs and to make appropriate adjustments in school practices—that is, to have the capacity for continuous improvement.

Figure 3.1 shows the type of training and the typical distribution of effort for each type of professional development activity at MRSH sites. Generally, members of MRSH's technical assistance team are on-site 20 to 30 days per year primarily working with teachers in small groups. Organizational and leadership training constitutes about a third of the overall effort.

Adapting to student needs has implications for school leadership and organization: First and foremost, it requires some level of autonomy from district and state mandates—which we refer to as site-based decision-making. Evidence from research in cognitive psychology regarding effective instruction (Bransford, Brown, & Cocking, 1999) as well as evidence from organizational literature (Darling-Hammond, 1990; Deming & Walton, 1988;

Hall, 1982; Senge, 1990) would suggest that many decisions are better made (both in terms of efficiency and quality) at a school site than as a district-wide policy. Every school is situated in a unique environment with varying types of resources (community service agencies, business partners, and volunteer profiles). To mandate, then, that all schools will hire, say, a school psychologist may create redundancies in some schools but not others—redundancies will occur in this instance where a school is serviced by a community psychologist from an agency residing in their office building or neighborhood. Thus, the design developers seek to find ways that schools can exercise some meaningful control over staffing, the organization of the school day, the design of instruction, and the acquisition of materials and equipment.

Separate from site-based decision-making is the issue of participative management, that is, involving some or all of the staff in the decision-making process. The effects of participative management on the quality of decisions are unclear (Chapman & Boyd, 1986; Chrispeels, 1992; Friedkin & Slater, 1994; Murphy & Beck, 1995; Rosenholtz, 1985; Weiss & Cambone, 1994) and the effect on student achievement mixed (Leithwood & Menzies, 1998; Robertson & Briggs, 1998), but its effect on the implementation of decisions is clear. Research on school reform (McLaughlin, 1987; Rosenholtz, 1985; Sebring & Bryk, 2000) as well as organizational studies (Coch & French, 1948; Drucker, 1986; March & Simon, 1958; Pfeffer, 1997) are consistent: Participative management—even of limited scope—increases the likelihood that decisions will be implemented and appropriate changes occur.

Urban school districts, under pressure for quick change, are most likely to have leaders who rely heavily on top-down decision-making strategies. Yet, research on urban school reform is littered with instances where principals sought to buffer teachers from new expectations or where teachers found ways to close their doors and maintain their practices. School staff reason, often quite sensibly, that the pressure for change will disappear as leadership changes. At best, staff can (and likely should) mold a new mandate to create the least disturbance to existing practice (McLaughlin, 1987).

The inability of leaders to convert mandates or new policies into action, MRSH developers claim, is a critical barrier in most efforts to change practices in public schooling. For action to occur, those implementing the decision must own it. As Drucker (1986) explains, "it requires that any decision become "our decision" to the people who have to convert it into action. This in turn means that they have to participate responsibly in making it" (p. 365). If people are able to evaluate alternatives in terms of how it will improve the quality and efficiency of their work, it is likely that the decision will be better than one devised in isolation by a manager.

More generally, then, the Modern Red design calls for changes from a bureaucratically organized school to one based on participative management. A change from top-down to participative decision-making decreases formalization (or written rules and procedures) to allow more flexibility, increased communication among all personnel, greater professionalism among teachers, and improved collaboration and cross-training (or a decrease in specialization).

These organizational changes constitute a radical departure from the way schools traditionally have been structured. Dan Lortie in his study of *The Schoolteacher* (1975) vividly describes a teacher's role in the traditional school and classroom. Schools were characterized as egg crates with teachers instructing their students in isolation from other classrooms and principals making decisions with no input from teachers. Teachers were portrayed as focusing on the pursuit of the intrinsic rewards of teaching the children assigned them and buffering themselves from the demands and expectations of a bureaucratic organization. The MRSH design seeks to break down the egg crate structure and help teachers create greater coherence and transparency of instruction within and across grades (and subjects). Through the use of participative management, principals will engage in more consultation. Creating a culture that nurtures collegial review builds the capacity for educators to devise their own strategies for continuous improvement.

DEVELOPING A STRATEGY FOR IMPLEMENTING MRSH LEADERSHIP COMPONENT

Having set these principles for school leadership and organization, the tough questions begin: How does one help leaders implement change in practices? The scope of autonomy varies across districts. Even in instances where district superintendents are committed to site-based decision-making, barriers remain. Tradition and habit often drive the actions of central office staff; the new responsibilities create risks that principals may want to avoid; and many state laws set tight boundaries on the range of autonomy schools can exercise. MRSH developers generally work within the scope of autonomy accorded schools and help principals identify whatever site-based authority exists. Even in highly bureaucratized school districts, some meaningful measure of control over the school practices can be achieved by astute manipulation of a district's policies (as in staffing) or by direct requests for a specific change in practice (such as bus schedules). For participative management, on the other hand, the developers impose some minimum consultative role for a leadership team and task forces regardless of the principal's current practice. Given that principals do vary in their leadership styles and dispositions, the model developers allow for considerable variation across sites in the level of influence and control given to teachers.

In addition to site decision-making and participative management, MRSH developers seek to address the principal's role as an instructional leader. Elmore (2000) defines the responsibilities of an administrative leader as: "enhancing the skills and knowledge of people in the organization, creating a common culture of expectations about the use of those skills and knowledge, and holding people accountable for their contributions to the collective results" (p. 15).

What remains unclear is the degree to which these responsibilities can be delegated. Do principals, for instance, only need to ensure that the structure and resources needed to enhance skills and knowledge are present, or do they need to engage personally in enhancing that knowledge? Friedkin and Slater (1994), for instance, find that the degree to which teachers seek advice from their principal affects school performance, whereas teacher-to-teacher advice-giving shows no independent effect on school performance. Thus, the research suggests that not all aspects of instructional leadership can be delegated; rather, the principal needs some personal involvement. Moreover, accountability systems, of most any sort, place "the buck stops here" signs on the principal's desk by requiring some direct engagement with those outcomes that directly affect their success.

On the other hand, Stinchcombe's (1965) more general analysis of organizations would suggest that there are multiple ways to meet certain essential organizational functions. And clearly, good leaders do hire staff that compensate for their weaknesses, so why could principals not do that for instructional leadership? In urban areas, people qualified to hold principalships often lack the training and preparation to assume every responsibility associated with instructional leadership. More often, they deliver the resources and create the culture needed for teachers to provide powerful instruction. Certainly, state and district policies during the past 50 years have removed considerable amounts of authority from principals—in staffing and instruction—so it should be no surprise to find many administrators selected for their abilities in other areas, such as facilities management.

MRSH developers choose to find ways that the function is assumed by someone, whether by the principal or others. Experience suggests, though, that principals must convey personally the importance they attach to the quality of instruction by attending training and curriculum work sessions, using faculty meetings to discuss instructional issues, and finding ways to recognize success stories in student learning.

The use of task forces is a critical instrument for acquiring commitment and cultivating energy among MRSH faculty. Teachers often claim that their long-term commitment to the Modern Red design began with their experience on a task force. Similarly, that structure allows schools to recruit politically significant people in their neighborhoods—people from social or medical services, small businessmen, and area school board members. These community representatives can become not only active committee members but also ardent advocates of the school and its chosen design in the often turbulent environment of urban schools. Not surprisingly, the role and effectiveness of these task forces has proven to be dependent on the support and direction of the principal and other significant administrators (Hallinger, Murphy, & Hausman, 1992). They are, however, central to effective implementation of the design.

That said, the particular skills and knowledge needed by school staff were not fully appreciated until the pilot phase of MRSH began in 1993. For instance, events at a weekend retreat for teachers at an elementary pilot site forced the developers to give much greater attention to the skills required for managing meetings. One of the MRSH interns attended the retreat and reported on what happened. Anticipating numerous materials from MRSH, teachers spent several hours deciding *where* the materials would be located and, after due deliberation, selected a room in the basement. Then, another two hours were devoted to whether or not the room that held these materials would be locked or unlocked. Finally, after deciding that the room would be locked, another hour or so was spent deciding who would keep the key to this room with materials.

The MRSH developers realized that a few more meetings like that would place the participative decision-making process at great risk. It was, in fact, meetings such as this one that had rightfully reduced teachers' desire to participate. Helping team leaders to become more skilled in managing meetings, as well as conflict, became essential parts of MRSH training. With greater investment in building leadership skills, greater direction on organizational structure emerged. Teams are expected to use staggered terms of membership to ensure continuity and promote mentoring. And, with little effect, contracts with districts specified the developers' expectation that principals at implementing sites should remain at the school for at least three years.

COACHING AND TRAINING
SUPPORT FOR MRSH LEADERSHIP COMPONENT

During the first year of implementation, the technical assistance designed to support and develop school leadership specifically includes strategies for organizational change, diagnostics and coaching, and task force training.

Strategies for Organizational Change

School staff learn to anticipate the peaks and valleys of enthusiasm and frustration they will encounter as they adopt new practices and technologies. Teachers identify strategies they can use to help themselves and others through those periods of frustration.

Given that teachers are expected to work more intimately and routinely with their colleagues, the school staff also learn about the strengths and needs of different personality types. With the use of the Myers-Briggs Temperament Indicator (MBTI), teachers acquire ways of understanding their own behavior and that of others—giving them a shared vocabulary for understanding differences and fostering effective strategies for dealing with them. Principals use the MBTI data to form task forces—enhancing the likelihood that a balance of various talents exists within each group.

Leadership Diagnostics and Support

Before beginning any work at a school, the MRSH team conducts a diagnostic visit to profile student achievement and existing practices at the school. Teacher and administrator interviews, classroom visits, and a building walk-through provide data for the MRSH team to develop a plan of work for the first year that not only advances implementation of the design but also addresses pressing needs—most often in one or more areas of student achievement.

For the implementation phase, each principal is assigned a mentor who is also responsible for the training and support of the school's leadership team. The content of the principal mentoring varies, depending on the experience, skill, and disposition of the administrator. For novices, it may focus initially on the fundamentals of setting expectations for teachers and students. More sophisticated and experienced principals may begin with efforts to refine skills in monitoring standards-driven classrooms and managing the larger environment. In all cases, though, coaches or mentors work with principals to establish and orient the leadership team and task forces—seeking to ensure that the membership is inclusive of various social and structural networks among teachers and balances the skills and talents within each task force. It is not uncommon for the mentor to become a confidante to the principal, providing a safe venue to express frustrations, confess weaknesses, and develop strategies to remedy both.

As with principal mentoring, leadership team training is customized to match the level of sophistication and experience of team members. Topics may include conflict resolution, development of task force agendas, communication plans, decision-making procedures, problem-solving strategies, and development of coalitions to support change. A critical component of this training is to establish consensus on the respective roles and responsibilities of the team and principal and to ensure a shared understanding of the sphere of influence accorded to the leadership team. State and district policies, as well as the dispositions of principals, influence variation in the shape and form of the leadership team.

Task Force Training

Some or all members of the leadership team serve as chairpersons of task forces. Although the Modern Red design proposes six task forces (standards and assessment, curriculum, technology, community involvement, organization and finance, and professional development), schools are allowed to vary the number (combining or adding) as long as all essential functions are covered. During the first two years of implementation, task forces are provided extensive assistance in developing a plan of action that supports student learning. Technical assistance, again, is customized and can be both procedural and substantive.

Embedded in the work of the task forces are core elements of the design. General goals are shared across task forces in a given school at each stage of implementation—supporting teachers as they design instruction, for instance, the school organization task force should evaluate ways to increase common planning time for teachers, while the technology task force should identify ways for all teacher teams to have the hardware, software, and skills for designing instructional units. However, specific activities at each site are only partially shared with other sites. For instance, curriculum and parent involvement task forces almost always work together to establish routine practices that allow parents to support student learning and community members to support teachers' work in designing instruction. Beyond that, participating sites develop different approaches to community and parent involvement that reflect the needs of students and the resources of communities they serve. MRSH provides assistance in identifying those diverse factors, developing a comprehensive plan of involvement that reflects the interest and skills of parents, and tailoring strategies to address the students' academic needs. Community volunteers support the instructional program, help establish a consortium for early childhood education or social service support, and mentor students.

IMPLEMENTING THE MRSH DESIGN FOR SCHOOL LEADERSHIP: A CASE STUDY

In the summer of 1998, when MRSH's strategy for developing leadership at implementing sites was well established, work began with three elementary schools in a midsized urban school district in the southern part of the United States. During the second and third years of MRSH implementation, one of the authors of this chapter agreed to pursue an independent case study of the three sites.

The three schools are among many in the district with low achievement records although they varied in their district ranking when they began implementation. Nearly all of the students in each of the schools are African American, and those eligible for a free or reduced lunch range from 71% to 97%. One school is located in a fairly stable working to lower middle-class neighborhood and began implementation in the lowest quartile of the district in terms of student performance. Another school is in a neighborhood changing from an established middle-class neighborhood to a more working-class neighborhood and was positioned above the district average in student performance. Finally, the third is located in an area populated by lower income residents with substandard housing. Student mobility is high, and achievement is one of the lowest in the district. Taken collectively, students at these Modern Red schools completed the second year of implementation showing greater achievement gains than students at other schools within the district who were either implementing another CSR model or not implementing any CSR model.

Throughout the period of study, district leadership remained stable. Schools had fairly broad discretion in designing instruction, hiring staff, and allocating material resources. In the third year, however, the district mandated eight-week testing cycles in reading and math. Neither the district nor the state had any policies regarding participative management.

During the third year of implementation (2000–2001), interviews were conducted with the principals, assistant principals, or their equivalents in each school. In addition, the MRSH facilitator, members of the leadership team (and therefore task force leaders), the curriculum leader for each grade, and parents in each school were interviewed. Leadership team, task force, and faculty meetings were observed at each school. If the organization and leadership elements of the Modern Red design had been adopted, one should find credible evidence at these meetings. Finally, to obtain a more complete picture of leadership at the three schools, key district level administrators were interviewed for their perceptions on how MRSH was working, the nature of the relationship between the central district administration and the Modern Red schools, the administration of the schools, and the comparative characteristics of teachers and students at each school.

Leadership and Implementation in School A

Over the course of two years, the principal of School A institutionalized many aspects of participative management. For example, the leadership team, not the principal, exercised control over hiring teachers or other staff members. The principal usually assisted in making interview arrangements, as well as obtaining and organizing credentials, but the choice was made by the members of the team. While this principal may have had considerable informal influence in hiring decisions, it was not evident in meetings or interviews.

Budget information was distributed to all leadership team members in its first meeting of the year, including the amount and sources of revenue and projected expenses—mostly curricular in nature. All members of the team were invited to make recommendations on how to use revenue yet to be allocated—not a trivial amount.

A teacher conducted School A's leadership team meetings and, from the evidence available, it appeared that the agenda was generated by that teacher-chairperson. Members of the leadership team, however, frequently asked the principal questions about the procedures and substantive issues.

Interviews with the task force leaders suggested that they did seek a lot of guidance from the principal, but the teacher-chairperson set the agenda for their meetings. Task force leaders thought that their teams' recommendations were consistently honored by the leadership team and principal. We probed the principal several times about the scope of authority and decision-making she had delegated to her teachers. Her response was consistent: "No problem." In describing how her role had changed, the principal noted: "In the past my work was done when I announced a decision. Now, when the leadership team makes a decision, my work has just begun."

The principal's commitment to participative management was also evident at faculty meetings. Although these meetings are conducted by the principal, much of the agenda consisted of progress reports from the various task forces. At the meetings observed, fellow teachers prodded each other to do more or supply a task force with additional information or data. Team leaders were the ones pushing their colleagues to do their part, not the principal.

The principal consistently used meetings to express her confidence in the staff's ability to solve problems. Having established the leadership team without defining staggered terms, for instance, the team confronted the problem of how to transmit their wisdom and routines to an entirely new collection of members. One initial proposal was to have the principal orient the new members. Tempting as that role might be for many principals, this principal refocused the group on their ability to solve the problem. And, indeed, they did, choosing to extend their terms and mentor new members for one year.

School A was the first to obtain much of the computer equipment and related software stipulated by MRSH. All of the lesson plans they had developed were online and available to all teachers. Coupled with this transparency in instructional plans was an increase in the communication among teachers across grade levels. Teachers became more focused on the critical foundations that their students needed to succeed in subsequent grades. Fostering the knowledge of substance and skills taught in adjacent grades was also facilitated by looping,[1] a practice of one teacher maintaining the same class of students for two or more years. Adopted by only some[2] teachers at this school, looping, as reported by teachers, is similar to what other organizations call cross-training. It increases flexibility in a previously bureaucratically structured organization. Indeed, when someone was hired for a teaching position in this school, that person agreed to teach wherever he or she might be needed. The school, then, could react and adjust quickly to changes in enrollment or attendance boundaries with little compromise to the quality of instruction. Organizational continuity was also enhanced.

The principal, teachers, and aides all collaborated to increase the effectiveness of their teaching efforts. Each grade level shared a scope and sequence for the year's work that had been developed by the staff. The collaboration and planning necessary to execute such instructional units effectively were most evident in the materials sent to parents before new units were launched: Parents were informed of the standards to be addressed in the upcoming unit, the activities planned for that unit, when specific materials would be needed by students, and suggested activities for parents to complete at home to reinforce what students would be learning. Teachers at most grade levels, then, demonstrated a level of professionalism found among highly educated and skilled employees engaged in complex tasks; that is, they were productive without constant monitoring and supervision.

Finally, the principal in School A directed much of her energy in developing relationships within the environment of the school, that is, the school district and the larger community. These relations allowed her to learn about resources that were available to schools, but not well-publicized. On one day, devoted to celebrating the pleasures of reading, the principal recruited more than 40 people to read in various classrooms. At least five were from the central office and many others were corporate and civic leaders. The principal greeted each reader at the school entrance, handing them the book she had personally selected for them and hanging name tags, customized for the occasion, around their shoulders. On this and other occasions, the principal provided suggestions to community and district leaders on the roles they could assume in School A. Her queries to these leaders also gave her information about potential resources available to schools in the district.

The principal also guided teachers in writing proposals to local organizations to fund various class activities. As a result of these relationships and the efforts of teachers, contributions of time, money, and materials were evident everywhere. Clearly, this school leader understood the potential benefits of creating strong external relations and the good will of the community.

Participative management and implementation of the Modern Red design were well underway in this school. The teachers on the leadership team had taken the reins of leadership, albeit tentatively at times, and were anxious to have other teachers get involved in leadership positions.

Leadership and Implementation in School B

Before the MRSH partnership, several principals at School B had left abruptly with innuendos of financial mismanagement. Teachers were embarrassed by the public attention and skeptical that the new principal—having joined them only months earlier—would remain long enough to achieve any improvement. The turnover rate of teachers was high and their attendance and attention to instruction, spotty. After some deliberation and with some doubts remaining, the faculty selected the Modern Red design. Although the principal had favored the design, she was anxious to acquire meaningful commitment from her faculty.

Two years later, the principal's office is draped and cluttered with MRSH signs, handbooks, and other MRSH materials. While her demonstrated commitment is high, indicators of participative management are not as apparent in this school as in School A. The principal insisted that authority was distributed throughout the school much differently than before MRSH and that she was comfortable in delegating many decisions. It was a burden she was willing to share. At this school the MRSH facilitator, who also served as the assistant principal, was more visible, more active in steering and monitoring the Modern Red design than her counterparts at the other schools.

Other school leaders—such as task force chairs—gave evidence that they were clearly making decisions on their own. The task forces were operational and doing their work. Issues were often given to them by the principal or leadership team for them to make recommendations to the leadership team for resolution. Thus, teachers were participating in the management of the school. But limits to that engagement were also evident—such as a full review of the school's budget.

The leadership team—whose membership changed some each year—was consulted about hiring decisions, but was not at liberty to make the final decision. With respect to the school budget, teachers were invited to recommend ways to spend money over which the school has discretion and occasionally made the final decisions about their use. No evidence, however, suggested that the complete school budget was shared with the teachers. Most teachers, though, thought that the principal spent school funds wisely.

In other areas, such as scheduling, teachers at the grade level made the decisions—an alternative never considered by the MRSH developers. When the school began implementation of Modern Red, teachers had ample planning time set aside by the principal, but now, a couple of years later, teachers schedule common planning time with their grade-level colleagues. Having allowed grade-level teams to determine when they would have grade-level planning has led some grade levels to schedule no meetings—in particular, the one grade level taught exclusively by persons opposed to the design rarely, if ever, convene meetings.

Unlike School A, where teachers routinely set expectations for each other, seek professional advice from one another, and freely participate in enforcing deadlines and norms, School B teachers—even those serving as task force leaders—were often (but not always) hesitant to set expectations. While at least one task force set expectations and goals for the staff, most did not. "Teachers are not used to telling each other what to do," said the assistant principal, "and it is hard to get them to do what needs doing to fully implement Modern Red." Both the leadership team and the school administrators, it seems, opted to avoid confrontation with those not meeting expectations.

Most teachers were enthusiastic about implementing—showing evidence of the collaboration expected within and across grades. In fact,

School B had some of the most fervent supporters of the design in the city. On the other hand, several teachers were equally fervent dissenters. Unfortunately, this resistance was housed almost exclusively in one grade—where teachers would not participate on task forces or align the curriculum with Modern Red or state standards. (Thus, students at School B spend their initial years with teachers implementing the Modern Red design, but then they miss a year or so before returning to Modern Red classrooms.) Teachers who were task force leaders would attempt to persuade the recalcitrant teachers by stating in faculty meetings that the curriculum work was not yet completed (despite the approaching due date) and making a general appeal to all faculty to provide copies of their instructional units. The nonparticipants remained so.

The principal was reluctant to intervene in this situation. She regarded (incorrectly) the design of instruction as the province of teachers as stipulated by the design, and thus she viewed setting expectations about it as outside her scope of authority. In the absence of her active support, though, the teachers had neither carrot nor stick to encourage participation.

Committed teachers moved ahead quickly with collaborative curricular alignment and development, and left their "not on board" peers seriously behind. Committed teachers were also the ones that used the computers in their classroom for designing instruction and benefit from sharing it. Yet, the resistors were frequently part of their conversation. Even with these challenges, School B completed their second year of implementation showing the greatest achievement gains of the three Modern Red schools in the city.

The School B principal leaves the cultivation of community support exclusively to the community involvement task force. Most of their school partners are neighborhood churches whose members support the school with their time—in mentoring and tutoring—but are not viewed as sources of other resources. The principal at School B perceived the district office as an external agency with very few resources. Administrators and teachers at School B viewed themselves as constrained by district policy and the district staff as unable to help the school achieve its objectives.

Overall, School B has critical elements of the participative management structure envisioned by the Modern Red design. Consistency in how and when teachers participate is lacking, and many teacher-leaders remain hesitant to set expectations for their colleagues. At the same time, the principal's decision to delegate many instructional leadership decisions to grade-level and task force team members has led to a stalemate with resistant teachers.

Leadership and Implementation in School C

Entering School C, one was hard-pressed to recognize the existing partnership that implementation of the Modern Red design was underway.

No signs or displays revealed the MRSH affiliation; very little of students' work was displayed in the halls, and standards—whether of the state or MRSH—were not posted in classrooms. In fact, marks of comprehensive school reform were entirely lacking.

The area from which this school drew students was somewhat different from either of the other two schools. All of the students were eligible for a free or reduced cost lunch in contrast to the other two schools where between 70% and 94% were eligible. Student mobility was high, perhaps because the neighborhood was a high crime and low-income area of the city. Historically, this school had not had the resources available to it that were evident at the other two schools. The physical circumstances of this school were also very unlike the other two schools. Several portable classrooms (trailers) were adjacent to the permanent school building. While lacking much external appeal, these portables were clean and looked similar to any other classroom on the inside with the temperature being comfortable inside regardless of the weather outside. Finally, this school lacked an auditorium for assemblies and special occasions. The cafeteria was sometimes used, but all the students could not fit into it at the same time. Consequently, when a local dignitary visited the school, students and teachers assembled outdoors—assuming the weather was pleasant, which it often was.

Generally, teachers in this school seemed less aware of all the changes that would be required for full implementation of the Modern Red design. They were aware of the basic structural outlines of MRSH but the understanding, insight, and benefits that might accrue to students, teachers, and administrators was not as appreciated here as in the other two schools. Interviews with teachers at this school revealed some teacher opposition to MRSH that varied from being explicitly to more subtly expressed. A few were not yet convinced that every child is capable of learning and instead were more concerned about gifted students in their midst. Others, especially new teachers, were very surprised to find out how eager their students were to learn (this contradicted their stereotypes) and were somewhat more favorable to implementing Modern Red thoroughly.

Operations at School C were fairly bureaucratic. For instance, the principal had developed and distributed rules and procedures for the faculty in booklet form with the MRSH logo on the cover. The principal conducted faculty meetings, which focused on announcements and instructions. The principal entertained questions but generally devoted most of the time to reading memos from the central office. Teachers did not seek clarification of those announcements, nor were initiatives by teachers apparent.

The principal also conducted the leadership team meetings in a similar fashion, i.e., with announcements and notices. Most of the task force leaders also made reports on projects on which they were working. All seemed to undertake their tasks competently with the exception of one—the curriculum task force. They had postponed their work to those days scheduled for professional development at the end of the school year. The principal did not share the budget with this team nor gave them a voice in how discretionary funds might be used.

Evidence suggested that this principal understood her instructional leadership responsibilities as one of resource acquisition and resisted encouragement to visit classes in the school or to set expectations for staff. Over the course of two years, she acquired classroom tables that allowed for small-group discussions and computers for every classroom. When teachers expressed frustration with designing instruction, she purchased instructional units for teachers to use. On the other hand, in the third year of implementation, when the district first began providing classroom-level data on student performance to principals, she was observed counseling a low-performing teacher by comparing her classroom scores with those teachers known to be successful implementers of MRSH strategies—a clear case of communicating some expectations to teachers.

The principal at School C maintained weak to hostile relations with a number of central office staff. For her, advocacy was exercised by sending protest letters to one or more members of the office staff—challenging decisions or making demands. No evidence of community volunteers or corporate sponsors was apparent.

Collegiality was evident in some grades and its benefits were valued by those teachers. Where this collegiality was developing, teachers were beginning to think for themselves and creating strategies for collaboration with other teachers. While this collegiality was isolated, it could lead some to experience the stirrings of professionalism.

Implementation of Modern Red came to a halt in the third year and was reinstated for a fourth year (2001–2002). With the district's introduction of eight-week assessments, the principal and the teachers narrowed their focus to student performance on these assessments. Accreditation and, perhaps, their jobs, were at risk if their scores did not improve that year. The principal purchased texts with fairly scripted instructional units and put them in place for language arts and math instruction. These curricula were deemed as especially useful for the population of students in attendance at the school; they also were seen as a means of structuring instruction. New teachers were especially appreciative of these curricula as they provided a blueprint of what to do every step of the way. But the principal also thought the texts would help overcome the resistance to change that was apparent among the older teachers. Student achievement in these teachers' classes was significantly lower than that of other students in the same grade in other classrooms.

In sum, School C's implementation of the Modern Red design has been marginal, with some incremental movement toward a more participative management structure. Authority is still largely exercised by the principal's issuing rules and procedures, a practice that fosters a formal set of relationships between the principal and the teachers. This style of leadership likely explains the lukewarm enthusiasm exhibited by teachers for the design's governance strategy.

Finally, the evidence shows that the principal at School C was not indifferent to student performance, but rather her strategies for exercising political and instructional leadership were not sufficient to transform instructional outcomes and student performance. The prospects for full implementation of the Modern Red design were dim. An officer elsewhere in the district noted that the teachers in School C were not as well-prepared as the teachers in the other two schools. Still, the situation was not totally hopeless. Progress was being made, and some changes in the structure of the district administration may be significant for this school, which had had several disadvantages compared to Schools A and B. These district changes are discussed below.

District Support

The importance of central administration support for successful implementation of New American Schools' comprehensive school reform designs has been noted by others (Berends, Kirby, Naftel, & McKelvey, 2001). School leadership affects and is affected by district support. The principals in Schools B and C both indicated that district support had let them down at critical junctures and in significant ways. The district delayed purchasing—and in some instances, failed to purchase—the necessary hardware and software to support the Modern Red design. One central district administrator confessed that the district had not delivered as needed and expected, and that this had some unfortunate consequences, especially for School C. The district was a year late with this equipment and this stymied curricular development to some extent in these two schools. (It is also true, however, that the principal at School C had initiated requests for this equipment in ways that angered members of the central office staff.)

A second shortcoming in central district support concerned the administrative liaison to the Modern Red schools. The quality of her relationship with principals varied. And, by the third year, no central office administrator had liaison responsibilities. Our interviews with central district administrators revealed an absence of solid familiarity with the Modern Red design, despite the fact that they felt MRSH was a central item on the agenda of the district and had shown the strongest achievement gains of any design in the district.

The district gave Modern Red schools considerable discretion in pursuing implementation of the design. This "hands-off" approach, however, extended into the expectations they set for principals as well as the structure for moving teachers who do not wish to implement a design to a school more congruent with their approach.

During the third year of implementation, the district organized all the schools in the district by feeder patterns into its high schools. In each feeder pattern, an experienced elementary school principal was designated as the executive principal who will work with all other elementary school principals in the feeder pattern. Although this arrangement may provide a better structural connection between the Modern Red schools and the central district administration than existed before, its effect on Modern Red implementation remains unclear.

CONCLUSION

As these cases suggest, the degree to which schools acquire participative management practices varies even when a strategy and technical support are available. In the cases shown here, the MRSH contribution varied from providing a structure and strategy for an able and flexible leader to ramp up the leadership skills of her talented but docile staff and to transfer considerable authority to them (School A); to providing an earnest and dedicated leader with a concept of participative management that was adapted, somewhat incongruously, to match her disposition and the level of professionalism at her school (School B); to adding another forum for maintaining a leadership structure focused on procedural compliance (School C).

Given the degree to which principals varied in their adoption of participative management, one must return to the now tiresome question: Can participative management work in schools?

Drucker's (1986) work suggests why early attempts at participative management often failed. For Drucker, participative management requires managers to define the problem, set objectives, and spell out the rules. Early trials of participative management in schools often lacked such boundaries (Weiss, 1994). With the introduction of state accountability systems, district and school leaders focused on student learning, especially in urban systems. Defining the problem and objectives, then, became easier.

Although these changing conditions can explain the greater viability of participative management in the 1990s compared to prior decades, it cannot fully explain the variation across schools in this case study. Student achievement was understood to be "the problem"; yet, the specific objectives were hard to establish when diagnostic data from state assessments were largely absent in the first two years of implementation. The district's introduction of eight-week assessments in the third year of implementation did provide data that prompted the principal at School C to confer with individual teachers. While the principal might argue that the district had failed to provide needed tools in a timely fashion, it is also the case that the district failed to place any accountability on the principal for meeting achievement objectives until the end of the third year.

Other explanations can be considered, however, by assessing contextual differences, especially at Schools A and B. School A began its implementation of the design with the fundamentals of professionalism already in place. At School B, the principal's need to strictly follow norms regarding attendance, supervision, and instruction may have sent conflicting messages to her staff. Smylie (1992) finds that teachers are more willing to participate in decision-making if "they perceive their relationship with the principal to be open, collaborative, facilitative, and supportive." Some strategies for enforcing professional norms may compromise such a relationship. On the other hand, the principal at School B may have limited participative management because she lacked confidence in her staff.

Limited evidence suggests also that the leadership team at School B drew disproportionately from some social groupings in the school. Yet, sociological research (Coleman, 1957; Laumann, 1987) would suggest that divisions among staff (by age, race, or gender) should not be reinforced by the composition of various teams—be they leadership, task forces, or grade-level teams. Instead, school teams should be organized in ways that develop cross-cutting ties across whatever social cleavages exist in the school. It can mean the difference between a school where the ownership of reform is broadly shared and one that has intense support among a more limited subset of teachers.

The case studies provided here obscure one of the greatest challenges to school improvement in urban areas: the constant churning of personnel (Hess, 1999) in leadership positions—at the school as well as at the district level. It is not uncommon for principals at implementing sites to leave because the district needed the principal's solid leadership elsewhere to turn around a disaster at another school, because the principal decided to retire, because the principal's frequent reprimands had raised the ire of the teachers' association, or because the principal was clearly inept. In each instance, implementation of the design was compromised—in some instances it was impossible to proceed. For low-performing schools, MRSH loses a third of the principals during a three-year implementation period. Urban school superintendents have a similarly fragile tenure, and that change generally has an even greater impact than shifts in principals as everyone takes stock of the new superintendent's commitment to and understanding of comprehensive school reform. Such changes in leadership seldom, if ever, enhance the level of implementation, and always slow its pace.

Since the work in this southern city, MRSH developers have become more direct in their expectations for principals, especially in the area of instructional leadership. For as this case study suggests, its absence is far more consequential than variations in participative management structure. MRSH developers have sought, however, to increase the efficacy of participative management in a variety of school contexts by giving greater emphasis on producing small wins and analyzing student data. Weick (1984) emphasizes the importance of identifying "small wins" for organizations engaged in substantial change to their culture and structure. Applying this concept to the participative management in schools, we encourage all principals (not just those positively disposed) to identify some decisions that can be entirely delegated to task forces or the leadership team (i.e., he or she could "live with the decision"). In this instance "small wins" not only allow staff to identify increments of progress, but, equally important, we think, help establish the efficacy of participative management for both teachers and administrators.

Given the increasing number of states requiring advisory councils or leadership teams for every school, allowing principals to shape advisory groups to fit their style of leadership is not a sensible option. Instead, they must be given the tools to create advisory groups (of teachers and parents) that increase the commitment of educators and improve the capacity of the school to make all children high achievers.

REFERENCES

Berends, M., Kirby, S. J., Naftel, S., & McKelvey, C. (2001). *Setting expectations for comprehensive school reform: The experience of New American Schools.* Santa Monica, CA: RAND.

Bransford, J. D., Brown, A. L., & Cocking, R. (Eds.). (1999). *How people learn: Brain, mind, experience, and school.* Washington, DC: National Academy Press.

Chapman, J., & Boyd, W. I. (1986). Decentralization, devolution and the school principal: Australian lessons on statewide educational reform. *Educational Administration Quarterly* 22(1), 28–58.

Chrispeels, J. H. (1992). *Purposeful restructuring: Creating a culture for learning and achievement in elementary schools.* London: Falmer.

Coch, L., & French, J. R. P., Jr. (1948). Overcoming resistance to change. *Human Relations 1*, 512–532.

Coleman, J. S. (1957). *Community conflict.* New York: Free Press of Glencoe.

Darling-Hammond, L. (1990). Instructional policy into practice: The power of the bottom over the top. *Education, Evaluation, and Policy Analysis, 12*(3), 339–347.

Deming, W. E., & Walton, M. (1988). *The Deming management method.* Cambridge, MA: Perigee.

Drucker, P. F. (1986). *The practice of management.* New York: Harper.

Elmore, R. F. (2000). *Building a new structure for school leadership.* Washington, DC: Albert Shanker Institute.

Friedkin, N., & Slater, M. R. (1994). School leadership and performance. *Sociology of Education, 67*(2), 139–157.

Hall, R. H. (1982). *Organizations: Structure and process.* Englewood Cliffs, NJ: Prentice-Hall.

Hallinger, P., Murphy, J., & Hausman, C. (1992). Restructuring schools: Principals' perceptions of fundamental educational reform. *Educational Administration Quarterly, 28*(3), 330–349.

Hess, F. M. (1999). *Spinning wheels: The politics of urban school reform.* Washington, DC: Brookings Institution.

Kilgore, S. B., & Pendleton, W. W. (1993). The organizational context of learning: Framework for understanding the acquisition of knowledge. *Sociology of Education, 66*(1), 63–87.

Laumann, E. O. (1987). *Networks of collective action: A perspective on community influence systems*. San Diego, CA: Academic Press.

Leithwood, K., & Menzies, T. (1998). A review of research concerning the implementation of site-based management. *School Effectiveness and School Improvement 9*(3), 233–285.

Lortie, D. C. (1975). *Schoolteacher: A sociological study*. Chicago: The University of Chicago Press.

March, J. G., & Simon, H. (1958). *Organizations*. New York: Wiley.

McLaughlin, M. W. (1987). Learning from experience: Lessons from policy implementation. *Educational Evaluation and Policy Analysis, 9*(2), 171–178.

Murphy, J., & Beck, L. (1995). *School-based management as school reform: Taking stock*. Thousand Oaks, CA: Corwin Press.

Pfeffer, J. (1997). *New directions for organization theory: Problems and prospects*. New York: Oxford University Press.

Robertson, P. J., & Briggs, K. L. (1998). Improving schools through school-based management: An examination of the process of change. *School Effectiveness and School Improvement, 9*(1), 28–57.

Rosenholtz, S. J. (1985). Effective schools: Interpreting the evidence." *American Journal of Education, 9*(3), 352–388.

Sebring, P. B., & Bryk, A. (2000). School leadership and the bottom line in Chicago. *Phi Delta Kappan, 81*(6), 440–443.

Senge, P. M. (1990). *The fifth discipline: The art and practice of the learning organization*. New York: Doubleday.

Smylie, M. A. (1992). Teacher participation in school decision making: Assessing willingness to participate. *Educational Evaluation and Policy Analysis, 14*(1).

Stinchcombe, A. L. (1965). Social structure and organizations. In J. G. March (Ed.), *Handbook of organizations* (pp. 142–193). Chicago: Rand-McNally.

Weick, K. E. (1984). Small wins: Redefining the scale of social problems. *American Psychologist, 39*(4), 40–49.

Weiss, C. H., & Cambone, J. (1994). Principals, shared decision making and school reform. *Educational Evaluation and Policy Analysis, 16*(3), 287–301.

NOTES

1. Although this is not the primary purpose of looping, it is the outcome most frequently articulated by teachers.

2. At any given time only a few teachers were looping because curriculum development was at different stages among the grades.

CHAPTER FOUR

Co-Nect

Purpose, Accountability, and School Leadership

BRUCE GOLDBERG AND DONALD M. MORRISON

A practitioner who reflects-in-action tends to question the definition of his task, the theories-in-action that he brings to it, and the measures of performance by which it is controlled. And as he questions these things, he also questions elements of the organizational knowledge structure in which his functions are embedded.

—Daniel Schon, *The Reflective Practitioner*

For many reasons—economic, social, demographic, and techno-logical—our nation has been engaged for more than 20 years in an intense and historic debate concerning the state of public education, the purposes of public schools, and strategies and policies that may help to change our schools for the better. There is now general agreement that many schools, especially those in low-wealth urban and rural communities, are failing to adequately prepare all students for life in a modern, democratic society. Most people would also agree that there are many schools in this country that rank among the best in the world, and that in between these two poles are a very large number of schools that exhibit varying degrees of mediocrity, where some students predictably succeed and others predictably fail. As a society we seem to have reached consensus that there are varying degrees of potential and progress—and that the ultimate goal for supporters of public education must be to help all schools become as good as the best schools in this country.

There is less agreement about what to do to help schools get better. In recent years, of the many different[1] approaches that have been offered, two are especially interesting because they seem so different. One of these is the idea that schools become better when emphasis is placed on the role of the school as a community of learners. In this version, making schools "better" means creating and nurturing local culture. The focus is on the social relationships that adhere among the various people that play a vital role in the everyday life of the school—teachers, administrators, students, parents, and other community members.

A second approach emphasizes the role of the school as an organization within a larger system. This approach views schools not primarily as communities to be created, but organizations to be changed, primarily through a focus on outcomes. Borrowing, as is often the case, from the world of business, and viewing schools as part of the education "industry," advocates argue that all schools, especially low-performing schools, ought to be shepherded along the path to success through a three-part strategy: high academic standards for all students; standards-based tests designed to measure the degree to which students have mastered these standards; and a system of accountability that rewards success and sanctions failure.

Interestingly, advocates of both approaches employ similar tactics, but different strategies. Both, for example, emphasize the importance of decentralized decision-making, which community advocates see as needed to build a supportive culture for learning, and change advocates see as needed to improve standard measures of academic performance. Both groups cite similar "best practices" in schools where faculties work together to continually assess progress and intervene when necessary; where collaboration is the rule, not the exception; and where research-based instructional practice is encouraged and no finger-pointing or excuses tolerated.

Strategies, however, differ. Where school improvement is seen as a matter of strengthening relationships, the strategic emphasis is one that values and preserves culture, creating and nurturing community. Where the goal is to improve academic performance on a large scale, the strategy is to establish policies that encourage teachers and school leaders to improve their performance so that they can meet the standards to which they are held accountable. One approach emphasizes the importance of "reculturing" the school (Fullan, 2000); the other, of "reorganizing" it. Similar tactics, different strategies.

To the extent that both approaches have taken hold, school leaders now find themselves at a fork in the education road. One path implores them to "reculture" their schools, be responsive primarily to local conditions and values, spurn intervention redolent of outside formulaic approaches, eschew bureaucratic red tape, and initiate self-regulating communities of practice so that local schools become genuine and vibrant places of learning. The other path calls for a "restructuring" of the organization of schools around a set of academic standards. This path leaves little time or space for responding creatively to local needs and conditions, and views the progress of schools through the lens of externally devised and graded testing instruments. One road split in two paths.

This is the geography in which today's school leaders map their strategies. At the fork between external demands for standards and the community's insistence on uniqueness, many are following the sage advice of Yogi Berra: "When faced with a fork in the road, take it." Successful school leaders somehow manage to take both paths. They focus the collective resources and energies of all adult members of the school community—teachers, families, business partners, and other allies and stakeholders—in a concerted, day-to-day, year-to-year effort to ensure that each young person passing through the school, whether for 10 days or 10 years, makes progress toward standards and receives the best education possible. Remarkably, these leaders are also able to knot together rigorous external accountability systems and local capacity-building.

To accomplish this feat, successful leaders manage to forge a consensus around three questions: Who's in charge? Where are we headed? What values do we believe in and practice? They bring to life a sense of mission and purpose and a shared understanding of the means by which school community members will be held accountable, and hold each other accountable, for helping to achieve it. When teachers, students, families, and other stakeholders are focused on a set of shared goals, there is a possibility of concerted action to achieve these goals. When there is a common agreement as to how progress toward these goals will be measured and evaluated, and a willingness to *fully share responsibility* for meeting these goals, the likelihood of success migrates from the realm of the possible to the probable.

This is not an easy thing to do, especially in a "fuzzy" environment that both encourages and undervalues local knowledge and initiative. Leaders who succeed must have a clear sense of purpose, a deep understanding of the role of the many different, and sometimes conflicting, accountability processes at work in schools, and a toolbox of effective strategies for change and coordination amongst the work of internal and external actors.

We offer this discussion in the hope that it may be of some help to those in the trenches of school reform, in full knowledge that we cannot do full justice to the complexity of actual situations in the field. Our method is to expose the deep roots of the issues in the abstract, trusting that in doing so, we may help to clarify relationships that are otherwise obscured by complexity. In particular, we invite the reader to join us in an examination of three simple, fundamental questions:

- What kind of educational results really matter—what is the purpose of our institutions of public education from the perspective of the stakeholders the school serves?
- What kinds of accountability processes and strategies for change are most likely to help schools fulfill their purpose in the eyes of their stakeholders?
- What kinds of reform and leadership are required to develop and sustain these processes in schools?

We bring to this discussion 10 years of experience with Co-nect, a national school reform network and one of the original New American Schools "design teams" (Goldberg & Morrison, 1999). We work currently in more than 175 schools in 60 districts and 30 states, primarily in so-called "low-performing or under-performing" schools. Our work involves a facilitated process of comprehensive reform aimed at dramatically improving the quality of teaching and learning in every classroom, leading to an exceptional education for every young person. That, at least, is the vision.

In reality, we have found that the conflicting pressures described above complicate our mission. Working inside schools, side by side with principals and instructional leadership teams, we understand what Fullan (2000) calls the "inside story" of school reform, with its necessary focus on developing a strong professional community that is capable of taking collective action to help all students achieve at the highest possible level. And because we are often employed by school districts, we also see the problems of schools from the "outside in" perspective, where the focus is often on establishing procedures to ensure consistency and quality of educational programs over large numbers of schools and an incredibly mobile student population.

Here, we take the perspective of school leadership. Indeed, we dedicate this chapter, in humility and respect, to the hundreds of principals and lead teachers we have had the privilege of working with over the past 10 years, and also those we hope to work with in the future—committed educators who find themselves grappling with deep issues of educational accountability and instructional leadership *while at the same time* finding money to pay substitutes, keeping buses running, providing a safe haven for children, and maintaining some semblance of a personal life.

While we realize the words we offer here will not make your working lives easier, we hope they may give you a different way of thinking about the problems you face. Standards and high-stakes accountability systems have their place. Yet, isolated from the people and communities that sustain them, they lack the almost ineffable element that animates change, the *élan vital* necessary to inspire us all to make a difference. And as the philosopher William James once noted, there is no difference if it does not make a difference.

THE QUESTION OF PURPOSE

Public schools are social organizations in service to a local community and collectively to our country. Successful leaders are those who manage to rally local efforts around national purpose, and who make national purpose fit local needs. When there is no national purpose for education, no general will about what it is or should be, schools still have the mission of being in service to their local communities. When a mission is shared among members of a community, those who are charged with carrying out the mission can draw on an underlying store of social capital, including trusting, collaborative relationships that allow various civic, neighborhood, and other groups in society to work together toward realization of individual and group purposes. To the extent that individuals and organizations work together to successfully accomplish these purposes, relationships are strengthened and extended, further trust is built, and social capital increases.

The most obvious purpose of schooling is to prepare young people for a lifetime of learning, productive work, and responsible citizenship. This is the promise of our public system of education, that all Americans, no matter what their starting place in life, will have an equal opportunity to become, as the Army puts it, "all that they can be." This function of schooling is vital to our economy, vital to our democracy, and a vital individual right for all of us—to share in knowledge of the world that others have discovered, and to discover it afresh for ourselves, with help from others. In short, public education is what Goodlad (2000, p. 86) refers to as "a moral endeavor, serving both the individual and the common."

Adequate preparation for life in a complex, democratic society includes, but goes far beyond, the "basics" of reading, writing, and arithmetic. To be fully prepared for life after school, young people must have learned to work in teams, to apply academic knowledge to complex problems for which there is no obvious solution, to use technology wisely, to speak well in front of groups, and to understand and be prepared to fulfill the responsibilities of citizenship. Beyond this, the common good requires that large numbers of Americans will have learned to speak second and foreign languages, will be prepared for careers in science and engineering, and will, speaking more generally, have had opportunities to develop their own unique strengths, interests, and aspirations. The fact is, while it may be possible to identify a core set of academic standards that all students should master, it is wrong, even dangerous, to limit learning to only this core set. Our nation and its communities depend on a diversity of talent and expertise, and it is therefore essential that schools provide young people with opportunities to develop and pursue their special interests and talents.

Schools can also serve as learning communities for adults. In good schools, teachers and educational leaders develop and contribute their professional knowledge and skills, through active participation in a community of professional practice. In this sense, schools are (or should be) similar to teaching hospitals, which are valued as much for their contribution to research and the training of new generations of doctors as they are for patient care.

Good schools also tend to form multiple, mutually beneficial relationships with external individuals and organizations who unite around collaborative projects and shared goals. They become centers of community life, generating opportunities for learning, service, and public discourse, for all members of the local community. For example, one of the schools we work with, the Accelerated Learning Laboratory in Worcester, Massachusetts, enjoys active working relationships with more than 100 community organizations, many of which are involved in the school's internship program. A school such as this, which has multiple relationships with its surrounding community, is more valuable to the community, and draws more value from the community, than a school that does not take part in such relationships.

In summary, successful schools generate value for a community, and for the society at large, in the form of *human capital* (the growing skills and knowledge of the members of the community, teachers as well as students), and *social capital* (the strengthening of collaborative relationships and trust among the school and outside individuals and organizations). The challenge for local school leadership is to facilitate change in the organization and culture of schools so that they are capable of enhancing their value and rendering an account of that value generated for their community and for our society as a whole. Only in such an organization and culture can members of the school community and its stakeholders hold each other accountable for helping the school fulfill these core functions.

WHAT IS ACCOUNTABILITY?

As with many words in the English language, the term "accountability" bears a long history of usage, and thus carries with it many meanings, not all of which we commonly recognize or make use of now. In recent years, especially in educational parlance, the term has come to assume a particularly narrow meaning, something like, "being subject to sanctions for substandard outcomes and behavior." Thus, when a policy maker says that teachers "ought to be held accountable for results," many people understand this as a call for sanctions against poor teaching, not necessarily as a call for teachers to "give an account" of their professional activities. More generally, the "accountability movement" is seen as focused on defining standards, creating standards-based tests, and promoting policies that impose sanctions for substandard performance and provide monetary rewards for exceeding standard performance expectations.

In fact, the primary dictionary meaning of the term "accountable" has much less to do with consequences than it does with explaining one's actions. To be accountable means "subject to giving an account," by which is meant an explanation, reckoning, report, or narrative. All of these meanings are more or less connected to the root of the word, which means "to count." English speakers feel this meaning most powerfully in the term "accountant"—that is, someone whose profession it is to document an organization's business activities by "counting" money involved in financial transactions.

In the following discussion, we ask the reader to think of the root meanings of the word and conceive of accountability in a broader, deeper sense than the word is generally used today. Generally speaking, we want to say that accountability is the willingness and ability to give an *account* of one's actions, to fully describe and explain; it is also the willingness to accept the consequences of one's actions according to agreed-upon commitments. A system of accountability has standards of behavior or performance, an implied commitment to these standards, mechanisms for measuring value and adherence to standards (the "counting" part), mechanisms for reporting (the explanation part), a way of providing feedback (the consequences part), and an assignment of power.

Accountability processes and mechanisms differ in the degree to which these various features of accountability are developed and have weight. They also differ depending on the degree to which they are parts of a group, practice, or formal or informal social or political institution. Some forms of accountability emphasize consequences, while others emphasize counting and reporting. The members of all social organizations, from families to armies, are subject to at least one form of accountability, and often to several different forms at once.

Those who work in schools, of course, are no exception. Schools are involved in multiple forms of accountability—bureaucratic, political, legal, professional, and market accountability (Darling-Hammond & Ascher, 1991). Here we review three types of accountability that have particular relevance to the present argument: bureaucratic accountability, professional accountability, and community accountability.

Bureaucratic Accountability

By bureaucratic accountability, we refer to two equally defining characteristics, one traditional, the other of more recent vintage. Bureaucratic accountability has been historically a kind of hierarchical map of rules, roles, and regulations that is exercised within large organizations or systems of organizations and to which individuals within the system position themselves. This "process" stream of bureaucratic accountability reveres compliance and defines success by the degree to which the system functions smoothly and efficiently. A second, more recent stream of bureaucratic accountability can be characterized by the degree to which the success of the system can be measured in student achievement data—a stream of bureaucratic accountability that can be called "outcome-based."

Taken together as one accountability system with two streams, the locus of control (that is, the power to wield consequences) tends to be top-down within the organization, while reporting is bottom-up. Performance measures, part of the "outcome" emphasis, tend to be highly standardized and applied more or less arbitrarily, according to clearly established guidelines. A person is subject to bureaucratic accountability simply by belonging to the organization that has adopted bureaucratic accountability as part of its culture. In such organizations, leadership is "positional." It exists by virtue of the place one holds in the organization and is accountable in various ways to positions above and below in the organizational hierarchy, while the system as a whole is accountable for the standardized outcome measures the smooth-functioning bureaucracy is intended to produce

Bureaucratic accountability is, in itself, neither good nor bad. In large organizations, some amount of bureaucratic accountability can be an effective management tool, especially when goals and standards of performance are clearly stated, measures of behavior and output are accurate, and consequences are dealt out in a predictable and equitable manner. Bureaucratic accountability is especially important in large, diverse organizations, or systems of organizations that would not function well otherwise, and where simple *trust* is not enough.

The dominant force in school accountability is, for the time being, primarily bureaucratic. As noted above, the school reform movement during the past few years has led to a growing consensus among politicians and educational policy makers (though not necessarily among school-based educators), that the solution to the problem of poor student and school performance is to hold local educators accountable for ensuring that all students meet high academic standards, as measured by performance on standardized tests.

This kind of accountability is hierarchically arranged, with a locus of control external to the school. Principals and faculty members are subject to rules and regulations, personnel policies, and the like. Typically, the performance of the school is assessed through an impersonal system of measures based on a single standardized test created by outside vendors. The measures or tests may be more or less aligned with a set of content and performance standards designed by committees of educators at the state level. Students in the school sit for tests sometime during the second half of the school year, often in March or April. (Other tests may be given, but there is usually a single one with high-stakes implications.) Tests are mailed off to an outside vendor, who scores them and sends the results to state or district officials. With some of the better state tests—for example, those in Maryland and Massachusetts—the tests include both machine-scoreable, multiple-choice items, as well as items that require written answers and short essays. In this case, these portions of the tests are scored by trained raters.

Policy makers at the state or district level decide on cut points, determining what will constitute an acceptable or passing score for individual students, for groups of students in a school, or for the school itself. They also determine the consequences of performance outcomes. Students may be required to take the test again, held back, or refused diplomas; teachers may receive, or fail to receive bonuses; entire faculties may be asked to resign and reapply. Test results are published in local newspapers and posted on state or district Web sites.

In sum, the prevailing mode of bureaucratic accountability in schools involves a top-down, external locus of control. Members of the school community are *held* accountable for outcomes, in the sense that they are subject to sanctions if they fail to meet performance expectations. The system's requirements for improved performance on these measures does not necessarily translate into having each member of the school community hold one another accountable in any meaningful way—a situation that if it were to occur, could conceivably upset the existing hierarchy established to avoid problems through compliance with rules and leadership positions that emanate from above. Change is encouraged instead, through a system involving a single measure of accountability, the standardized test, which is administered once each year. There is a public reporting of results. And although there may be some public discussion of results, this discussion is seen as a biproduct of the accountability system, not a necessary component. Finally, the results of the tests often have high-stakes consequences for individual members of the school community.

Most importantly, the prevailing model of school accountability is one that ignores social capital as a resource for nurturing, leveraging, and sustaining change, and fails to take the generation of social capital into account as an added value of community collaboration. Rather, it promotes a change strategy that at best is neutral and at worst de-emphasizes the role of trust and collaboration as a condition for continued improvement. Instead, it substitutes the hierarchical rules, roles, and regulations inherent in the modern "rational" organization.

Professional Accountability

Professional accountability is the kind of accountability that governs the professional behavior and actions of doctors, lawyers, engineers, teachers, and other professionals. It is based on a body of professional knowledge, and a set of rules, many of which may be unwritten, regarding how professionals treat each other and their clients (Darling-Hammond & Ascher, 1991). The Hippocratic oath, with its commitment to the welfare of patients and sharing of professional knowledge, is a simple statement of professional accountability standards.

Unlike bureaucratic accountability, professional accountability depends on the deployment of a sophisticated body of knowledge amassed by individuals, and implemented and enforced collectively by recognized professional bodies. Professionals are required to have obtained a level of individual knowledge (and hopefully wisdom) that enables them to make critical decisions for the sake of their clients. Professionals, however, do not "do their own thing." Rather, they are required to undergo a rigorous course of study, often followed by an examination, before gaining entry to the profession. Once admitted, professionals are obligated by the rules of the profession (written or unwritten) to apply their knowledge and skill in service to clients, to consult with one another, to share information, and to speak out if the behavior of a colleague violates agreed-upon principles of professional practice.

The locus of control in professional accountability is internal to the profession, played out through both formal and informal processes of peer review. Performance is evaluated more or less continuously, based on results achieved for clients. If results are very far below what is expected (i.e., attracting a suspicion of malpractice), then professionals may be banished from the profession by other members. They may also be subject to legal action—a completely different form of accountability that is outside the realm of this discussion.

School teachers and leaders demonstrate elements of professional accountability when they: (a) work actively to keep up with the latest research in their fields; (b) participate in reviews of educational quality with colleagues, including taking part in peer evaluations; (c) employ and continuously monitor the effects of research-based instructional strategies; (d) continuously work to improve their qualifications, such as working toward National Teaching Board Certification; and, most tellingly, (e) undertake actions that can be at odds with other types of accountability (for example, union rules or prevailing community norms), but are consistent with professional "best practices."

As we acknowledge below, mechanisms for professional accountability are underdeveloped in this country; as a result, and unfortunately, professional accountability is a weaker force in schools than bureaucratic accountability.

Community Accountability

Community accountability is a kind of voluntary accountability practiced by social organizations in respect to the larger community within which they are embedded. Community accountability is to community organizations what interpersonal accountability is to the individual members of informal groups such as families. Community accountability allows and requires businesses, sports clubs, service groups, and other such organizations to express and shape their relationship with the community of which they are a part.

Community accountability exists alongside other forms of accountability—including legal, political, and bureaucratic accountability—that regulate the relationships between individual community organizations and the larger community. As practiced by schools, community accountability is a "strategy for school improvement that relies on an open flow of information between public educators and the general public" (Henry, 1996).

We recognize that community accountability is far less developed, as a concept and a practice, than the other two kinds of accountability discussed here. Unlike the case of bureaucratic or professional accountability, there are no commonly agreed on standards of performance that govern the practice of community accountability. And to the extent that schools often serve multiple and overlapping communities, often with different agendas, the question of who is accountable to whom, and for what, does not always have an easy answer. It is also hard to separate out community accountability from other forms of public accountability, such as political accountability or legal accountability.

Nevertheless, many schools engage in accountability practices that go beyond the requirements of bureaucratic, legal, and political accountability. These schools identify a community of stakeholders and potential allies (primarily parents, but also including local businesses and other community organizations), then engage these stakeholders in a process of accountability that emphasizes reporting and community engagement. It is a process built on trust that seeks to strengthen trust by inviting community members to help review and examine the effectiveness of the school's instructional programs.

Here is one example of how community accountability can work: At the start of a new academic year, the school's instructional leadership team prepares a public statement of goals and objectives, perhaps presented in the form of a "State of the School" address at a school open house or other such forum. This statement identifies known problem areas (for example, poor reading comprehension for certain groups of students), sets ambitious goals addressing these problem areas, and identifies strategies that will be used in pursuit of these goals.

A cyclical and open process of goal setting, strategizing, and regular reviewing of progress unfolds throughout the school year. Groups of teachers regularly meet together to identify areas of strength and weaknesses, to set goals for student learning, and to work together to achieve these goals. Teachers periodically meet together to review student work and discuss implications for instruction. Teachers and members of the instructional leadership team regularly visit classrooms to observe and give feedback on instructional methods.

The school is aided in its review of progress by a panel of community members who periodically take part in school "walk arounds," visiting classrooms, interviewing teachers and students, and examining student work. The results of this review are documented and become part of the body of evidence that the school and community use to judge the quality of the school's educational offerings.

At the end of the school year, the school leadership team makes another public presentation, this time presenting evidence of progress toward the school's stated goals. If the school has fallen short of its goals, this is discussed and reasons given. Citizens are invited to engage in a public discussion of the school's accomplishments and failings, and suggestions for improvement are invited.

Community accountability processes such as those above focus largely on the "accounting" part of accountability, on the school's responsibility to keep a community fully informed of its accomplishments, its challenges, and the strategies it is undertaking to overcome these challenges.

As such, community accountability is fundamentally different from other kinds of accountability, especially bureaucratic accountability. As an organization within a larger system of organizations governed by local education agencies, a school has little choice but to participate in and comply with the accountability mechanisms the district, state, or federal government establishes. And those who work in the school, as employees of a larger, hierarchical organization, are accountable *to* those above them in the organization, as those who have less power are accountable to those who have more.

Community accountability is different, or can be. Whereas bureaucratic accountability is a matter of compliance, community accountability is creative and voluntary, an important part of an "inside-out" engagement strategy aimed at strengthening relationships with community stakeholders, gaining additional external allies, and generally building trust and support through open communication and full disclosure of goals, strategies, and results. Unlike the case of bureaucratic accountability, the locus of control for community accountability is internal to the school. The school, while responsive to the many influences on it from the "outside," drives the process and shapes the conversation, inviting participation as it sees fit. The school chooses to put itself in a position of accountability to its stakeholders, in the sense of a willingness to give an account of itself to the community—or at least those who care to listen. Community accountability is, in a deep sense, an existential, self-actualizing process through which a school seeks to define its relationship with its surroundings by claiming a status for itself that it might not be accorded otherwise.

Ideally, the relationship becomes two-way. The school is accountable to the community, in the sense that it assumes an obligation to publicly explain and justify the measures that are being undertaken using taxpayer dollars to ensure that all students are getting the best education possible.

The community is accountable to the school, in the sense that community members are responsible for hearing and understanding the school's account of its activities, asking hard questions when necessary, and doing what they can to support the school in its efforts on behalf of young people and their families. Most importantly, by using and developing collaborative relationships built on trust, community accountability draws on, and adds to, a community's store of social capital.

CHALLENGES FOR SCHOOL LEADERSHIP

It should be clear that no single form of accountability is the "right one" for schools. Each has its benefits and weaknesses, and the strengths of one has the potential to compensate for the weaknesses of another.

There can be no argument, for example, that external accountability mechanisms have, in many ways, been good for pubic education. The establishment of rigorous academic standards; reliable, standardized measures of student achievement; and incentives for schools to meet these standards have led to improvements in educational quality in many areas of our country. And of course, external accountability is what enables resources to be allocated, and safety and health standards to be upheld. Nonetheless, external, bureaucratic accountability without professional accountability can no more ensure educational excellence at the classroom level than building codes can ensure safe buildings without fully trained and certified civil engineers, plumbers, and electricians. Professional accountability for teachers entails necessary processes of training and certification, a growing body of research on educational practices, and, perhaps most importantly, a sense of professional obligation that puts the needs of clients (young people and their families) first.

A well-established professional community in a school can also compensate for the vulnerable "Achilles heel" of bureaucratic accountability— the inability of a standardized process to foresee every situation and meet unique local needs as they arise. But, while rules may indeed be "meant to be broken," it takes a level of professional knowledge and accountability to know when to follow guidelines and when to depart from them. A "do-it-yourself" electrician breaks rules out of ignorance, and thereby puts lives at risk—a trained, certified electrician breaks rules to improve safety. Similarly, a school leader, perhaps in consultation with colleagues, can and must decide when to depart from bureaucratic curriculum guidelines to make sure that the children in her classroom learn what they need to know, even if it means taking time away from other topics that are, in her professional judgment, less important.

Finally, community accountability provides a necessary arena in which professional educators can communicate and justify difficult decisions such as these to those who are most closely affected—students, families, and other stakeholders. By explaining not only what they are doing, but why, and for what purpose, that is, by opening their work up to public scrutiny, school-based educators can attempt to ensure that their efforts on behalf of young people are fully understood, if not always fully endorsed, by the different communities that schools serve.

At any point in time, any school organization, including its leadership and members, may be involved in a mix of these and other accountability mechanisms and processes. Leaders need to ask whether the accountability mechanisms in place help to ensure they are responsive to promoting and sustaining the school's purpose. In particular:

- Do existing accountability mechanisms and strategies for change lead to adequate preparation of young people for life after school?
- Do existing accountability mechanisms and strategies for change encourage faculty and staff to grow in their professional knowledge, take part in the life of a professional community, and publicly apply professional knowledge to decisions about how best to prepare young people for life after school?
- Do existing accountability mechanisms and strategies for change create opportunities to strengthen ties between the school and other organizations within the community, resulting in net gains in social capital?

In the following sections we address these issues in respect to the use of accountability systems in changing and sustaining improvement in schools, with a special emphasis on professional, community, and bureaucratic accountability. We focus on strategies that leaders can use to: (a) strengthen professional and community accountability; (b) work more effectively with the mechanisms and resources provided by standards-based bureaucratic accountability; and (c) mediate when demands of these different forms of accountability come in conflict.

CREATE A SHARED SENSE OF PURPOSE

Most schools have mission statements, but not all mission statements are taken seriously. A well-crafted mission statement, one that clearly states the school's purpose, can become the crown jewels of a strong, "inside-out" accountability culture. Take, for example, the following:

> Our entire school community holds itself accountable for ensuring that all students are fully prepared for a lifetime of learning, productive work, and responsible citizenship—in ways that are consistent with each individual's special strengths, interests, and aspirations.

A mission statement such as this, by publicly clarifying a school's purpose, serves as a touchstone for discussions of school quality. Questions about curriculum and instructional practice can be judged in the context of the school's stated purpose.

A truly valuable mission statement is not just a "vision"—it is a public commitment for which a school may ask to be held accountable. A statement such as this, for example, clearly implies that a "standards-based" curriculum may not be a sufficient guarantee that young people in the school are afforded opportunities to pursue individual interests that take them beyond core standards into other important realms of knowledge and its creation. A public accounting of this school's educational programs will presumably include evidence that the school is indeed providing opportunities for personal pursuits that allow individuals to develop individual "strengths, interests, and aspirations."

When a mission statement is taken seriously, leaders manage resources so that the time and money allocated to meeting the mission is disproportionately greater than time and money spent on activities less central to the mission. This might mean that a personal learning plan is available for each student (and personal growth plans available to each teacher). If it turns out, for example, that this is not the case—that the data leaders routinely gather on student learning indicate that students are learning the same "content" in third grade that they learned in second, that the nature of student work is largely repetitive and drill-oriented—then leaders can invite the school community to revisit the mission and devise plans to better align the learning in the school to the mission. Even very young students can contribute to the gathering of this data through their own student drawings of what "school is like" (Tovey, 1996). Teachers can then interpret the drawings to get a better "picture" of whether the school mission is alive and well.

There will, of course, be conflicts over mission. Often, they will come from the requests of the "outside" actors inviting themselves inside. Sometimes, they will arise because individuals inside the school bring pet programs that conflict with or detract from the overall mission. Even more innocently, these conflicts can be subterranean and grow quietly from without. They will take the more innocent form of well-intentioned "programs" externally imposed to meet needs that local, state, or federal governments might think critical to education. These programs, if left to grow, may nibble away at the mission until gradually it becomes unrecognizable.

MAKE GOOD USE OF ACADEMIC STANDARDS

The attempt to identify a comprehensive set of content and performance standards, a laudable effort begun in the mid-1980s by professional organizations such as the National Council of Teachers of Mathematics

(NCTM), was originally intended to identify a body of critical skills and content knowledge in areas such as mathematics, history, language arts, and social studies that students could be expected to master and teachers could be expected to teach. The rapidly expanding standards movement led to the creation of countless committees of local experts at the state and district level who have taken on the task of preparing comprehensive lists of facts and skills in their specialties.

Recent research suggests that states that have managed to combine carefully crafted standards with tests aligned to the standards manage to promote "more adventurous teaching" than states that do not have such mechanisms in place (Blank, Porter, & Smithson, 2001). Nevertheless, the faults of standards documents are well-known, and there is a growing recognition that we need to have "standards for standards." Recently, for example, the Commission on Instructionally Supportive Assessment, a group of well-known assessment, curriculum, and instruction experts convened by five leading educational organizations and chaired by W. James Popham, issued a report detailing nine requirements "to ensure *a responsible educational assessment system for the improvement of learning*" (italics original). The first requirement stipulates that "a state's content standards must be prioritized to support effective instruction and assessment." The commission's other requirements include the state's provision of optional assessment procedures that can measure student progress in attaining standards not assessed by state tests, and the monitoring of the breadth of the curriculum to ensure that instructional attention is given to all content standards and subject areas, including those that are not assessed by state tests (Commission on Instructionally Supportive Assessment, 2001).

The question is, what should school leaders do in localities where standards documents may in fact hinder improvement of learning—for example, by insisting on broad curriculum coverage at the cost of deep understanding, by emphasizing facts over "big ideas," by failing to identify cross-cutting themes that serve to unify what would otherwise be fragments of knowledge, or by failing to make allowances for addressing important content and skills that are not necessarily tested? In these situations, leaders must fall back on their own professional judgment, the collective professional judgment of the faculty and the profession at large, to ensure that the school's curriculum is sufficiently cohesive, conceptual, and compelling—and, perhaps most importantly, in full alignment with the school's stated mission.

A schoolwide process of "curriculum mapping" (Jacobs, 1997) can help to ensure that local standards lead to improvements in classroom instruction. As teachers work together to map out exactly who is teaching what, and when, they begin to identify gaps, redundancies, and missed opportunities for interdisciplinary connections. For example, in a recent curriculum mapping process in one of our Co-nect schools, the faculty discovered that the mathematics text they were using covered only about half of the standards on the state test. Missing topics, including statistics and probability, were exactly those topics that students were having the most difficulty with.

Initiating and overseeing such a process is an important and proper function of instructional leadership. The resulting curriculum map itself can become a public document; the act of making this process public can become an important expression of community accountability.

MAKE GOOD USE OF DATA
FROM STANDARDIZED TESTS

Standards-based tests of the type that are currently being developed and implemented by most states are useful to schools in a number of ways. We have found that in Co-nect schools these tests provide reasonably reliable estimates of the extent to which individual students, and groups of students, have "mastered" local academic standards. As such, they can be used to identify students in need of special help, areas of the curriculum that may need increased instructional support, or (more problematically) teachers who require increased professional support. These tests can also be used as a measure of progress against goals. Results can be compared to results that have been achieved by similar schools, and also to results from previous years; in this way, school leaders can get some measure of the effectiveness of internal reforms.

These potential benefits, however, do not come automatically. Furthermore, harmful effects of the tests can offset them, if these are not managed appropriately.

First of all, schools must be knowledgeable consumers of test data. This means knowing, as a simple example, that the significance of differences in test scores among groups of students, and among schools, is largely dependent on the number of students tested. If relatively small numbers of students are tested at a given grade level, changes in test scores for just a few students can have a large impact on the group mean. If we do not understand this, we may draw unwarranted inferences from annual fluctuations in test scores. To cite another example, it is important to understand that tests measure only a *sample* of what students know and do, and are, therefore, subject to error. Not everything that is taught during an academic year can be tested in a single sitting. Therefore, test results are imperfect measures of curriculum coverage. When schools are sophisticated consumers of test data, they are more likely to use the data in ways that lead to instructional improvement.

Second, knowledgeable consumers of test data will want to have the data supplied in a form that lends itself to careful analysis. Often this means having access to student-level electronic data in a form that can be imported into analytical tools such as an electronic spreadsheet or statistical package. The data can then be merged with data from other sources (such as course grades) to get a more complete picture of student achievement than is available from the test data alone. This can lead to the creation and maintenance of a data set that allows the schools to track progress of individual students from one year to the next, analyze the performance of subgroups, and correlate results of standardized tests with other measures.

Simple access to the data is not enough. It is important to create an organizational environment in which standardized test data is taken seriously by all members of the school community, including, most importantly, teachers and students. Among other things, this means setting up processes that engage the faculty as a whole in the analysis of the data, and developing strategies for continuing instructional improvement based on the results. This is more likely to happen within the context of a strong professional community that is knowledgeable about the tests, and treats the data seriously, with a good mix of curiosity and skepticism.

We have found that when test data is used in this way in Co-nect schools, it has the potential to strengthen professional and community accountability. It strengthens professional accountability because it gives teachers an external, standards-based measure to use in judging the effectiveness of their practices. And it strengthens community accountability because it provides a base of evidence that the school can point to in relating both accomplishments and remaining challenges.

WORK WITH TEACHERS TO IMPROVE ON THE RELIABILITY AND VALIDITY OF LOCAL ASSESSMENTS

While externally developed standardized tests provide useful diagnostic data to schools, they are lacking in many ways and must be supplemented by locally developed forms of assessment. The leadership challenge is to ensure that these local assessments are as valid and reliable as possible.

Data from standardized tests is limited in a number of ways. For one thing, tests are usually given only once each year, usually in the spring. The length of time it takes for results to become available to the school depends on the complexity of the test. For example, for our Co-nect schools in Maryland, where the state tests includes many open-ended questions that must be scored by hand, results are not available before November of the following year, at the earliest. At best, in most states results are available for analysis and discussion by September, at which time many teachers and students will have gone on to other schools. Clearly, schools cannot wait this long to know how well students are doing.

Another problem with standardized tests is that they tend to measure only what can be easily tested. They are good at measuring reading comprehension, vocabulary, command of mathematical procedures, and command of factual knowledge. Some tests also measure the ability to work through a multistep problem, and to produce short written answers to questions on demand. However, few such tests even attempt to measure other important skills and accomplishments such as: *breadth of reading*; effective use of technology; ability to communicate in a second or foreign language; ability to plan and carry out an extensive project; or, most fundamentally, the ability and willingness to exercise the rights and responsibilities of citizenship.

Two possibilities exist. One is to ignore these important outcomes and focus only on the results of standardized tests. The other is to develop methods of assessment that measure these other outcomes.

One may be tempted to argue that schools do not have the capacity to develop alternative assessment measures, and that even if they did, there would be serious questions of validity and reliability. In answer to the first objection, the fact is that almost all teachers *already* develop and use a wide variety of assessments (including tests, quizzes, homework assignments, etc.) to judge student achievement. The problem is that these assessments are not valued in the same way that standardized tests are valued. What can be done to make local assessments more valid and reliable?

Many Co-nect schools are in the process of developing schoolwide portfolio systems. Each student in the school accumulates a collection of samples of authentic work in certain specified genres, for example: a design proposal; a reading log; a file of correspondence; a report on an original science investigation; a report on an investigation in the social sciences; an extended piece of creative writing; and so on. For each of these generic pieces, the faculty develops a set of scoring guidelines, together with examples of work at the different scoring levels. The simple availability of these guidelines does not, in itself, make the assessment more reliable or valid. However, as explained below, it is the first step in increasing reliability and validity of local assessments.

During the course of the year, students produce work as part of curriculum projects in the different content areas. Teachers (and sometimes students themselves) score this work using the school's generic scoring guidelines and "anchoring samples." Also, from time to time, teachers meet together in groups to look over the student portfolios and score the work together. Finally, at the end of the year, the school may pull a random selection of portfolios and score them, possibly with the assistance of an external panel of community raters (see below). The data from these portfolio audits becomes part of the body of evidence, along with data from standardized tests, and together these help the school understand how well it is doing in respect to improving student achievement.

Assessments such as these, based as they are on authentic student work, enjoy a high degree of "face validity" because they measure performance on authentic tasks quite directly. (A reasonable measure of a student's ability to carry out and report on an original science investigation is the report itself. A reasonable measure of the breadth of a student's reading is a reading log.)

Reliability of scoring is another matter. Reliability can be pursued through the use of generic, schoolwide rubrics that are developed and used by faculty members as a group. By using a common set of scoring rubrics, and, more importantly, by meeting periodically to review and score student work together, faculty members gradually develop a common understanding of what the rubrics mean, and how to use them. These kinds of conversations lead to higher levels of inter-rater reliability. In other words, the reliability of such assessments should eventually fall somewhere between the reliability of standardized tests (highly reliable from a technical standpoint), and the noted unreliability of assessments that are developed and administered by individual teachers in isolation.

The point here is not that these locally developed assessments should come to be viewed as alternatives to standardized tests, or that they can be as "reliable" or "generalizable" as standardized tests. Rather, the goal for school leaders should be to supplement tests that are infrequent but highly reliable and (by some measures) valid with regular, local assessments that are as valid and reliable as possible.

LEVERAGE AND PROMOTE SOCIAL CAPITAL IN THE SCHOOL AND ITS COMMUNITY AS A FUNDAMENTAL CURRENCY OF ACCOUNTABILITY

Just as an exclusive focus on bureaucratic accountability may tend to weaken professional accountability, if only by leaving it undervalued and underused, so too can a focus on bureaucratic accountability weaken mechanisms of community accountability. As a result, opportunities to generate social capital are lost.

This is just a technical way of saying that community stakeholders ought to be asked to take an active role in accountability processes in a way that goes beyond simply reading reports of test results in the local newspaper.

In all Co-nect schools, our field staff helps local leaders organize annual "school progress reviews." An informal review panel—consisting of local business partners, district and state education officials, parents, and other stakeholders—spends a day or two in the school visiting classrooms, interviewing students and teachers, and reviewing student work. At the end of the visit, the panel puts together a brief report identifying what they see as the school's most salient "strengths" and "challenges." This report then becomes input, along with other inputs, to the school improvement process.

Other such "community accountability events" in Co-nect schools include community project fairs (in which students present examples of their work), community portfolio audits, and presentations of test results for public discussion at school open houses. These kinds of events depend on, and help to build, multiple, productive relationships among the school and outside individuals and organizations. In this way, the school expresses its accountability to the community, while community members arrive at a deeper understanding of what is going on in the school, including both accomplishments and needs. These events strengthen school-community relationships, thus adding to the community's store of social capital.

This, of course, is seldom as easy as it sounds. Community accountability is more straightforward in communities where students are drawn from a single, well-bounded geographical area, where community engagement is already at a high level, and where parents send their children to the same school, support the school directly through taxes, and already take part in school governance—in other words, communities with an abundance of focused social capital. Community accountability is less straightforward when schools serve multiple communities with different interests, where students are drawn from all parts of a city (as in a magnet school), where community engagement is low, for example, because families have difficulty finding time to take part in "community accountability events," or where business partnerships are difficult—in other words, where social capital is relatively scarce and more diversified.

The challenge for leadership in these more difficult situations is to find a suitable starting point. Principals in Co-nect schools sometimes begin by organizing a parent night featuring a simple demonstration of student learning, or by inviting a local newspaper reporter to visit the school and learn about a new technology initiative. Even these small steps put "social capital pennies" in the bank, opening an account that may eventually grow to become a significant investment.

CREATE A STRONG PROFESSIONAL COMMUNITY

In theory, the professional educators in a school can and should hold themselves accountable for ensuring that all students have opportunities to develop the knowledge and skills they need to be successful in the world that lies before them. When mechanisms of professional accountability are fully developed, teachers apply and share their professional knowledge in ways that meet the needs of students and their families. Teachers review each other's work, keep up to date on the latest research, and apply guidelines developed by professional bodies such as the NCTM, the International Reading Association, and the National Science Teachers Association. In this case teachers are not just "doing their best"—they are applying the best practices the profession has to offer.

The strength and effectiveness of professional accountability in a school's community of practice depends on a range of factors, including the training and professional qualifications of local teachers, professional development opportunities, and the presence of mechanisms and structures enforcing and encouraging the growth of a professional community. School leaders have varying degrees of control over these factors. For example, principals have limited hiring and firing responsibility, and even if they have some control over hiring, the pool of applicants may be limited. There may be limited time in the schedule for professional development and common planning. And there may be limited funding for or availability of substitutes, thus making it difficult to free up teachers for professional development opportunities, even if there is time in the schedule. These factors are difficult, if not impossible, to deal with from the inside out.

Clearly, one of the biggest challenges of leadership is to create a professional community where there has been none before; and where there is one, to sustain it over time, in the face of external obstacles. Professional communities and collaborative work cultures, of course, do not just happen. They are consciously created and nurtured. Exactly how they come into existence is somewhat mysterious. "Indeed," Fullan writes, ". . . even if you knew how particular schools become collaborative, you could never tell precisely how you should go about it in your own school. There is no magic bullet" (Fullan, 2000, p. 582).

As noted above, professional accountability requires that teachers make day-to-day decisions in the interests of the children and young people in their charge, based on their own knowledge and skill, the advice of colleagues, and the knowledge base of the profession. They must know their students. The only way to strengthen professional accountability from the inside out is to build up the school as a professional community of learners.

While it is true, as Fullan points out, that there is no single "magic bullet," school leaders can take steps to encourage the development of a strong professional community in their schools. Strategies used in Co-nect schools include: stocking and maintaining a library of professional journals in the teacher's lounge, creating time in the schedule for common planning and reflection, organizing faculty members in teams to work with a selected number of students over a period of years, inviting specialists from a local university to come in and give talks, providing workshops and other kinds of professional development opportunities, making sure teachers have access to professional resources on the Internet, and finding funding for teachers to attend and make presentations at conferences. Leaders can also organize a series of "research lessons" whereby faculty members observe an experienced teacher teach a lesson, then discuss what they have seen and how the lesson might be improved (Stigler & Hiebert, 1999)—and so forth.

The main idea is to work at (a) making sure that faculty members are plugged into a wider community of professionals in their content areas; and (b) creating opportunities for public examination of educational issues within the school, so that teachers are not just doing their own thing, but working *with* others to provide the best possible education for every young person in the school, by implementing recognized "best practices."

Strengthening the school as a professional community also strengthens professional accountability. Teachers who keep themselves up-to-date on current research in their areas of expertise, and who do their best to apply known best practices, are, in an important sense, more accountable to their profession than teachers who shut the door and teach what they have always taught, as they have taught it. Similarly, professional accountability is at play when teachers share their knowledge with others, invite review of their instructional strategies, and willingly speak out when their professional judgment tells them they must.

Of course, the simple existence of a strong professional community in the school does not mean that *all* teachers will hold themselves accountable to the profession in these ways. Nor does it follow that all teachers who *do* hold themselves accountable will be good teachers. As David Cohen has shown in his famous study of "Miss Oublier," teachers who *think* they are implementing best practices do not always do so (Cohen, 1990). Given this research, it is certainly possible to imagine a group of teachers who read the journals, visit each others' classrooms, and regularly discuss important instructional issues—but who, collectively and individually, fail to provide a high quality of education for the young people in their charge. Professional community does not necessarily lead to professional accountability, and professional accountability of the kind we are describing here does not necessarily lead to excellence in teaching—which is why both alone are insufficient.

Further, the requirements of professional accountability and the communities that sustain it can sometimes be at odds with the requirements of bureaucratic and external accountability. For example, in some of the districts we work with, teachers are required by district guidelines to teach a set curriculum, guided by a system of "pacing charts" in mathematics and other subjects. Students are tested on the material at set intervals, and district supervisors visit classrooms to ensure that teachers are on schedule with their lessons. This system works well if the pacing chart is so well designed that students and teachers can move easily through curriculum together at the designed pace. But what if a teacher discovers that it is time to move on to computing averages and students have not yet mastered the basics of long division? In such a situation, the teacher may find herself caught between the conflicting demands of two different accountability systems. As a professional, she may feel obligated to take extra time to help students understand what they need to know before going on to the next level. As an employee subject to bureaucratic accountability, she may feel obligated to move on to the next topic, against her professional judgment.

Equally plausible as the above "pacing chart" example are instances in which teachers might unknowingly employ strategies that evidence-based research, research endorsed by national professional organizations, has shown to be ineffective. Teachers might not be aware of the most recent discoveries regarding the teaching of reading, or how to recognize various learning disabilities early on so that children are not misdiagnosed or placed into special programs that can harm rather than help them. In schools without a strong professional community, teachers may be forced to make these kinds of decisions on their own, and who knows whether they are making the right decision? Strong professional communities help guard against both instances. They are places in which teachers' work as well as students' work is made public and subject to rigorous standards established by the larger professional community of teachers. In schools with a strong professional community, issues such as these can be illustrated and discussed publicly and collectively. Decisions can be made therefore on the basis of the public evidence and collective professional judgment of the entire faculty. When hard instructional decisions are made in this way, they are more likely to be the right ones.

CONCLUSION

School leadership is the taking of responsibility for achieving educational goals and purposes through local reforms. To do this leaders must take account of three contexts for educational change and accountability. They must take account of the "inside story" of schools, and, in particular, of the collaboration and trust that is essential to the functioning of successful communities of professional practice. Leaders must also take into account the institutions of civil society, including families, businesses, and community and professional organizations. To be successful here, leaders must be able to ward off fragmentation of their efforts while being responsive to the needs of the larger world the school inhabits. Finally, leaders must take account of local, state, and federal governments, of their mandates and measures of performance. They must be responsive to policies that can influence their school's future but insist on making those policies preserve and build on the social capital necessary to sustain their efforts. It is the local school that creates and sustains net increases in human and social capital. Accountability systems that fail to promote this kind of leadership are deficient or incomplete.

Success is never easy nor obvious. School leaders must somehow weave together mechanisms and processes of accountability that are based on a clear sense of where they are headed, who is in charge of getting them there, and the values they will not only abide by but live by along the way. To do this, they must journey through an often barren and lonely accountability terrain, the interstices of a complex system whose loosely coupled parts are out of alignment. Where there is collaboration and trust, they must seize it by its roots. They must leverage the social capital already invested in their schools' professional practice, families, and communities, and build schools, as Michael Fullan has said, "worth fighting for" (Fullan & Hargreaves, 1996). This is the only path worth traveling in preparing young people to be productive workers, lifelong learners, and responsible citizens.

External forms of accountability, ushered along by various bureaucratic mandates, national standards, and high stakes might be necessary, but they are clearly not sufficient. Taken piecemeal, they cannot foster the ongoing culture and momentum to change and improve schools. As of this writing, external forms of accountability seem to have overshadowed the importance of other forms and all but drowned out the legitimate and necessary voices of other stakeholders. When policy makers speak about accountability, they usually seem to have in mind the kind of top-down, bureaucratic accountability implied in the call to "hold schools accountable." The objects of this external accountability—primarily principals, teachers, and students—have little to say and much to lose by bucking the system. And yet, paradoxically, the power to sustain changes in the prevailing system lies in the hands of school and district leadership.

Negotiating the rocky terrain of the present accountability landscape is arduous and potentially treacherous. It requires a creative and courageous kind of educational leadership. Whereas changing organizations has championed the *change skills* of modern rational systems, community accountability calls for the *conserving skills* of those who know how to create and sustain the culture of community. Both kinds of skills are required for effective leadership in today's schools. Leaders must change the system but simultaneously create, nurture, and sustain a local culture in doing so.

Changing the "organizational knowledge structure" is the job of leadership. If successful, we will once again know and inhabit our institutions better than they come to know or inhabit us. The education of our young people will take place in engaged local communities, communities that find themselves as culturally proximate to their schools and their values as are their neighborhoods. It is this kind of accountability that encourages teamwork and educational excellence, makes good use of local knowledge (including, most importantly, teachers' knowledge of the children and young people in their charge), allows for flexibility in rewards and sanctions comprising high-stakes decisions, and strengthens the relationship between a school and its surrounding community.

REFERENCES

Blank, R., Porter, A., & Smithson, J. (2001). *New tools for analyzing teaching, curriculum and standards in mathematics & science: Results from survey of enacted curriculum project.* Washington, DC: Council of Chief State School Officers.

Cohen, D. K. (1990). The case of Ms. Oublier. *Educational Evaluation and Policy Analysis, 12*(3), 327–345.

Commission on Instructionally Supportive Assessment (2001). *Building Tests to Support Instruction and Accountability.* **Publisher?**

Darling-Hammond, L., & Ascher, C. (1991). *Creating accountability in big city schools.* New York: Columbia University, ERIC Clearinghouse on Urban Education, and National Center for Restructuring Education, Schools and Teaching.

Fullan, M. (2000). The three stories of education reform. *Phi Delta Kappan. 81*(8).

Fullan, M., & Hargreaves, A. (1996). *What's worth fighting for in your school.* New York: Teacher's College Press.

Goldberg, B., & Morrison, D. (1999). Co-nect schools. In J. Block et al. (Eds.), *Comprehensive school reform: A program perspective.* Dubuque, IA: Kendall/Hunt.

Goodlad, J. (2000). Education and democracy: Advancing the agenda. *Phi Delta Kappan, 82*(1), 86–89.

Henry, G. (1996). Community accountability: A theory of information, accountability, and school improvement. *Phi Delta Kappan, 78*(1).

Jacobs, H. (1997). *Mapping the big picture: Integrating curriculum and assessment K-12.* ASCD.

Schere, M. (2001). How and why standards can improve student achievement: A conversation with Robert J. Marzano. *Educational Leadership, 59*(1).

Shon, D. (1987). *The reflective practitioner: How professionals think in action.* San Francisco: Jossey-Bass.

Stigler, J., & Hiebert, J. (1999). *The teaching gap: Best ideas from the world's teachers for improving education in the classroom.* New York: Free Press.

Tovey, R. (1996). Getting kids into the picture: Student drawings help teachers see themselves more clearly. *Harvard Education Letter*, Nov/Dec, 5–6.

NOTE

1. The growing charter school movement, along with increased support for new forms of school governance, organization, and financing, further complicates the issue of leadership and accountability. While we recognize that what we have to say in this chapter may not apply, or may apply in different ways to these new settings, we have chosen to focus our attention here on the overwhelming majority of public schools that continue to exist within the traditional school district framework.

CHAPTER FIVE

The Accelerated Schools Project

*Can a Leader Change
the Culture and Embed Reform?*

CHRISTINE FINNAN AND JAMES MEZA, JR.

Originally this chapter was to focus on the synergy of leadership at the district, school, and classroom levels needed to successfully implement and sustain the Accelerated Schools Project (ASP). We planned to use the scale-up of school reform in Memphis, Tennessee, as the case since early indications were that the Memphis reform experiment was promising (Berends, Kirby, Naftel, & McKelvey, 2000; Bodilly, 1998; Ross, Alberg, & Wang, 2001; Stringfield & Datnow, 1998). The cohort of schools implementing the ASP model in 1995 and 1996 showed promise both in terms of student achievement gains and in meeting standards for implementing the model (Memphis City Schools, unpublished data; Ross, Wang, Sanders, Wright, & Stringfield, 2000). We had to reconsider the focus of this chapter when Memphis City Schools (MCS) discontinued all comprehensive school reform models, including the ASP, in June 2001. This decision raises several critical questions. How can such a promising experiment in school reform end so decisively? Why did people within the schools not rise up in support of the reforms they had worked so hard to implement? What does this situation illustrate about the ability of school reform efforts to survive a change in leadership at the school or district level?

Despite the abrupt end of comprehensive school reform in Memphis, we decided to continue to use Memphis as our case, albeit with a different focus, because of what this experience tells us about organizational culture, leadership, and school reform. Our focus also broadens to address implementation of multiple reform models, not just the ASP. This chapter addresses three sets of questions. The first set deals with culture. What do we need to know about district, school, and classroom culture to embed reform into these cultures? How do we work within existing cultures to make reforms a part of them? The second set deals with leadership. How can leaders change the culture in the unit they lead? How does a trans-forming culture change once a leader leaves? The third set of questions deals with educational reform. Will reform last if it is mandated from above? Is it better to focus reform efforts on the classroom rather than the school? This chapter examines the relationship between culture, leader-ship, and reform, presenting a conceptual framework that ties together these three elements. This case focuses specifically on schools implement-ing the ASP within the context of a district-wide effort to implement comprehensive school reform models.

The ASP is one of the oldest comprehensive school reform models. Developed in the mid-1980s by then Stanford University professor Henry M. Levin, ASP is designed to improve the effectiveness of schools serving large numbers of students who have been underserved by traditional schools. From years of research, Levin found that many students, espe-cially minority students and students living in poverty, rarely had access to the kind of challenging and exciting curriculum and instruction usually reserved for students identified as gifted (Accelerated Schools, 2002; Levin, 1987, 1996).

ASP is implemented at the school level through a specified governance structure and a research-based inquiry process. Both the structure and process are grounded in three principles (unity of purpose, empowerment coupled with responsibility, and building on strengths), nine values (equity, participation, communication and collaboration, community spirit, experimentation and discovery, trust, reflection, risk taking, and school as the center of expertise), and a commitment to teach all children as if they are gifted and talented (Finnan, St. John, McCarthy, & Slovacek, 1996; Hopfenberg, Levin, & Associates, 1993). This commitment is trans-lated into a concept of powerful learning that defines ASP's approach to changing classroom practice. Learning is powerful if it is authentic, inter-active, learner-centered, inclusive, and continuous (Finnan & Swanson, 2000; Keller & Huebner, 1997). ASP does not provide a packaged curricu-lum or prescribe instructional strategies. Rather, it gives school community members a decision-making process and analysis tools to make appropri-ate decisions about teaching and learning.

The ASP serves schools through a national center (now located at the University of Connecticut) and a network of regional satellite centers. Staff from these centers train leadership teams (the principal, an external coach, and an internal coaching team) and provide ongoing training and field support. The goal of training and support is to internalize the ASP philosophy and process into the school culture within five years. The University of New Orleans Accelerated Schools Center served the ASP schools in Memphis.

CONCEPTUAL FRAMEWORK

Culture and Culture Change[1]

Efforts to reform education are actually efforts to change the culture of districts, schools, and classrooms. Culture is something that surrounds us, gives meaning to our world, and is constantly being constructed both through our interactions with others and through our reflections on life and our world (Finnan & Swanson, 2000, p. 65).

Six characteristics of culture impact reform efforts. First, while culture provides meaning, it also restricts our objectivity and shapes our preferences (McQuillan, 1998; Spindler & Spindler, 1987). Within a school, the culture determines what can be expected of students, what curriculum and instructional methods are right for the students, appropriate discipline methods, and interaction and discourse patterns. Teachers in some schools respond to new ideas by saying, "That won't work with our students," and the culture of the school supports them in this belief.

Second, culture is also both conservative and ever-changing (Schëin, 1992; Wax, 1993). It provides a conservative shield against the unknown, but it can also adapt to influences from other cultures and from changes in the physical, social, and political environment. School cultures are often characterized as resistant to reform because of this conservative tendency (Cuban, 1990; Sarason, 1996; Tyack & Cuban, 1995), when, in fact, school cultures change frequently to accommodate changes in student populations, district and state policies, curriculum and instructional innovations, and changes in administration. School cultures are not resistant to change if the change effort builds on the existing culture (Finnan & Levin, 2000).

Third, boundaries between cultures are permeable allowing multiple cultures to interact and allowing individuals to be members of multiple cultural groups. School cultures are relatively unbounded. Teachers, administrators, parents, and students bring different cultural assumptions together within the context of the school culture. Teachers work side by side with colleagues who have very different assumptions about teaching and learning. They establish very different classroom cultures that influence and are influenced by the school culture. Classrooms, on the other hand, are relatively bounded. Teachers, because of their role and authority, have considerable control over the classroom culture (Finnan, Schnepel, & Anderson, no date).

Fourth, culture is experienced through one's role or position (Spindler & Spindler, 1993). A teacher's experience of the school culture is different from that of a student or the principal. Overlap in expectations and assumptions occur, but the school becomes a social system and has a culture through an orchestration of differences and similarities of individuals with distinct roles and different levels and degrees of authority (Spindler, 1999).

Fifth, culture is transmitted, shaped, and maintained through language and dialogue. Within schools, culture is created and maintained by what is talked about and what topics are avoided, by how language is used, by whose language is encouraged, and by who has control of the discourse (Florio-Ruane, 1989). A common vocabulary develops within a school to ease communication among those within the culture, and, in some cases, to exclude those who are not in it.

Finally, culture functions primarily through the shared assumptions, beliefs, and values that shape the actions people within a culture take (Evans, 1996; McQuillan, 1998). School cultures are shaped by assumptions adults hold about students, by assumptions students hold for themselves and their peers, and by assumptions that are held about adult roles, about appropriate educational practices, and about the value of change (Finnan & Swanson, 2000).

The literature on reform tends to treat district culture less as a mere context influencing school culture and more as an active force in influencing the direction of school reform (Elmore & McLaughlin, 1988; Fullan, 2001b; Tyack & Cuban, 1995). Politics and power relationships influence implementation at the school level but are even more influential at the district level (Timar, 1989 in Desimone, 2000). School district cultures are even more permeable than those of schools. The school district is highly visible in most communities. Cultural and political conflicts existing in the community often find their way into the district culture. Although district cultures are permeable and open to influences from diverse sectors of the community, district level staff and administrators share assumptions that shape what and how students learn and that profoundly influence school reform.

Leaders and Leadership

Given the considerable attention paid to the importance of leaders in educational change and in shaping organizational cultures (Deal & Peterson, 1999; Evans, 1996; Fullan, 2001a; Sergiovanni, 2000), a clear consensus exists that leaders do play an important role in changing culture. The literature identifies the beliefs, knowledge, interaction patterns, and actions that characterize effective leaders, especially principals. Principals are expected to manage the instructional program, promote a positive school climate, and define a mission or vision for the school. Specific tasks within each of these functions have also been identified (Copland, 2001; Hallinger & McCary, 1990; Hallinger & Murphy, 1985). Principals are also expected to shape culture so that teachers are able to teach and students can learn (Deal & Peterson, 1999, p. 10). They are expected to simultaneously manage the status quo while leading for change (Firestone, 1996).

Although the literature is clear that school leadership is a daunting task and that a single leader cannot reform a school or a district, the pressure to make immediate change still falls heavily on principals and superintendents (Copland, 2001). It is very appealing to think that decisive answers, clear steps, and a map of the future are the characteristics of an effective leader, but the literature increasingly recognizes that leaders should not be expected to address the complex problems in education in this way (Fullan, 2001a, p. 3). The characteristics of effective school leaders identified by Deal and Peterson (1999), Sergiovanni (2000), Evans (1996), and Fullan (2001a) call for leaders who build the capacity of everyone in the school or district, create a climate that allows everyone to do their work effectively and efficiently, and recognize the importance of working within the school's or district's culture.

Recognizing that a single leader cannot reform a school or district has led to an awareness of the potential of teacher leadership (Ayers, 1992; Schlechty, 1997; Sergiovanni, 1994). Increasingly, teachers are being recognized for their knowledge of curriculum and instruction and of their students. They are being asked to take on responsibilities formerly assumed by administrators (e.g., curriculum development, communication with the community) while being held accountable for their students' learning. While many teachers welcome being asked to assume a broader role in their schools, they are now sharing in the sense of overload felt by the principal. Roles and responsibilities are often not clearly defined, which can lead to miscommunication and confusion (Datnow & Castellano, chap. 9, this volume). It is often unclear how the multiple leaders within a school and district come together to make change happen at the school or district level. Recognizing the importance of leaders is not the same as creating a synergy among them so that real reform can take place.

The new conceptualization of leadership as distributed within the culture of the school or district provides a compelling framework for understanding the interaction between leadership and culture. Distributed leadership theory (see Distributed Leadership Project, 2001) emphasizes the importance of the social context in shaping intelligent activity (e.g., leadership), not just contextualizing it (Spillane, Halverson, & Diamond, 1999, 2001). The emphasis is on leadership practice, which is best understood as "practice distributed over leaders, followers, and their situation," rather than "solely a function of an individual's ability, skill, charisma, and cognition" (Spillane, Halverson, & Diamond, 1999, p. 13). This theory places leadership practice within the cultural context. In the context of school reform or school "reculturing" (Fullan, 2001b), distributed leadership provides an effective framework to analyze why reform works in some situations and not others. In the case of Memphis, it helps to explain why this promising experiment officially ended so abruptly but its effects linger within the district and schools.

Linking Culture, Leadership, and Reform

As the above illustrates, changing schools through comprehensive school reform models is a complex process. District, school, and classroom culture is more than a context for implementation; it is essentially what is being reformed. Leadership is more than roles, responsibilities, and styles. It is a process that involves an interplay between leaders, followers, and the situation. Reform models are more than programs to be implemented. If implemented properly, they involve individual and collective change in assumptions, beliefs, values, and actions. Culture, leadership, and reform are dependent on each other. They are dynamic, multifaceted, and not rational. A key characteristic of all three components is that individuals use their prior knowledge, current role or position, and their hopes and aspirations to make meaning of culture, leadership, and reform. In other words, individuals view culture, leadership, and reform through their own eyes. Collective meaning emerges as people work together within a culture, using leadership practices to bring reform to their school or district. The process and outcomes are unlikely to be those envisioned by model developers and advocates for educational reform, but they make sense to those within the districts or schools. As the following case illustrates, culture, leadership, and reform cannot be treated simply and rationally. Implementation plans, leadership checklists, and organizational charts assume a simpler context than exists in schools and districts.

METHODOLOGY

The research conducted for this chapter essentially started when the University of New Orleans Accelerated Schools Center began working with schools in Memphis in 1995. The University of New Orleans center maintains extensive records of training, field visits, and end-of-year assessments. These data were augmented by interviews conducted between July and December 2001 with staff members in MCS, researchers at the University of Memphis, and staff of the University of New Orleans Accelerated Schools Center. The MCS Office of Research and Evaluation provided data from implementation satisfaction surveys completed by all current accelerated schools in 2001. Because of the prominence of the Memphis commitment to comprehensive school reform, considerable data are available through numerous publications by the RAND Corporation (Berends, 1999; Berends, Kirby, Naftel, & McKelvey, 2000; Bodilly, 1996, 1998, 1999) and the Center for Research in Educational Policy at the University of Memphis (Ross, Alberg, & Wang, 2001; Ross, Sanders, Wright, & Stringfield,

1998; Ross, Wang, Sanders, Wright, & Stringfield, 1999; Ross, Wang, Wright, & Stringfield, 2000).

The conceptual framework was developed through the authors' involvement in research and leadership within the ASP (Finnan & Levin, 2000; Finnan & Swanson, 2000; Finnan, 1995; Meza, St John, Davidson, & Allen-Haynes, 1993/1994). Data from the Memphis interviews, site visit reports, end-of-year assessments, and document reviews were synthesized and analyzed through the lens of the conceptual framework.

CULTURE, LEADERSHIP, AND REFORM: MEMPHIS CITY SCHOOLS

Memphis City Schools: Prereform

When N. Gerry House came to MCS as superintendent in 1992, the district was one of the poorest performing districts in Tennessee, serving a population of primarily poor (71% qualify for free/reduced price lunch) African American (87%) students (School System Report Card, 2001). Although some small-scale innovations had been attempted before House's arrival (Etheridge & Collins, 1992; Etheridge, Terrell, & Watson, 1990), the district and the city did not have a reputation for innovation. An Education Week Special Report published in 1998 describes Memphis as having:

> a reputation as a generally sleepy Southern city, conservative in the sense that it is leery of outsiders and tends to resist change. While there have been pockets of innovation over the years, the district's officials remained largely untouched by the school reform movement. Its administrative culture was authoritarian, its curriculum regimented. (Sommerfeld, 1998, p. 245)

Most of the teachers and administrators had been educated in Tennessee, many of them in MCS, and there was a prevailing belief that, as one district office staff member said, "if the schools were good enough for me, they are good enough for today's students." However, the schools were clearly not serving the needs of its students. As late as 1998, 35.2% of the 9th grade students who started high school dropped out before they graduated; student attendance was low; and performance on the Tennessee Comprehensive Assessment Program, a standardized test given annually in second through eighth grade, was below state average in all subjects (Sommerfeld, 1998).

The culture of MCS was conservative and relatively bounded; most people within the district had few experiences with other educational systems and other ways of viewing the teaching and learning process. Because of their shared assumptions, beliefs, and values, it is likely that they did not realize that their expectations for students were low and that alternative approaches to education were possible. Role expectations were clear: leaders made decisions and followers carried them out. It was generally agreed that poverty, high student mobility, and lack of parental involvement were the cause of students' poor performance. Although most people in the district wanted the best for all students, their expectations for student performance were generally low, and there were few examples of concerted efforts to improve student achievement.

The superintendent, Willie W. Herenton, was prominent in the community, serving as superintendent from 1979 to 1991. He was politically active and was elected mayor of Memphis in November 1991. The central administration was described as top heavy with a superintendent, a level of deputy superintendents, another level of assistant superintendents, as well as several area offices, and additional district office staff (House, 1997). Decision-making was centralized and highly bureaucratic.

MCS had little experience with reform before House's arrival (Sommerfeld, 1998). In response to the poor performance of inner-city schools and loss of middle-class families to the suburbs, the district initiated several initiatives: one to deregulate seven inner-city schools (Etheridge & Collins, 1992), and the other to establish Optional Schools, a magnet school program designed to offer options to students and parents. With the exception of these initiatives, the administration encouraged people to maintain the status quo. The district ethos was one of recognizing what can't be done, rather than encouraging people to find innovative ways to make change (Sommerfeld, 1998, p. 246).

Memphis City Schools: The Reform Years

MCS may not have realized that they were to become a high-profile school district when they hired House in 1992. House had limited experience as a superintendent and no experience with an urban district; he came to Memphis from a much smaller, more affluent district in Chapel Hill-Carrboro, North Carolina. She had the reputation of being "an energetic, hands-on, methodical, and determined leader" (Hill, Campbell, & Harvey, 2000, p. 144). She immediately applied these traits to the problems she found in Memphis. She came to Memphis with a vision that she described through an imaginary school, Promise Street School. Promise Street set a vision that all schools were to emulate: high expectations for all students, active parental involvement, challenging and balanced curriculum and instruction, and highly collaborative teachers (House, 1997, pp. 239–241).

House welcomed the New American Schools Development Corporation (NASDC)[2] initiative to implement comprehensive school reform models on a large scale. The aims of the NASDC initiative were consistent with the goals she and a planning group developed, and she saw the school reform models brought by this initiative as providing research-based, systematic approaches to meeting many of her goals. House embraced comprehensive school reform whole-heartedly. Where other jurisdictions chose to scale up, but not involve all schools in the reform, House pledged that all 164 schools would eventually select a model. She gave schools three years to select a model. In hindsight, this pledge may have been a large part of the undoing of comprehensive school reform in Memphis (Viadero, 2001b). The first cohort of 34 schools received grants to implement models in 1995. A second cohort of 14 schools began implementing models in 1996; the remaining schools selected models in 1997 and 1998 (Center for Research in Educational Policy, 2002, p. 4). Schools were encouraged to select a model from a menu of NAS models and independent models (at this time the ASP was an independent model[3]).

The scale of implementation of comprehensive school reform in Memphis, House's energy and presence, and early positive reports on the effect of the models on student achievement and school climate (Ross, Sanders, Wright, & Stringfield, 1998; Ross et al., 1997; Bodilly, Purnell, Reichardt, & Schuyler, 1998) led to considerable attention from researchers, policy makers, and politicians. Memphis was considered the model for states and districts interested in school reform. Robert E. Slavin, founder of Success for All, told a reporter for *Education Week* "When people ask me, 'Where is an urban system with a vision of where it is going, and a plausible plan of how it's going to get there?' then Memphis would be at the top of my list" (Sommerfeld, 1998, p. 245).

On the whole, the schools choosing models in the first two years were more interested in and committed to comprehensive reform than those selecting in the last two years. In addition, more resources were available through MCS and NAS. Most of the schools in the early cohorts were excited about the support and resources provided to implement a model of their choice. Other schools, especially the schools in the later cohorts that hoped to "wait out this fad," tended to select models that appeared to require the least work (Datnow, 2000). Even among the schools in the first two cohorts, buy-in by teachers was not always as strong as model developers recommend; although people appreciated having an opportunity to select a model, they knew that they did not have the option to choose not to participate. While some teachers resented the additional work required of implementing a school reform model and found the professional development offerings insufficient (Calaway, 2001), others appreciated the opportunity for professional growth, teacher empowerment, and the focus on student achievement offered by the models. In addition, principal leadership was not always consistent with effective implementation (Center for Research in Educational Policy, 2002).

As additional schools were adopting models, the cost of scale-up increased. At the point when the more resistant schools were adopting models, the resources to support training and follow-up were reduced. As part of a cost-saving effort and to build local capacity, MCS relied increasingly on district staff to provide training and follow up support for the models. Many of the models provided what they later referred to as "model lite" support in order to remain involved in Memphis. The district staff selected to represent the models were trained and knowledgeable, but staff often wore more than one hat when working with a school. For example, some district model liaisons also served as teacher evaluators in the same schools where they worked as a facilitator or coach for the model. This confused teachers because they felt they could not trust the primary link to their model.

How did this total commitment to district-wide implementation of comprehensive school reform affect the district culture? The commitment to comprehensive school reform definitely challenged the assumptions, values, and beliefs held by people in the district. However, it is impossible to ascertain the degree to which people actually changed their assumptions, values, and beliefs in line with House's vision and the underlying philosophy of the reforms. With comprehensive school reform came people from outside MCS who had different ideas and beliefs concerning teaching and learning and how schools should be organized. Rather than reinforcing the existing culture, House and the reform models encouraged people to transform the culture.

The closed, self-referential system that existed before House's arrival was opened up to multiple influences. Role expectations shifted. There was a real emphasis on collaborative decision-making; principals were expected to assume different roles in their buildings, and teachers were expected to take on more leadership roles. Communication channels flattened. Rather than communicating to schools what they should do, district office staff members were assigned to schools to help them implement designs. They were expected to listen to the requests of schools rather than tell schools what to do. Room in the communication network had to be made for the model developers. Possibly the most important impact on the existing district culture involved assumptions about students and their ability to learn, about who should be involved in decision-making, about the teaching and learning process, and about the value of change. These changes in organizational structures, expectations, and opportunities to interact with people from outside the district initiated culture change in the district.

Leadership during this period changed considerably. House led very differently than her predecessor. Herenton was an authoritarian, traditional superintendent, but he was also very attuned to the concerns and issues in the community. People trusted him and felt that he listened to them; he was very well-connected within the local political setting. He supported the growth and advancement of people within the district. House, on the other hand, was intelligent, innovative, analytic, and methodical. She expected a lot from the people working under her and was described as impatient and somewhat detached. According to a MCS staff member, a local newspaper described her as a "wine and cheese superintendent in a cold-cut town." House was also very political, but her focus was more national than local.

She became a rising star in educational administration and school reform circles. In 1999, she was voted Superintendent of the Year by the American Association of School Administrators. She brought bright, dedicated, and innovative people into the district, but many of them became discouraged as their enthusiasm about change met the resistance and skepticism lying beneath the surface in the district.

Reform was "the name of the game" during the House years. Where change was incremental and small-scale before House, it was intentional, rapid, and ubiquitous during her superintendency. The primary focus of reform was on schools and on teaching and learning. As teachers and principals were expected to improve their schools and their teaching, the district office was also expected to change. Many jobs were eliminated; central office staff and administrators were either let go or reassigned to jobs that worked more closely with schools, the reform models, and professional development. Most district office personnel worked directly with schools under House. The Teaching and Learning Academy was established to provide state-of-the-art professional development to teachers in all MCS schools. Reform was seen as a positive, exciting adventure away from the status quo. It was easy for people brought in from the outside to get excited about the focus on reform, but it was challenging and unsettling for many of the people within the district. By committing to reform, the district was implicitly saying that prior practice was wrong. House was careful to not criticize Mayor Herenton, but it was transparent he left serious problems that House set out to rectify.

Memphis Accelerated Schools: The Reform Years

Each school affiliating with the ASP brought its own culture, leadership practice, and experience with reform to the process. The schools were typical of Memphis schools. Few had experience with reform. They served predominantly low-income (average of 81% of students receive free or reduced price lunch) Black (average of 92%) students (Memphis City Schools, 2000). Most of the administrators and teachers were educated in Tennessee, many of them in Memphis. Between 1995 and 1998, 18 schools affiliated with the ASP. It is best to describe the ASP schools in two cohorts. Schools joining ASP in 1995 (three schools) and 1996 (three schools) were, with two exceptions,[4] eager to embrace change and most had strong leadership. Four of the principals had many social and professional ties; they lived in Tennessee all of their lives and worked in MCS for many years. Two of these schools were located in relatively affluent areas of Memphis and benefited from strong teaching staffs and solid parental support. Most of this cohort welcomed a change in focus from what students cannot do to what they can do.

The second cohort includes schools joining ASP in 1997 (five schools) and 1998 (seven schools). These schools either delayed affiliation with ASP because the district did not think they were ready to implement the model (e.g., their applications to implement a model were not funded), or they joined ASP reluctantly and only because they were told they had to select a model. They were not familiar with reform and had little interest in change. With three exceptions, these schools had serious problems implementing ASP. The culture in many of these schools justified resistance to reform, as did ineffective leadership patterns and chronic teacher turnover.

Memphis schools were introduced to comprehensive school reform through a Design Fair held in the spring of 1995.[5] All Memphis schools were required to send representatives to the Design Fair. Each model held information sessions throughout the day to give the school representatives an overview of the model. Staff from the University of New Orleans Accelerated Schools Center participated in the fair and provided training and follow up to Memphis Accelerated Schools until June 2001. Following the Design Fair, schools interested in implementing a model the next year completed an application process. Some schools applied immediately, others prepared applications that were not funded until later cohorts, and some waited until they had to apply. See Table 5.1 for more information on the schools that implemented the ASP in Memphis.

ASP schools in the first cohort participated eagerly in training, and they selected strong coaches to work within their schools to implement the project. Three of the principals were strong, well connected in the community, and committed to ASP. Many of the teachers in this cohort participated actively in the network of ASP schools in Memphis, in the University of New Orleans Accelerated Schools Center network, and nationally. Teachers presented at conferences and helped provide training for other ASP schools in Memphis. They also used the resources of the Teaching and Learning Academy frequently.

The second cohort of schools embraced ASP less enthusiastically and had a lower level of readiness to implement school reform. With several exceptions, the principals lacked the commitment to the project or did not have leadership styles compatible with ASP; coaching teams were not as strong as those in the first cohort, and interest and enthusiasm to implement ASP was not as evident among the teaching staff. This is strikingly illustrated in a study conducted by MCS in 2001. Teachers and administrators in all schools were asked to complete a survey on the effectiveness of implementation of the reform models adopted at their schools. Part of the survey was generic to all reform models and involved eight characteristics of effective organizations (Calaway, 2001, pp. 12–13). The findings show a marked difference between the 1995/1996 cohorts and the 1997/1998 cohorts in terms of reported effectiveness of implementation along these dimensions. As Table 5.2 illustrates, where the early cohort is uniformly well above the norm (calculated from the responses of all schools), the later cohort is below the norm. The difference in satisfaction is attributable in part to the lack of readiness and interest of these schools

Table 5.1 Characteristics of ASP Schools in Memphis

School	Year Joined ASP	Percentage of Black & Hispanic Students*	Percentage of Free or Reduced Lunch	Initial Interest in ASP	Principal Rating	Coach Rating	MCS Implementation Rating**	Student Achievement Gains***	Left ASP Before June 2001
1995 A	1995	100%	89%	high	not strong with teachers.	strong	0.459	n/a	yes, in 2000
1995 B	1995	100%	99%	high	strong but focus on public relations	multiple turnover	n/a	significant decrease	no
1995 C	1995	100%	100%	mixed	lax leadership	initially strong	not included	not included	yes - SFA in 1998
1996 A	1996	100%	84%	high	strong	strong	0.759	n/a	no
1996 B	1996	85%	75%	high	strong	strong	0.557	significant increase	yes, in 2000
1996 C	1996	43%	41%	high	strong, well connected	strong	0.605	significant increase	yes, in 2000
1997 A	1997	92%	79%	high	strong	strong but unorganized	0.358	decrease	no
1997 B	1997	99%	88%	mixed	strong, but intimidating	weak—coach changes	0.342	n/a	no
1997 C	1997	99%	75%	low	no commitment	organized but inflexible	−0.215	n/a	no
1997 D	1997	100%	92%	mixed	traditional	inflexible & controlling	0.459	significant decrease	no

(Continued)

Table 5.1 Continued

School	Year Joined ASP	Percentage of Black & Hispanic Students*	Percentage of Free or Reduced Lunch	Initial Interest in ASP	Principal Rating	Coach Rating	MCS Implementation Rating**	Student Achievement Gains***	Left ASP Before June 2001
1997 E	1997	92%	70%	high	strong	strong & methodical	0.112	significant increase	no
1998 A	1998	n/a	n/a	high	strong	strong	n/a	n/a	no
1998 B	1998	96%	75%	low	strong & no nonsense	weak	−0.421	n/a	no
1998 C	1998	100%	79%	mixed	weak	weak	n/a		no
1998 D	1998	100%	87%	mixed	gone 1st year. No commitment	organized, no knowledge	n/a	n/a	no
1998 E	1998	100%	92%	low	weak	weak	−0.208	significant decrease	no
1998 F	1998	98%	93%	low	average—no nonsense	weak	−0.249	n/a	no
1998 G	1998	99%	69%	low	weak—didn't want ASP	not allowed to coach	n/a	n/a	no

*Memphis City Schools (2000).
**Memphis City Schools (no date).
***Center for Research in Educational Policy (2002)

Table 5.2   Scale Means and Item Frequencies for General Implementation
             Questions by Implementation Cohort—Elementary Schools*

	Implementing 1995 & 1996**	Implementing 1997 & 1998**	ASP Average	Norm
Productivity	.572	−.031	.092	0
Direction	.650	−.075	.071	0
Coordination	.593	−.114	.020	0
Monitoring	.524	−.098	.016	0
Facilitation	.620	−.106	.029	0
Mentoring	.581	−.072	.061	0
Innovation	.662	.019	.152	0
Brokering	.549	−.076	.057	0

*The survey was developed by Memphis City Schools Office of Research and
Development. The scales are derived from research on effective organizations.
**Average score for all schools that began implementation during these two years. Two
schools are not included because of low response rate; one school dropped ASP in
1998, and another is not included because it serves a special population. N for 1995 &
1996 = 4 schools. N for 1997 and 1998 = 8 schools. The norm is calculated for all
schools implementing reform.

to implement the model, but it also reflects the limited time the schools
had been involved with the model.

A 2002 report conducted by the Center for Research in Educational
Policy at the University of Memphis examines the factors that most strongly
influenced Memphis schools' success or lack of success in improving
student achievement over time (p. 2). According to the report, "schools rated
by MCS evaluators as being more successful in implementing a reform
model were significantly more likely to have higher 1995–2000 achievement change scores once school background variables were controlled"
(p. 11). The study found that three ASP schools were highly successful (had
significant student achievement gains following implementation) and four
were less successful (demonstrated the least progress in raising achievement over time) (p. 14); schools falling between highly successful and less
successful were not analyzed. Of those found to be most successful, two of
the three were in the first cohort. Of those found to be least successful,
three of the four were in the second cohort.

ASP challenged the assumptions, values, and beliefs underlying the
culture of all of the schools implementing the project in Memphis. In some
cases, there was compatibility between the existing culture and that of
ASP, and the school community embraced the project as a way to make
desired changes (Finnan, 2000). In many cases, some components of ASP
were embraced, while others were ignored or avoided. For example, one

school implemented the governance structure and used the inquiry process, but classroom practice never reflected ASP's commitment to powerful learning. In other cases, especially among schools implementing ASP in 1998, some schools only went through the motions of implementing ASP, and the school culture did not change.

Shared leadership was the norm among the Memphis Accelerated Schools. Coaches (teachers selected to support the project internally) embraced this new opportunity for teacher leadership. Teachers assumed additional decision-making roles through their work on cadres, the steering committee, and School As A Whole (meetings of the whole school community that are more inclusive than traditional faculty meetings). Although all of the principals were trained and mentored within a hierarchical system, some of them embraced the more facilitative leadership style necessary to implement ASP. They welcomed the opportunity to build on the strengths of teachers and other staff members. Other principals were unwilling to relinquish control; this was very frustrating to teachers excited by the promise of having a voice in decision-making. Others had been ineffective prior to joining ASP, and they remained ineffective despite growth opportunities offered through ASP training and networking.

Although all of the schools implemented ASP, it served to reform each school in a unique way. Because ASP is a process reform, not prescribing curriculum or instructional strategies, each school adapted ASP to its own needs and goals. Schools also varied in their fidelity to the model and in their capacity to implement it. They chose to implement some ASP components more fully than others. In some cases, ASP was evident in teachers' classroom practice with many teachers embracing the concept of powerful learning and adapting gifted and talented strategies for their students. In other cases, the reform focused primarily on making the school's governance structure more inclusive and on making decision-making more systematic. In other cases, it was barely evident in any aspect of the school. Reform, although not uniform, occurred in almost all of the schools implementing ASP. The same cannot be said about all classrooms, but the focus of ASP has been on reforming classrooms by first reforming schools.

Memphis City Schools: Postreform

House left MCS in April 2000 to head the Institute for Student Achievement, a public-private partnership in Long Island, New York. Johnnie B. Watson, a former deputy superintendent under Willie W. Herenton, was selected as interim superintendent in spring 2000 and became superintendent in October 2000, with the strong backing of the mayor. Watson is a veteran of the MCS system, leaving the district only during the House years. House's departure led many in the district to question the future of comprehensive school reform, and schools not fully committed to models began to slack off implementation as soon as they knew she was leaving. Test scores released by the end of the school year were discouraging, providing opponents of comprehensive school reform evidence that the models were not working.

Soon after taking over as superintendent, Watson commissioned a study of the reforms that showed that they had little or no positive effect on student achievement (Calaway, 2001). In June 2001, Watson announced to the school board that he wanted to discontinue supporting the reform models. Watson justified this decision saying, "When you look at the expenditure and the results we were getting, it did not seem to me to be worth it" (Viadero, 2001a, p. 1). The board agreed with the decision, as did many people in the district. According to newspaper accounts, many teachers thanked Watson for his decision because it allowed them to return to teaching (Edmonson & Erskine, 2001). The MCS report has been externally reviewed and found to be flawed, but the decision to discontinue all comprehensive school reform holds (Vaidero, 2001b).

Superintendent Watson has developed an eight-point plan to improve the schools. The plan involves a new curriculum framework developed by the district, an emphasis on reading, and purchase of new reading textbooks. Professional development is geared to meeting the Tennessee curriculum standards, as is teacher support and assessment. Attention is also shifting to help schools better "monitor, mentor, and coach their teachers" (Viadero, 2001a, p. 19). Missing from the plan are all comprehensive school reform models.

What is the culture of MCS now that the district no longer supports comprehensive school reform? As one district office staff member said, "People are hailing Watson's decision as a 'return to normalcy.'" The backlash against the reforms was sufficient to make many in the district long for the days before Memphis was under the spotlight for reform; they have gotten what they longed for. The district has turned inward for direction and support. Almost all of the professional development offered to teachers is done through staff assigned to the Teaching and Learning Academy. Expectations that all students can excel at high levels have been replaced by an emphasis on basic skills development. Because the Tennessee standards encourage a blend of basic skills and higher order skills, expectations for students cannot revert completely to prereform levels. A commitment to innovation and risk taking has been replaced with a commitment to uniformity across all schools. All schools must complete a strategic plan, assess teachers in the same way, and provide the same reading curriculum to all students in the district. The conservative nature of MCS's culture is evident in its current organization and in the assumptions guiding policies and procedures.

Leadership at the district level reverted back to many of the same patterns and structures that existed before the reform years. Whereas House encouraged shared leadership, recognizing that leadership is an interactive process involving leaders and followers within a school or district, Watson is a top-down leader, designing programs and determining directions for the district that principals and teachers are expected to follow. Watson enjoys the support of Mayor Herenton whose influence in the city is undeniable. Herenton has been referred to as the "Richard Dailey of Memphis," controlling all aspects of the city while benefiting from the considerable support from the majority of Memphis citizens.

MCS continues to change; reforms are underway. Yet now these reforms are "homegrown" and divorced from national comprehensive school reform models. The reforms are geared to meeting state standards and creating more uniformity in the direction of reform. Reform is more accepted in the district than it was before House's arrival; MCS is aware that it cannot totally isolate itself from outside influences and that schools must change to better serve the students. Experience with reform accounts for some of this willingness to engage in reform, but pressure from the state to improve student achievement and to integrate curriculum standards into the teaching and learning process also drive current reform efforts. Where reform expertise was sought from the outside under House, it now emanates from within the district. This is consistent with the orientation of the two superintendents—House sought support and encouragement at the national level; Watson seeks it at the local level.

Memphis Accelerated Schools: Postreform

When Gerry House left Memphis and Johnny B. Watson took over as superintendent, the schools that implemented the ASP only because they were forced to stopped all pretense of involvement. Schools that were committed to ASP assumed that they would be allowed to continue involvement with it. Principals from eight Memphis schools registered to attend a Principals' Academy at the National Center for the ASP in late June 2001. They arrived at University of Connecticut days after Watson made the announcement that Memphis would no longer support or encourage involvement in comprehensive reform. Needless to say, these principals were in shock, realizing that the Principals' Academy would be the last ASP event they would attend.

Did involvement with the ASP change school culture for these schools? Clearly, the answer depends on the school. In schools that demonstrated readiness and the capacity to implement ASP, the school cultures have been changed. The "way of doing business" in these schools is different. In many of them, decision-making remains shared; teachers, staff, and parents are involved in the decisions schools are allowed to make. Schools are allowed to retain the best practices from ASP and include these in their strategic plans. Most importantly, the ASP principles and values, the commitment to high expectations for all students, and the focus on powerful learning challenged or reinforced the assumptions held by administrators, teachers, staff, and parents in the ASP schools.

Because culture change is essentially collective individual change, school cultures will reflect ASP as long as people who were truly committed to ASP remain at the schools. Will the cultures be changed permanently? The school cultures are unlikely to return to what they were like before schools joined ASP, but they are also not likely to stay as they were during the reform period. As described at the beginning of this chapter, cultures are conservative and ever-changing. Where the conservative nature of culture made it difficult to make rapid changes in the schools, it will serve to retain influences from ASP. Where the ever-changing nature of culture led to changes in these schools, it will also accommodate future changes.

Some changes in the leadership patterns in the schools that embraced ASP are likely to remain as long as the principals remain at the schools. Some principals demonstrated true changes in leadership style during the years they were involved with ASP. The district expects more hierarchical leadership, and principals who were more inclined to this leadership style are likely to revert back to this style, but they have experienced a different way of leading. Shared leadership will be stifled by the expectation of the superintendent that decisions flow from the top down. Leadership will remain distributed as described by Spillane, Halverson, and Diamond (1999, 2001), but it is likely to be distributed among fewer leaders and more followers.

Reform will also continue in the former ASP schools. The reform will not emanate from the ASP or from networking with other ASP schools. Reform in Memphis schools will come through initiatives designed by the district and the state. These reforms retain some of the focus of the ASP, with an emphasis on holding all students to high standards and assuming that all students should be expected to master basic and higher order skills. The support provided to the schools to meet these goals is quite different. Where during the reform period, the accelerated schools received support from the ASP (at the national level, through the University of New Orleans Accelerated Schools Center, and through local liaisons) and from resources at the Teaching and Learning Academy, support now is primarily offered through the Teaching and Learning Academy, with some funding available for approved consultants. The national reform spotlight is no longer turned on Memphis, but reform will continue because of Tennessee's and the nation's commitment to accountability.

CONCLUSION

We began this chapter with three sets of questions related to culture, leadership, and reform. The Memphis experiment provides answers to these questions related not only to ASP implementation, but also to the implementation of all models. The following are some lessons that can be drawn from this case.

What Do We Need to Know About District, School, and Classroom Culture to Embed Reform Into These Cultures?

- Understand how the six characteristics of culture interact within the district, school, or classroom.
- Realize that culture change can be supported and encouraged, but it cannot be forced or mandated.
- Expect "two steps forward, one step back" change; culture change is not linear; new ideas and assumptions need to meld with established ways of thinking and doing for cultures to change.
- Understand that culture change involves individual change since culture resides within people.

How Do We Work Within Existing Cultures to Make Reforms a Part of Them?

- The key is to work "within" existing cultures and recognize the influence of the existing culture.
- Do not expect change to occur quickly and smoothly.
- Recognize and build on existing strengths in the culture.
- Understand the power and political structure within the culture.
- Realize that changing cultures involves changing people, and that personal change can be difficult if it is not adequately supported.

How Can Leaders Change Culture in the Unit They Lead?

- Understand that viewing leadership as practices distributed among leaders, followers, and the situation is more compatible with changing culture than other ways of viewing leadership.
- Realize that superintendents or principals alone cannot change district or school cultures, but they can create conditions that encourage change.
- Realize that teachers have more opportunity to change their classroom culture than superintendents and principals have to change district or school culture.

How Does a Transforming Culture Change Once a Leader Leaves?

- Recognize that, at some level, culture changes do remain as long as the changes reach people's assumptions, values, and beliefs.
- Some changes in school culture can survive leadership change at the district level if they are truly embedded in the school culture.
- Changes in classroom culture follow the teacher; a classroom culture does not remain once a teacher leaves.

Will Reform Last If It Is Mandated From Above?

- It can if the people being asked to change support the reform.
- Reform needs to be nurtured through provision of resources, stable leadership, and supportive district and state policies.

- It needs to be seen as a culture change process that takes time.
- Attention needs to be paid to the political and power structure for reforms to be accepted and nurtured.

Is It Better to Focus Reform on the Classroom Rather Than the School?

- Yes, because the classroom is buffered from outside influences.
- It is easier to improve student achievement if reform focuses on the classroom.
- If the focus of reform is shifted to the classroom, attention still needs to be paid to the school so that it creates conditions to foster change in classrooms.
- Whether the focus is on the school or the classroom, the principals must provide opportunities for effective professional development.

We began this chapter by asking how school reform could end so decisively and why people in Memphis did not mobilize to retain the comprehensive school reform models. As this chapter illustrates, the reforms did not end as decisively as it seemed. They remain within the individuals committed to them and within the cultures of schools that have a collective commitment to the reforms. One administrative decision cannot wipe out five years of effort and individual and collective transformations of assumptions, values, and beliefs. Why did model supporters not mobilize to fight Watson's decision to discontinue support for comprehensive school reform models? First, the decision took most people by surprise, and they did not have time to mobilize support. Second, support for the models was far from universal; many people within schools were happy to see their involvement with the model end. Third, the models were so different in focus and support that collective action was difficult. The question remaining to be answered is how long will the influence of the Memphis experiment with comprehensive school reform remain in the teaching and leadership practices of people who participated in reform. Teaching and learning will continue to change in Memphis, as in the rest of the nation, and this experience with comprehensive school reform will remain an important influence for those in Memphis who embraced reform.

REFERENCES

Accelerated Schools Project (2002). Retrieved June 21, 2002, from: www.accelerated-schools.net.

Ayers, W. (1992). Work that is real: Why teachers should be empowered. In G. A. Hess Jr. (Ed.), *Empowering teachers and parents: School restructuring through the eyes of anthropologists* (pp. 13–28). Westport, CT: Bergin & Garvey.

Berends, M. (1999). *Assessing the progress of New American Schools: A status report.* Santa Monica, CA: RAND.

Berends, M., Kirby, S., Naftel, S., & McKelvey, C. (2000). *Implementation and performance in New American Schools: Three years after scale-up.* Santa Monica, CA: RAND, MD-1145-EDU.

Bodilly, S. J. (1996). *Lessons from New American Schools Development Corporation's demonstration phase.* Santa Monica, CA: RAND.

Bodilly, S. J. (1998). *Lessons from New American Schools' scale-up phase: Prospects for bringing designs to multiple schools.* Santa Monica, CA: RAND, MR-942-NAS.

Bodilly, S. J. (1999, April). *District support needed to promote reform at scale.* Paper presented at the American Education Research Association, Montreal.

Bodilly, S. J., Keltner, B., Purnell, S., Reichardt, R., & Schuyler, G. (1998). *Lessons from New American Schools' scale-up phase: Prospects for bringing designs to multiple schools.* Santa Monica, CA: RAND, MR-942.0-NAS.

Calaway, F. (2001, June). *Evaluation of the comprehensive school reform models in the Memphis City Schools.* TN: Memphis City Schools Office of Research & Evaluation.

Center for Research in Educational Policy. (2002, January). *Using comprehensive school reform models to raise student achievement: Factors associated with success in Memphis schools.* Report prepared for New American Schools. University of Memphis.

Copland, M. A. (2001). The myth of the superprincipal. *Phi Delta Kappan, 82*(7), 528.

Cuban, L. (1990). Reforming again, again, and again. *Educational Researcher, 19*(1), 3–13.

Datnow, A. (2000). Power and politics in the adoption of school reform models. *Educational Evaluation and Policy Analysis, 22*(4), 357–374.

Deal, T. E., & Peterson, K. D. (1999). *Shaping school culture: The heart of leadership.* San Francisco: Jossey-Bass.

Desimone, L. (2000). *Making comprehensive school reform work.* ERIC/CUE Monograph. Retrieved June 21, 2002, from http://eric-web.tc.columbia.edu/monographs/uds112/index.html

Distributed Leadership Project (2001). Retrieved June 21, 2002, from www/letus.org/dls/indes.htm.

Edmonson, A., & Erskine, M. (2001). School reform put to test, now to rest. *The Commercial Appeal,* June 20.

Elmore, R. F., & McLaughlin, M. W. (1988). *Steady work: Policy, practice, and the reform of American education.* Santa Monica, CA: RAND.

Etheridge, C. P., & Collins, T. W. (1992). Conflict in restructuring the principal-teacher relationship in Memphis. In G. A. Hess, Jr. (Ed.), *Empowering teachers and parents: School restructuring through the eyes of anthropologists* (pp. 89–102). Westport, CT: Bergin & Garvey.

Etheridge, C. P., Terrell, L., & Watson, J. B. (1990). Teachers, administrators, and parents together: The Memphis model for managing schools through shared decision making. *Tennessee Educational Leadership, 17*(2), 43–48.

Evans, R. (1996). *The human side of school change: Reform, resistance, and the real-life problems of innovation.* San Francisco: Jossey-Bass.

Finnan, C. (2000, April). *Implementing school reform: Why is it so hard for some and easy for others?* Presented at the Annual Meeting of the American Educational Researchers Association. New Orleans. (ERIC Document Reproduction Service No. ED446356)

Finnan, C., & Levin, H. M. (2000). Changing school culture. In J. Elliott & H. Altrichter (Eds.), *Images of educational change* (pp. 87–98). Milton Keynes, UK: Open University Press.

Finnan, C., Schnelep, K. C., & Anderson, L. W. (n.d.). *Powerful learning environments: The critical link between changes in school culture and improvements in student learning.* Unpublished manuscript.

Finnan, C., St. John, E., McCarthy, J., & Slovacek, S. (Eds.). (1996). *Accelerated Schools in action: Lessons from the field.* Thousand Oaks, CA: Corwin Press.

Finnan, C., & Swanson, J. D. (2000). *Accelerating the learning of all students: Cultivating culture change in schools, classrooms, and individuals.* Boulder, CO: Westview Press.

Firestone, W. A. (1996). Leadership roles of functions? In K. Leithwood, J. Chapman, D. Corson, P. Hallinger, & A. Hart (Eds.), *Handbook of research on educational administration* (Vol. 2, pp. 395–418). Boston: Kluwer Academic.

Florio-Ruane, S. (1989). Social organization of classes and schools. In M. Reynolds (Ed.), *Knowledge base for the beginning teacher* (pp. 163–172). New York: Pergamon Press.

Fullan, M. (2001a). *Leading in a culture of change.* San Francisco: Jossey-Bass.

Fullan, M. (2001b). *The new meaning of educational change* (3rd ed.). New York: Teachers College Press.

Hallinger, P., & McCary, C. E. (1990) Developing the strategic thinking of instructional leaders. *Elementary School Journal, 91,* 89–107.

Hallinger, P., & Murphy, J. (1985). Assessing the instructional management behavior of principals. *Elementary School Journal, 86,* 217–247.

Hill, P. T., Campbell, C., & Harvey, J. (2000). *It takes a city: Getting serious about urban school reform.* Washington, DC: Brookings Institution.

Hopfenberg, W. S., Levin, H. M., & Associates (1993). *The Accelerated Schools resource guide.* San Francisco: Jossey-Bass.

House, N. G. (1997). Memphis City Schools, Memphis, Tennessee. In P. C. Schlechty (Ed.), *Inventing better schools: An action plan for educational reform* (pp. 239–255). San Francisco: Jossey-Bass.

Keller, B., & Huebner, T. (1997) *Powerful learning in Accelerated Schools: Opportunities for and impediments to implementation.* Paper presented at the annual meetings of the American Educational Research Association, March. Chicago.

Levin, H. M. (1987). *Accelerated schools for at-risk students* (CPRE Research Report RR-110). Paper commissioned by the Center for Policy Research in Education, Rutgers University.

Levin, H. M. (1996). Accelerated schools: The background. In C. Finnan, E. P. St. John, J. McCarthy, & S. P. Slovacek (Eds.), *Accelerated schools in action: Lessons from the field* (pp. 3–23). Thousand Oaks, CA: Corwin Press.

McQuillan, P. J. (1998). *Educational opportunity in an urban American high school: A cultural analysis.* Albany: State University of New York Press.

Memphis City Schools. (n.d.). unpublished data.

Memphis City Schools. (2000). *MCS School Profiles, 1999–2000.* Retrieved June 21, 2002, from http://www.memphis-schools.k12.tn.us/admin/communications/schools.html

Meza, J., Jr., St John, E. P., Davidson, B., & Allen-Haynes, L. (1993/1994). Discovering the meaning of empowerment. *Louisiana Educational Research Journal, 19*(2), 11–22.

Ross, S. M., Alberg, M., & Wang, L. W. (2001). *The impacts of alternative school restructuring designs on at-risk learners: A longitudinal study.* Memphis, TN: Center for Research in Educational Policy, University of Memphis.

Ross, S. M., Sanders, W. L., Wright, S. P., & Stringfield, S. (1998). *The Memphis restructuring initiative: Achievement results for years 1 and 2 on the Tennessee Value-Added Assessment System (TVAAS).* Memphis, TN: Center for Research in Educational Policy, University of Memphis.

Ross, S. M., Troutman, A., Horgan, D., Maxwell, S., Laitenin, R., & Lowther, D. (1997). The success of schools in implementing eight restructuring designs: A synthesis of first-year evaluation outcomes. *School Effectiveness and School Improvement, 8*(1), 125–150.

Ross, S. M., Wang, W., Sanders, W. L., Wright, S. P., & Stringfield, S. (1999). *Two- and three-year achievement results on the Tennessee value-added assessment system for restructuring schools in Memphis.* Memphis, TN: Center for Research in Educational Policy, University of Memphis.

Ross, S. M., Wang, L. W., Wright, S. P., & Stringfield, S. (2000). *The Memphis restructuring initiative: Achievement results for years 3 and 4 on the Tennessee Value-Added Assessment System (TVAAS).* Memphis, TN: Center for Research in Educational Policy, University of Memphis.

Sarason, S. (1996). *Revisiting "The culture of the school and the problem of change."* New York: Teachers College Press.

Schëin, E. (1992). *Organizational culture and leadership,* 2nd ed. San Francisco: Jossey-Bass.

Schlechty, P. C. (1997). *Inventing better schools: An action plan for educational reform.* San Francisco: Jossey-Bass.

School System Report Card (2001). Retrieved June 21, 2002, from http://www.k-12.state.tn.us/rptcrd01/school1.asp

Sergiovanni, T. J. (2000). *The lifeworld of leadership: Creating culture, community, and personal meaning in our schools.* San Francisco: Jossey-Bass.

Sommerfield, M. (1998). Solo performances. *Education Week Special Report: Quality Counts '89.* January 8, 244–247.

Spillane, J. P., Halverson, R., Diamond, J. B. (1999). *Distributed leadership: Toward a theory of school leadership practice.* Paper presented at the annual meeting of the American Educational Research Association, Montreal.

Spillane, J. P., Halverson, R., Diamond, J. B. (2001). Investigating school leadership practice: A distributed perspective. *Educational Researcher, 30*(3), 23–28.

Spindler, G. D. (1999). Personal communication. August 25.

Spindler, G., & Spindler, L. (1987). Cultural dialogue and schooling in Schöenhausen and Roseville: A comparative analysis. *Anthropology and Education Quarterly, 18*(1), 3–16.

Spindler, G., & Spindler, L. (1993). Cross-cultural, comparative, reflective interviewing in Schöenhausen and Roseville. In M. Schratz (Ed.), *Voices in educational research* (pp. 150–175). New York: Falmer.

Stringfield, S. C., & Datnow, A. (1998). Introduction: Scaling up school restructuring designs in urban schools. *Education and Urban Society, 30*(3).

Timar, T. (1989, December). The politics of school restructuring. *Phi Delta Kappan, 7*(4), 165–175.

Tyack, D., & Cuban, L. (1995). *Tinkering toward utophia: A century of public school reform.* Cambridge, MA: Harvard University Press.

Viadero, D. (2001a, July 11) Memphis scraps redesign models in all its schools. *Education Week, XXI,* 1, 19.

Viadero, D. (2001b, November 7). Whole-school projects show mixed results: Reform models suffer string of setbacks. *Education Week, XXI*(10), 1, 24–25.

Wax, M. L. (1993). How culture misdirects multiculturalism. *Anthropology and Education Quarterly, 24*(2), 99–115.

NOTES

1. This section draws from *Accelerating the Learning of All Students: Cultivating Culture Change in Schools, Classrooms, and Individuals* (Finnan & Swanson, 2000, pp. 63–74).

2. NASDC is now New American Schools (NAS).

3. The Accelerated Schools Project joined NAS in 2000.

4. One school ultimately found ASP incompatible with its school culture and affiliated with Success for All. Another school had strong teacher buy-in, but the principal was controlling and did not support teacher initiatives.

5. The comprehensive school reform scale-up in Memphis was supported by NASDC and the Education Commission of the States (ECS). ECS approached the Accelerated Schools Project and the Padeia Project to provide reform opportunities outside of NASDC models. NASDC funded implementation of its models, and the Memphis City Schools funded implementation of the other models. The funding available to the NASDC schools exceeded that offered to schools implementing the independent models. Funding disparities were evident to both NASDC and independent schools.

C H A P T E R   S I X

New American Schools

*District and School Leadership
for Whole-School Reform*

Mark Berends, Susan Bodilly,
and Sheila Nataraj Kirby

Throughout the history of educational reform efforts, a theme that has emerged is that the process of planned educational change is extremely complex, much more so than we anticipate or realize (Fullan, 2001; McLaughlin, 1991). This is largely because of the number of players involved and the number of factors that need to be aligned to support fundamental change in schools. A second theme that has emerged is the key role that leaders at the school, district, and state level play in bringing about such transformation (Elmore, 2000; Purkey & Smith, 1983; Sergiovanni, 2000).

This chapter addresses the complexities and challenges underlying reform of high-poverty schools through whole-school designs based on insights gained from RAND's assessment of New American Schools (NAS). In particular, we focus on the role of district and school leadership in initiating and implementing change at the school level. First, we provide a brief history of NAS and the leadership it provided in developing designs and distributing them widely to schools across the nation. Second, we describe RAND's assessment of NAS. Third, we provide an overview of the districts and schools that attempted to use NAS comprehensive school designs to improve their performance from 1995–1998 and the levels of implementation of reform models they achieved. Fourth, we use our findings to illustrate the importance of district, principal, and teacher leadership in the process of school change.

NEW AMERICAN SCHOOLS: LEADERSHIP FROM THE PRIVATE SECTOR

In conjunction with President George Bush's America 2000 initiative, the New American Schools (NAS) Development Corporation was established in 1991 as a nonprofit corporation funded by the private sector. NAS's main goal was to improve student performance in schools across the nation. Its core premise was that all high-quality schools possess a de facto unifying design that allows all staff to function to the best of their abilities and that provides a consistent and coherent education instructional program to all students. The best way to ensure that low-performing schools adopted successful designs was to create "break-the-mold" school designs that could be readily adopted by communities around the nation. A design "articulates a school's vision, mission, and goals; guides the instructional program; shapes the selection and socialization of staff; and establishes common expectations for performance and accountability among students, teachers, and parents" (Glennan, 1998, p. 11).

NAS founders thought that in the past many reforms were "programmatic," focused on a particular set of individuals in a school or a particular subject or grade level. They believed that adoption of multiple and unconnected approaches to address each area of schooling resulted in a fragmented education program and a balkanized school organization. In contrast, they meant for whole-school designs to integrate best practices into a coherent and mutually reinforcing set of effective approaches to teaching and learning for the entire school.

This whole-school approach to educational improvement was a dramatically different way of initiating and disseminating large-scale educational improvements. It was a unique combination of (a) private-sector involvement using a venture capitalist approach, (b) the choice of school designs as the vehicle for reform, and (c) the ambitious goal of scale-up across the nation. The involvement of the private sector also led to an ambitious timeline. The private-sector sponsors wanted results in the form of many schools adopting designs and showing improved student performance within a five-year period. At the end of five years, NAS was to go out of business as design teams became self-sustaining.

It is important to make clear here that NAS was also different in many respects from other types of reforms in that initially it did not want design teams to target specific populations, grades, or schools with peculiar characteristics. The designs were to cover grades K-12 for all schools and students.

To make its goal of improving student achievement a reality, NAS initially organized its work into several phases:[1]

- A competition phase to solicit proposals and select designs
- School settings
- A scale-up phase in which the designs would be widely diffused in partnering jurisdictions across the nation

NAS originally selected 11 teams with unique designs in its competition phase but reduced the number to nine during the demonstration phase. By the scale-up phase, which began in 1995, there were seven design teams:

- Audrey Cohen College [AC] (currently renamed Purpose-Centered Education)
- Authentic Teaching, Learning, and Assessment for All Students [AT]
- Co-nect Schools [CON]
- Expeditionary Learning Outward Bound [EL]
- Modern Red SchoolHouse [MRSH]
- National Alliance for Restructuring Education [NARE] (currently renamed America's Choice Design Network)[2]
- Roots & Wings [RW]

While each design had unique features, the designs tended to emphasize school change in the following areas: organization and governance; teacher professional development; content and performance standards; curriculum and instructional strategies; and parent and community involvement. Only one, Roots and Wings, was specifically developed to meet the needs of high-poverty schools, and it was the only one that had developed any materials for schools with significant proportions of students who spoke English as a second language.

One of the strongest lessons learned during the demonstration experience was that designs, by themselves, could not transform schools. Schools needed substantial amounts of professional development, technical assistance, and materials geared to the design. This "design-based assistance" (Bodilly, 1996) became a key component of the NAS initiative and distinguished it from the more traditional approaches to school reform. Such design-based assistance included providing: (a) schools with a choice of designs to partner with; (b) specified designs that clarify both the end outcomes for the school and also intermediate implementation steps; and (c) assistance by the team to the school in the form of professional development, training, materials, conferences, networks, curriculum and instruction packages, etc. Finally, NAS's intention was for schools to pay design teams for their services. This would allow design teams to become self-sustaining.

As NAS moved into the scale-up phase, it understood clearly that school transformation would not occur unless there was strong district support. Therefore, NAS decided to partner with a limited number of districts to develop "markets" for the designs. These markets were intended to be in jurisdictions supportive of the NAS initiative. In particular, NAS sought jurisdictions that would commit to five-year partnerships with NAS and the design teams to create a supportive environment for whole-school reform. NAS required that the partnering jurisdictions also commit to transforming 30% of their schools using design-based assistance because it thought that this percentage, although somewhat arbitrary, would establish a significant core of schools to propel further changes in districts and schools. NAS partnered with ten jurisdictions at the beginning of its scale-up phase: Cincinnati, Ohio; Dade County, Florida; several districts in Kentucky; the state of Maryland; Memphis, Tennessee; Pittsburgh, Pennsylvania; Philadelphia, Pennsylvania; San Antonio, Texas; San Diego, California; and several districts in Washington state.[3]

The analyses covered here focus on the RAND assessment of NAS-related activities in its scale-up phase in these jurisdictions.

RAND ASSESSMENT ACTIVITIES

In 1991, NAS contracted with RAND to provide analytical support.[4] In 1995, RAND began to assess the scale-up of NAS designs to schools in partnering jurisdictions. From 1995 to 1999, the RAND program of studies addressed three major questions:

- What is the level of implementation in NAS schools?
- What impedes or facilitates that implementation?
- Does the adoption of NAS designs result in any changes in student and school outcomes?

Over this time period, RAND studies included: a longitudinal sample of NAS schools that began implementing early on in the scale-up phase and including data on implementation and performance from principals, teachers, and districts; case studies to analyze implementation and the role that districts play in impeding or enabling comprehensive school reform; a description of how designs have evolved from the initial proposal stage to implementing at scale in schools across the nation; analyses in one urban school district of how designs promote changes in classroom instruction, teaching, and learning, and individual-level student achievement scores; an analysis of performance differences in high-implementing NAS sites; and ongoing discussions with NAS staff and design team leaders.

There are some important limitations of this research that need to be kept in mind. The schools analyzed here were, for most design teams, the first schools the teams had provided assistance to in implementing their designs on a fee-for-service basis. There were many changes in both the designs and the assistance provided as the teams and the schools gained experience (for an analysis of the evolution of these designs, see Bodilly, 2001). The fact that designs were evolving over time as they gained experience and adapted to local contexts makes a longitudinal evaluation difficult, so findings regarding progress in implementation over time need to be interpreted with some caution.

AN OVERVIEW OF NAS SCALE-UP SCHOOLS AND IMPLEMENTATION

After four years of studying schools in the scale-up phase, we concluded that implementation in the scale-up sites was problematic. In part this might simply be because of the fact that NAS was working in very challenged schools. This section discusses the schools' characteristics, the levels of implementation, and some findings on factors affecting implementation.

Characteristics of NAS Scale-Up Schools

Most of the schools receiving design team assistance during the scale-up phase were economically and academically disadvantaged in terms of poverty, racial-ethnic composition, climate, and student test scores. The NAS sites in our sample were below "average" on a variety of dimensions when compared against national norms (Berends, 1999). For example, the NAS schools in Cincinnati, Dade, Memphis, Pittsburgh, and San Antonio were serving mostly poor student populations—more than two-thirds of the students were eligible for free/reduced lunch at these NAS sites.

NAS schools in our sample were also serving a disproportionately high number of students of color. For example, about 35% of the nation's students were categorized as racial-ethnic minorities. In contrast, 57% of students in NAS schools were minorities. Excluding Kentucky and Washington schools, more than 80% of the students in NAS schools were students of color.

In general, our data indicated that the majority of NAS sites were in low-performing, urban school districts. With some exceptions (Washington and Kentucky schools), the NAS sites were scoring at or below the district test score averages before the NAS design began assisting these schools even in jurisdictions that are primarily low-performing when compared to state averages (Berends, 1999).

Implementation in NAS Schools

The most important finding of both the case study and the quantitative research was that schools varied considerably in the level of implementation. Two years after scale-up, only about half of the schools examined in the case study research were implementing at targeted levels (levels desired by teams, NAS, and districts) (Bodily, 1998). The level of implementation varied by design team, district, and school characteristics.

The longitudinal analysis that followed a sample of NAS schools over time found the following:

- Implementation appeared to increase and deepen over the first four years after schools adopted designs, although at a decreasing rate.
- The between-school variance of reported implementation decreased somewhat over time, but within-school variance increased.
- There were large differences in implementation by jurisdiction in 1999.
- There were differences in implementation by design team in 1999.

Factors Affecting Implementation

Several factors emerge from our research as fostering high-quality and coherent implementation in the types of schools in the sample (see Berends, Kirby, Nafel, & McKelvey, 2001; Kirby, Berends, & Naftel, 2001). The longitudinal sample of teachers supported the findings of the case studies showing lack of strong implementation and lack of increasing progress toward implementation:

- For the entire sample of schools we surveyed, implementation in the scale-up schools increased modestly from 1997 to 1999. The between-school variance in the level of implementation decreased somewhat over time, but the within-school variance increased. There was much greater variance in implementation *within* schools than between schools, suggesting that designs had failed to become "schoolwide."
- There were large differences in implementation by jurisdiction, by design, and across schools.
- For schools newly adopting designs, implementation increased and deepened over the first four years after schools adopted designs, although at a decreasing rate each year.

As expected, many factors influenced the level of implementation, and the different analyses identified similar conditions leading to higher levels of implementation. District, principal, and teacher leadership ranked high on this list of factors. The remainder of this chapter focuses on how leadership at these different levels enabled or did not enable the implementation of whole-school designs.

IMPORTANCE OF DISTRICT LEADERSHIP

Within the contemporary school reform movement, district leaders are operating in a world of ever-shifting priorities and complexity. This world requires that district leaders play several different types of leadership roles. They need to engage in *organizational leadership* to build organizational systems to support administrators and teachers to further expectations and norms for teaching and learning and to encourage a professional climate of continuous learning (Task Force on Principalship, 2000; Cohen, McLaughlin, & Talbert, 1993). Moreover, they must manage the role of *public leadership*—to effectively communicate among members of the school board, district office, school staffs, parents, students, and community members. They must also provide *instructional leadership*—to establish a clear vision for teaching and learning and provide guidance for other educational leaders throughout the district.

The history and experience of comprehensive school reform underscores the importance of these leadership skills. For example, Datnow and Stringfield (2000), in their comprehensive, longitudinal study of 300 schools implementing a variety of reforms, report:

> We found that clear, strong district support positively impacted reform implementation, and that lack thereof often negatively impacted implementation . . . schools that sustained reforms had district and state allies that protected reform efforts during periods of transition or crisis and secured resources (money, time, staff, and space) essential to reforms. (pp. 194–195)

RAND's early case studies identified several district and institutional factors that contributed to implementation in the NAS schools (Bodilly, 1998). These were leadership backing and stability at the district level; centrality of the NAS initiative to the district's agenda; lack of crisis situations; history of trust and cooperation; availability of resources for transformation; school level authority or autonomy; union support; and district accountability and assessment systems that were compatible with those of the designs.

In the NAS initiative, districts played several important roles in fostering/hindering implementation, including: (a) initial matching and selection of reform designs; (b) encouraging support by the design team; and (c) creating a supportive environment through political leadership, regulatory policies, and consistent, coherent funding streams.

Initial Matching and Selection of Reform Designs

During the initial selection of the reform design, central office leaders often failed to provide the organizational leadership necessary for the initial and sustained viability of the relationship between the school and the team. In every district in the sample, schools registered complaints about district administrators' poor planning and the fact that the administrators did not allow sufficient time for schools to make rational selection decisions, issues brought up in other assessments of the adoption of schoolwide programs (Wong & Meyer, 1998). Several districts imposed timelines that were suitable to NAS or to the district administrators but did not allow time for a thoughtful process of selection by the schools. Some schools indicated that district administrators told them what design the school would adopt based on the administrators' view of school context, not the school's view of its needs. These schools were well behind on implementation by the second year of scale-up and complained bitterly about the treatment they had received from district administrators. For example, in some schools in San Antonio, teachers felt that they had been pressured by district administrators into selecting a design quickly to ensure that they received funds from the district. Many reported not fully understanding, because of lack of information from the district administrators or from the design teams, how complex and labor-intensive design implementation really was.

Leadership in several districts negatively influenced the matching process in less visible ways by:

- Failing to provide information about choices and how to make them, the level of resources available for implementation, designs, and timelines for making choices and implementing them in a thoughtful, timely manner
- Implementing policies that called for the rotation of principals to other schools on a cyclical basis (every three to six years depending on the district)
- Failing to recognize severe problems in certain schools—poor leadership, political in-fighting, extremely low capacity in the school due to systematic resource allocation to other schools, or, in one instance, alleged malfeasance.

A reform design match thought to be well informed by both the design team and the school did not necessarily guarantee high levels of implementation. But, ill-informed decisions guaranteed low implementation levels.

Encouraging Support by the Design Team

Instances of poor support by specific design teams to schools were clearly the fault of teams in many instances and resulted from poor planning, lack of resources, and leadership turnover within the team. However, it was the districts, not the schools, which negotiated the contract for design team services and determined how much to pay the teams. Some district administrators recognized that assistance to transform an entire school would be more costly than the assistance offered to implement a single program within a school. In other districts, administrators attempted to get a cheaper package, more in line with what they were used to paying for individual, fragmented programs. Unfortunately, cheaper was indeed what districts and schools got in these instances. Our data indicated a strong positive relationship between the level of implementation and the amount of money district administrators dedicated to professional development and teacher planning in design-based schools (Bodily, 1998).

Creating a Supportive Environment

A crucial leadership role for district policy makers was to provide an environment where designs could flourish. Our findings revealed that this would include several types of support: political, regulatory, and financial. Principals and teachers looked to district leaders to provide this support, without which the school staff could not do the work of implementation. In many cases, this district leader did not provide the needed environment to encourage implementation.

Political and Leadership Support. Schools in districts characterized by stable leadership that placed a high priority on the reform effort, lack of a major budget crisis or other crisis, and a history of trust between the central office and the schools also had higher implementation levels. School-level respondents directly linked these factors to greater efforts at implementation. When these factors were missing, as is common in challenged urban schools, school respondents reported that their own efforts stalled or were less intense.

Pittsburgh is a clear example of failure of both organizational and public leadership. The superintendent announced the five-year commitment to the NAS effort at approximately the same time she announced her retirement in two years. Teachers and principals reported this sent them a "mixed message" about what level of effort they should give the initiative. Many asked, "Why should we commit to the superintendent's initiative, when the superintendent will not be around long enough to see it through?" In the first year of implementation, the same district put a redistricting initiative on the agenda that would have closed several of the implementing schools and reassigned students to others. In the second year of implementation, a severe budget crisis hit. Schools revised their budgets accordingly. Promised money for implementation of the designs did not arrive because of the budget crisis, and the attention of the central office support team for NAS was drawn to more pressing political problems. Again and again, teachers and principals indicated they interpreted these actions as showing the district leaders did not place a high priority on the NAS effort. Thus, the school-level leaders followed suit. It is no wonder then that the schools in this district showed low levels of implementation after two years. In fact, in our longitudinal study of schools, we dropped Pittsburgh schools from the final analysis because too few schools reported implementing a NAS design (see Berends, Kirby, Nafel, & McKelvey, 2001).

Yet, even in districts that provided initial political leadership, the key was to sustain this commitment over time. For example, after our research study in San Antonio ended in the spring of 1999, a critical moment occurred—the superintendent's departure and decline of the NAS initiative in San Antonio.[5] As so often happens in urban school districts, the superintendent's position was tenuous with the school board. After a school board election in May 1999, two new board members were elected—thus tipping the balance of the school board against her. Soon after, the superintendent accepted a generous buy-out and resigned. Her resignation was accepted by a 4 to 3 vote by the school board. Her success in improving the test scores in San Antonio schools relative to the state, yet still lagging far behind, assured her a position elsewhere. She moved on.

The stability of the NAS designs was deeply affected by the superintendent's departure. During the summer of 1999, teachers were asked to vote on whether or not to keep the designs. Whereas some schools initially adopted designs based on 60% of their teachers voting in favor of adoption, the new district superintendent required 80% of the teachers to vote in favor of keeping the design. The lack of support that existed in NAS schools, the overburden that NAS teachers reported, the political uncertainty, the tension within the district, and the lack of clear leadership and support likely led to the substantial number of schools that voted to drop the designs.

Memphis provided a similar story. What had been billed as the Memphis miracle in 1999 because of claims by some within the Memphis community of strong increases in tests scores, folded under a change in leadership (Berends, Bodilly, & Kirby, 2002; Berends, Kirby, Nafel, & McKelvey 2001; Ross, Sanders, Wright, & Stringfield, 1998; Ross, Wang, Sanders, Wright, & Stringfield, 1999; Ross, Sanders, Wright, 2000; Ross, Sanders, Wright, Stringfield, Wang, & Alberg, 2001) when the superintendent decided take a new position and left the district. Despite the promising indications of whole-school reform, the newly appointed superintendent decided to drop the NAS designs in favor of more curriculum-specific reforms.[6] In their place, he announced to the school board that the whole-school reform models would be discontinued in favor of new district-wide curriculum, beginning with a reading program in fall 2001. Similar to the situation in San Antonio, there were concerns about the effectiveness of designs and their ability to teach students more fundamental reading and writing skills.

These three examples highlight the fact that district leadership and support often rests on very tenuous ground—the beliefs of a single individual in positional authority. Once the superintendent changes, the reforms fall by the wayside.

Regulatory Support. While crucial for school reform, central office political support and attention must also be buttressed by significant changes in regulatory practices. Comprehensive school reform is not confined to the adoption of a new curriculum or a few new instructional strategies. Instead, it requires the rethinking and adoption at the school level of a whole new curriculum and instructional package that may be quite different than that which the district has mandated or approved for all its schools. In turn, this curriculum and instructional package cannot be developed or implemented without significant changes in resource allocation for instructional positions, materials, technology, professional development, etc. Thus, schools attempting comprehensive school reform to address their particular problems must have increased site-level control over their curriculum and instruction, their budgets, their positions and staffing, and most essentially their mission.

In our sample, district administrators varied significantly in their understanding and response to these needs for policies to support school transformation. In those districts that provided for budgetary and other types of autonomy, implementation progressed. In those that did not, implementation lagged. While we focus primarily on the central office, union actions or policies can also prohibit implementation.

San Antonio offers an example of the failure of organizational and instructional leadership to follow through on support for NAS designs. The district had originally provided extensive school-level control over curriculum and instruction and had the support of a strong superintendent committed to NAS designs, but also to raising the test scores of students in the district, which were abysmal. The district leadership introduced the NAS initiative to schools with hopes that the marketed "break-the-mold" designs would enable teachers and administrators to engage enthusiastically in comprehensive school reform. The thought was that external model providers would be more successful at pushing and sustaining change than the central office could ever be by itself. The district had every intention of fully supporting its NAS schools in all ways—including professional development, site-based facilitators (called instructional guides), and other resources for the schools to implement the designs.

The manner in which the district leaders chose to increase test scores, however, proved to be counter to the implementation of designs with their own sets of standards, assessment and curriculum, and instruction matched to those design specific standards. The district established an Office of Curriculum and Instruction responsible for developing a sequential, standards-aligned curriculum across grade levels in all schools throughout the district. The district leadership then required schools to implement specific mathematics, reading, and language arts programs in addition to the NAS designs. In the spring of 1996, all schools were implementing *Everyday Mathematics*—developed by the University of Chicago School Mathematics Project. The district leaders expected all schools throughout the district to follow a similar pace and developed pacing guides to ensure that this would happen. In addition, the district leaders required San Antonio elementary schools to begin implementing a reading initiative that involved a 90-minute block of time. In the 1998–1999 school year, the district required two 90-minute blocks of uninterrupted instructional time for reading and math, respectively, and teachers to manage time within these blocks in prescribed ways. Though not to the same degree, the district structured language arts activities (spelling, grammar, and writing) as well, totaling approximately 70 minutes of instruction time per day. Thus, the district leadership mapped out roughly four hours of instructional activities for all the district's elementary school teachers to follow (RW teachers were exempt from implementing the district's reading initiative[7]).

Within this context, the district leadership provided a substantial amount of professional development to teachers. Much of the in-service training revolved around the district's reading and mathematics initiatives. Because NAS teachers were obligated to attend as many of these various in-services as their colleagues in non-NAS schools, the amount of training activities served only to heighten frustrations. All of the designs, except RW, required teachers to develop units and write curriculum. While encouraging schools to implement NAS designs, the district leaders simultaneously constrained their ability to do so by telling teachers what to teach and how.

What we observed in San Antonio is not unique among high-poverty, high-stakes accountability districts and schools. Many schools are suffering the burden "of having a torrent of unwanted, uncoordinated policies and innovations raining down on them from hierarchical bureaucracies" (Fullan, 2001, p. 22). In a recent survey of schools in districts in California and Texas, Hatch (2000) reported that two-thirds of the schools were working with three or more improvement programs; over one-fifth were working with six or more. In short, barriers imposed by district leaders can significantly inhibit innovative ideas and reforms. Leaders must actively restructure existing mandates and regulations, in order that instructional reforms can flourish.

Financial Support. Our findings highlight the importance of leadership decisions regarding resources for implementation. These resources are spent on the following types of costs: payments to the design teams for assistance; personnel costs within the school, such as a facilitator or a coordinator; training and planning time for teachers; and materials and conference costs. Resources can come from different sources, depending on the districts.

RAND's research on NAS suggests that resource availability is more an issue of resource allocation. Keltner (1998) found that of the cost to implement a design during the 1996–1997 school year, nearly 40% of the resource burden was met through reallocation of budgets for personnel, substitute teachers, and materials. The remaining 60% came from resources external to the school (e.g., Title I, district, or grants).

We found several districts claimed to have increased school autonomy over the budget allowing for reallocation of budgets to promote implementation. As Odden notes in his analysis of NAS design costs, reallocation of funds is not always a straightforward exercise "because it usually involves 'trading in' or redefining the positions of current educational specialist staff for the needed NAS ingredients; however in terms of actively promoting and sustaining real reform, it is the most powerful and effective approach" (1997, p. 11). However, we found that reallocation authority was often limited to decisions on how to spend *within* particular, highly specified categories of funding, or stovepipes, but not *between* stovepipes. Thus, funding sources were narrow and fragmented (Bodilly, 1998; Keltner, 1998). Failure of district leaders to promote reallocations of existing funding streams to support whole-school reform resulted in poor implementation (Bodilly & Berends, 1999; King, 1994, 1999).

In short, district-level politics, policies, and practices—in terms of providing organizational, public, and instructional leadership—can promote or derail the effort to transform schools using comprehensive school reform models. Schools look to district leadership, climate, and regulations to understand if it is worth investing the necessary time and effort to transform themselves.

IMPORTANCE OF PRINCIPAL LEADERSHIP

Schools are changing dramatically: students are more numerous and more diverse; qualified teachers are often in short supply; technology is playing an ever-increasing role in education; schools are expected to become centers of community (Task Force on the Principalship, 2000). To guide such schools, we need principals who establish a vision, set goals, manage staff, rally the community, create effective learning environments, build support systems for students, and guide instruction.

Research has consistently shown that the principal strongly influences the likelihood of change (Bryk, Sebring, Kerbow, Rollow, Easton, 1998; Day, Harris, Hadfield, Toley, & Beresford, 2000; Fullan, 2001; McLaughlin & Talbert, 2001; Newmann, King, & Youngs, 2000). As Fullan writes, "I know of no improving school that doesn't have a principal who is good at leading improvement" (2001, p. 141). Without strong, supportive, visionary leadership, however, school capacity is seriously undermined. Elmore, for example, writes:

> [T]he job of administrative leaders is primarily about enhancing the skills and knowledge of people in the organization, creating a common culture of expectations around the use of those skills and knowledge, holding the various pieces of the organization

together in a productive relationship with each other, and holding individuals accountable for their contributions to the collective result. (2000, p. 15)

In our analysis of longitudinal data for schools implementing NAS designs four years into scale-up, we found that principal leadership was the single most important predictor of teacher-reported implementation level, both at the teacher level and the school level (Kirby, Berends, & Naftel, 2001). Principal leadership was measured in the longitudinal survey analysis as an index that included specific practical actions and more effective ones:

- Clearly communicated what was expected of teachers
- Was supportive and encouraging of staff
- Obtained resources for the school
- Enforced rules for student conduct
- Talked with teachers regarding instructional practices
- Had confidence in the expertise of the teachers
- Took a personal interest in the professional development of teachers

Schools in which teachers reported strong principal leadership also reported much higher levels of implementation, by more than half a standard deviation. Teachers who rated their principals higher than others in the same school also reported significantly higher levels of implementation (again by more than half a standard deviation).

This principal leadership effect was also present in our analyses of school and classroom effects on student achievement scores in a high-poverty district in Texas (Berends, Bodilly, & Kirby, 2002). Despite all that was going on the district and the overall similarity of instructional conditions, our analysis showed that reported levels of principal leadership using the same index was strongly related to elementary students' achievement scores on the state tests in reading and mathematics. Controlling for other student, teacher, classroom, and school factors, classrooms in which teachers reported greater principal leadership had significantly higher reading and mathematics scores.

Clearly then, teachers looked to their principals to guide them in their implementation of reform activities. The case studies indicated some very specific roles that principals played in encouraging the dedication of the teachers to the reform implementation. We describe several of these to enrich the survey findings: the role of the principal in the selection of the reform model; and the ability of the principal to bring resources to bear on implementation.

Role of Principal in Reform Model Selection

Interviews with school-level staff indicated that the principal played an important role in the selection process—sometimes ensuring a well-informed selection, in other cases preventing one. Notes from two schools illustrate contrasting cases from the scale-up case studies in years 1995–1996 that illustrate the role of principal leadership.

In one district, schools were exposed to the designs at a "design team fair" where teams of teachers and the principal could visit booths and hear presentations by the design teams. Schools then had to pick two candidate design teams that they could explore further. Schools were given limited funds to visit design sites or otherwise get information about the two designs. They then had to choose one, based on a collective process of school decision-making.

In one school, the principal chose a small group of teachers to go to the fair but told the teachers that his preference was for a particular design based on what he already knew and based on his perception of the design the district favored. The principal chose the teachers to attend. According to teacher reports, those selected were members of a close-knit group of teachers close to the principal. After the visit to the fair, the school did not visit design team sites, rather the selected teachers reported at a teacher meeting that they favored the design the principal had said was the best for the school. The larger group of teachers reported they received little information about the design or alternative designs. They reported that the principal then said they would be implementing his chosen design. Two years later, implementation was at very low levels and the teaching staff justified this low level by saying they had never accepted the design to begin with—it had been forced on them.

In a different school, the principal sent out notices to teachers asking for volunteers to attend the fair. Two different teacher teams went to the fair to accommodate the level of interest. This was followed by a whole-school discussion about the pros and cons of several designs as the attending teachers reported back. The principal then used the funds set aside by the district for teachers to visit nearby design team sites. Teachers reported back, again to the larger group, on what they learned from these visits. Finally a formal, but anonymous, vote was taken. Here, implementation was more positive after two years. One teacher reported, "In the past, we did not have to try to implement what the district told us; we would always say we were forced to implement something. This time we made the decision. We didn't have any excuses" (Bodilly, 1998).

Other examples abound of the principal's role in this process and how it can lead to teacher support or teacher retrenchment. For example, in more than one school, teachers reported the principal voicing his or her preference and then having a public vote with raised hands. The principal noted which teachers voted against his or her favored design. Few teachers had the courage to stand up for their views in this type of process. In short, the role of the principal in selection could encourage active involvement and inquiry by teachers or it could cut it off through hierarchical decision-making.

Role of Principal in Acquiring Resources for Implementation

Reform designs cannot be implemented without resources, especially time for teachers for professional development and training. The survey analysis found that teacher reports of the level of resources—in terms of materials, funds, and time—available to them to implement designs were strongly correlated with their reported level of implementation. Interviews with principals of schools dropping the designs indicated lack of resources to implement was the major reason for dropping a design (Kirby, Berends, & Naftel, 2001). Our case studies showed the important role played by principals in ensuring that resources needed to implement designs were available to the teachers. A few examples help to illuminate the role of the principal in ensuring adequacy and availability of resources.

Time, especially common planning time, is an essential resource needed for implementing many designs. Several designs required teachers to work together to develop curriculum. Even designs that did not require this often wanted teachers to meet in grade-level groups or other groupings to discuss students and their progress. The principal is largely responsible for setting school schedules. If the principal did not develop the schedule that allowed common planning time, implementation would often falter. In particular, some principals pointed to the district-determined schedules of the teachers who taught "specials" (computer lab, music, and art) around which they had to build the school schedule as the reason why implementation could not progress. But, in two closely associated elementary schools we visited, the principals had jointly applied to the district to allow them to change the "specials" schedules so as not to be held hostage to a few itinerant teachers' schedules. By banding together, they jointly pressured the district to accommodate their needs for common planning time. Several other principals approached design teams to join with them to exert pressure for this type of scheduling change.

Several designs also required that the school appoint and pay for additional positions. For example, the AC and RW designs involved a full-time design facilitator. The CON design originally entailed a technology coordinator. Funding these positions often required the principal to reallocate resources, perhaps reducing a traditional position of librarian or reading specialist. Some principals were successful in making these changes without rancor producing higher levels of implementation. Poor leadership resulted in these positions being funded at a part-time level or not at all, slowing implementation.

Finally, when district did not fully fund the design implementation effort, it fell to principals to elicit funds for design implementation. This either came from internal resource reallocation or external sources such as Title 1 or grants. It was clear from the case studies that some principals excelled at obtaining resources while others did not, the latter leading to lower level of implementation or the dropping of the designs (Bodily, 1998; Keltner, 1998).

Principal's Contribution to Consistent Effort

Interviews revealed that strong principal support combined with consistency appeared to be a major contributor to the implementation effort. School staff often pointed to turnovers in principal leadership as a contributor to slowed implementation, even when the new principal was supportive of the design. Leadership changes often cause disruptions as the new management team is put in place. This disruption slows implementation regardless of the leadership capability of the new principal. Our case study analysis of scale-up sites showed that schools reporting leadership turnover tended to have lower levels of implementation after two years (Bodily, 1998). In some cases, turnover was encouraged by the district, either through long-standing rotation, retirement policies, or specific superintendent "housecleaning."

IMPORTANCE OF TEACHER LEADERSHIP

Our analyses also found important roles for teachers as leaders. Schools were able to achieve strong implementation by using teacher leaders to enable other teachers to understand and implement the new curriculum and instructional practices. In one district, this took the specific form of instructional guides. In other schools associated with specific design teams, this took the form of facilitators.

In San Antonio, the superintendent created instructional guide positions to further facilitate communication and action around instructional practice and the reform designs. The instructional guides tended to be master teachers deemed highly competent, knowledgeable of curriculum and instruction, and able to readily communicate and anticipate the needs of others. They were hired to be their schools' instructional leaders, managing tasks for which principals did not have time. The instructional guides were also expected to serve as liaisons between the district and their schools, communicating the central office's ideas to teachers and learning the various district initiatives to take back to their respective campuses. Furthermore, they were to facilitate the implementation of all new programs and provide teachers with in-house follow-up to professional development.

Instructional guides received a great deal of credit for enabling the district office to push forward and implement ideas very rapidly. Quarterly meetings attended by instructional guides and central office staff served to further the budding lines of communication. During these meetings, the guides reportedly discussed what was working at their schools, what upset teachers, what needed to be improved upon, and what additional support systems were necessary.

Instructional guides were critical to advancing the professional development of other teachers within the same school. As stated, they were seen as the primary source of on-site instructional support. In the words of one district administrator,

> One of the things that we tried to do in supporting professional development was to make sure that we had some support right there on campus. So we really restructured Title I in saying, okay, we're going to put a person on every campus who's major job is to support teachers through providing professional development, doing model teaching, finding the materials or instructional things that teachers need.

In other places or with specific designs, a similar role evolved called design facilitators. Several designs, such as AC and RW, required the funding of facilitator positions—teachers in the school who lead the implementation of the design. They receive increased training from the teams in design and implementation issues. At the school site they are supposed to coach other teachers, answer questions about design practice, ensure everyone has the needed materials, and provide some level of faculty training in the design. Ideally, they contribute their full time to this function. In general, the facilitators were chosen from among the existing school staff. In some cases, the faculty chose the teacher who would be the facilitator.

In general, our case study analysis showed that the creation and full-time funding of the facilitator position enabled implementation (Bodilly, 1998). Nonfacilitator teachers credited the facilitators with providing motivation for and management of key implementation tasks. Indeed, the site visits impressed us with the notion that reforms in schools often depended heavily on the enthusiasm of the facilitators. Many teachers pointed to an important issue of trust. They could trust the facilitators more than the design team trainers because the faculty knew the facilitators and the facilitators understood the needs of the students and the past history of the schools' attempts at reform. When told how to do things by the facilitator, they listened and indicated they might not listen to "outsiders" as well. In addition, faculty pointed out that these facilitators provided them with onsite and immediate support—often noting it was practical and tangible support that was greatly valued. Such support was not always forthcoming from the teams but was reported as direly needed. As the design teams began to learn from each other over the demonstration and scale-up periods, more teams attempted to mimic this facilitator function or provision of more hands-on help—through regional facilitators or school site leads. Few schools, however, have been able to sustain this full-time funding of the teacher facilitator over time.

CONCLUSION

The NAS experience underscores the importance of district, principal, and teacher leadership and support in meaningful implementation of whole-school designs. Leadership involves balancing the organizational, public, and instructional goals and practices of the system over time. The role of district and school leaders is to meld these goals and practices into a coherent vision that can guide teachers in their daily practice. The NAS experience highlights the fact that while leadership can be found at all levels, seldom does it come together to create the coherent whole needed for meaningful school change.

Many of the NAS districts failed to provide organizational, public, and instructional leadership to the schools implementing the designs. Even where initial support existed, often support for NAS designs was limited to one individual, the superintendent, rather than to the central office staff. As a result, when the individual left, the reform was essentially abandoned. NAS failed to gain a strong foothold in their districts because it did not recognize the strong need to develop committed leaders throughout the system. Complex reforms require a broad base of support among the staff and community so that they will have continued support and be provided with the time and the resources necessary to mature. In many districts, the failure to protect the NAS reform effort from conflicting regulations and mandates put in place by district leaders anxious to show improvement again caused the reform to be virtually abandoned.

Quite apart from district leadership, schools need strong leaders—principals who can bring a unified sense of vision to the school and staff and who can provide instructional leadership and organizational leadership in terms of making sure the teachers have the necessary time, resources, and support to fully implement the designs.

Finally, last but certainly not least, are the teachers. Without willing and able teachers who embrace reform and provide the necessary leadership, no reform can be enacted, no matter how effective it may be. For teachers, policy goals and activities are part of a broader environment that presses on their classrooms. Their ability to correctly perceive what the leader's priorities are under these multiple pressures and demands determines their commitment to change and is crucial to coherent and sustained implementation reform. The teachers, as implementers, look to their leaders to help them decide whether, where, and to what extent they should focus their limited free time and energy. As Fullan has succinctly noted, educational change depends on "what teachers do and think—it's as simple and as complex as that" (Fullan, 2000, p. 115).

ACKNOWLEDGMENTS

Mark Berends and Susan Bodilly are coprincipal investigators for RAND's research on New American Schools. The order of authorship for this paper was alphabetical, and each contributed significantly to this paper. We would like to thank the Atlantic Philanthropies and the Ford Foundation for their support of this research on New American Schools. We are also grateful to the teachers and principals in the schools who gave of their time to respond to our questions, the staff in districts and states who helped us piece together relevant data, and the design teams who clarified issues along the way. Several members of RAND's research team contributed to the studies informing this paper, including R. J. Briggs, JoAn Chun, Brian Gill, Tom Glennan, Joann Heilbrunn, Brent Keltner, Christopher McKelvey, Scott Naftel, Susanna Purnell, Robert Reichardt, Gina Schuyler, and Sue Stockly. We thank the members of the Research Advisory Panel (funded by the Annenberg Foundation) who provide critical guidance to RAND's research on NAS. Members include Barbara Cervone, Paul Hill, Janice Petrovich, Andrew Porter, Karen Sheingold, and Carol Weiss. Of course, any errors remain the responsibility of the authors and not of these individuals or agencies.

REFERENCES

Ball, D. L., Camburn, E., Cohen, D. K., & Rowan, B. (1998). *Instructional improvement and disadvantaged students.* Unpublished manuscript, University of Michigan.

Berends, M. (1999). *Monitoring the progress of New American Schools: A description of implementing schools in a longitudinal sample.* Santa Monica, CA: RAND.

Berends, M. (2000). Teacher-reported effects of New American Schools' designs: Exploring relationships to teacher background and school context. *Educational Evaluation and Policy Analysis, 22*(1), 65–82.

Berends, M., Bodilly, S., & Kirby, S. N. (2002). *Challenges of whole-school reform: New American Schools after a decade.* Santa Monica, CA: RAND.

Berends, M., Chun, J., Schuyler, G., Stockly, S., & Riggs, R. J. (2002). *Challenges of conflicting school reforms: Effects of New American Schools in a high-poverty district.* Santa Monica, CA: RAND.

Berends, M., Kirby, S. N., Naftel, S., & McKelvey, C. (2001). *Implementation and performance in New American Schools: Three years into scale-up.* Santa Monica, CA, RAND.

Berends, M., Kirby, S. N., Naftel, S., & Sloan, J. S. (In Review). *The status of standards-based reforms in Title I schools: First-year findings from the National Longitudinal Study of Schools.* Washington, DC: U.S. Department of Education.

Bodilly, S. (1996). *Lessons from New American Schools Development Corporation's demonstration phase.* Santa Monica, CA: RAND.

Bodilly, S. (1998). *Lessons from New American Schools' scale-up phase: Prospects for bringing designs to multiple schools.* Santa Monica, CA: RAND.

Bodilly, S. (2001). *New American Schools' concept of break the mold designs: How designs evolved over time and why.* Santa Monica, CA: RAND.

Bodilly, S. J., & Berends, M. (1999). Necessary district support for comprehensive school reform. In G. Orfield & E. H. DeBray (Eds.), *Hard work for good schools: Facts not fads in Title I reform* (pp. 111–119). Boston: Civil Rights Project, Harvard University.

Bodilly, S., Purnell, S., Ramsey, K., & Smith, C. (1995). *Designing New American Schools: Baseline observations on nine design teams.* Santa Monica, CA: RAND.

Bryk, A., Sebring, P., Kerbow, D., Rollow, S., & Easton, J. (1998). *Charting Chicago school reform.* Boulder, CO: Westview Press.

Cohen, D. K., McLaughlin, M. W., & Talbert, J. E. (1993). (Eds.). *Teaching for understanding: Challenges for policy and practice.* San Francisco: Jossey-Bass.

Datnow, A. (2000). Power and politics in the adoption of school reform models. *Educational Evaluation and Policy Analysis, 22*(4), 357–374.

Datnow, A., & Castellano, J. (2000). Teachers' responses to Success for All: How beliefs, experiences, and adaptations shape implementation. *American Educational Research Journal, 37*(3), 775–799.

Datnow, A., & Stringfield, S. (1997). (Eds.). *School effectiveness and school improvement, 8*(1).

Datnow, A., & Stringfield, S. (2000). Working together for reliable school reform. *Journal of Education for Students Placed at Risk, 5*(1), 183–204.

Day, C., Harris, A., Hadfield, M., Toley, H., & Beresford, J. (2000). *Leading schools in times of change.* Buckingham, England: Open University Press.

Desimone, L. (2000). *Making comprehensive school reform work.* New York: ERIC Clearinghouse on Urban Education, Teachers College.

Elmore, R. F. (2000). Building a new structure for school leadership. Boston: Harvard University, Albert Shanker Institute.

Fullan, M. G. (2001). *The new meaning of educational change.* New York: Teachers College Press.

Glennan, T. K., Jr. (1998). *New American Schools after six years.* Santa Monica, CA: RAND.

Hatch, T. (2000). *What happens when multiple improvement initiatives collide.* Menlo Park, CA: Carnegie Foundation for the Advancement of Teaching.

Herman, R., et al. (1999). *An educators' guide to schoolwide reform.* Washington, DC: American Institutes for Research.

Keltner, B. (1998). *Resources for transforming New American Schools: First year findings.* Santa Monica, CA: RAND.

King, J. A. (1994). Meeting the needs of at-risk students: A cost-analysis of three models. *Educational Evaluation and Policy Analysis, 16*(1), 1–19.

King, J. A. (1999). *Making economically-grounded decisions about comprehensive school reform models: Considerations of costs, effects, and contexts.* Paper presented at the National Invitational Conference on Effective Title I Schoolwide Program Implementation, Laboratory for Student Success at Temple University Center for Research in Human Development and Education, May 10–11, Arlington, VA.

Kirby, S. N., Berends, M., & Naftel, S. (2001). *Implementation in New American Schools: Four years into scale-up.* Santa Monica, CA: RAND.

McLaughlin, M. W. (1991). Learning from experience: Lessons from policy implementation. In A. R. Odden (Ed.), *Education Policy Implementation* (pp. 185–195). Albany: State University of New York Press.

McLaughlin, M. W., & Talbert, J. (2001). *Professional communities and the work of high school teaching.* Chicago: University of Chicago Press.

Mitchell, K. (1996). *Reforming and conforming: NASDC principals discuss school accountability systems.* Santa Monica, CA: RAND.

Newmann, F. M., King, M. B., & Youngs, P. (2000). Professional development that addresses school capacity: Lessons from urban elementary schools. *American Journal of Education, 108*(4), 259–299.

Odden, A. (1997). *How to rethink school budgets to support school transformation.* Arlington, VA: New American Schools.

Purkey, S. C., & Smith, M. S. (1983). Effective schools: A review. *Elementary School Journal, 83*(4), 427–452.

Ross, S. M., Sanders, W. L., & Wright, S. P. (2000). *Fourth-year achievement results on the Tennessee Value-Added Assessment System for restructuring schools in Memphis.* Unpublished manuscript, Center for Research in Educational Policy, University of Memphis.

Ross, S. M., Sanders, W. L., Wright, S. P., Stringfield, S., Wang. L. W., & Alberg, M. (2001). Two- and three-year achievement results from the Memphis restructuring initiative. *School Effectiveness and School Improvement, 12*(3), 265–284.

Ross, S. M., Wang, L. W., Sanders, W. L., Wright, S. P., & Stringfield, S. (1999). *Two- and three-year achievement results for the Tennessee Value-Added Assessment System for restructuring schools in Memphis.* Unpublished manuscript, Center for Research in Educational Policy, University of Memphis.

Ross, S. M., Sanders, W. L., Wright, S. P., & Stringfield, S. (1998). *The Memphis restructuring initiative: Achievement results for years 1 and 2 on the Tennessee Value-Added Assessment System (TVAAS).* Unpublished manuscript, Center for Research in Educational Policy, University of Memphis.

Ross, S. M., Sanders, W. L., Wright, S. P., Stringfield, S., Wang, L. W., & Alberg, M. (2001). Two- and three-year achievement results from the Memphis restructuring initiative. *School Effectiveness and School Improvement, 12*(3), pp. 265–284.

Ross, S., Troutman, A., Horgan, D., Maxwell, S., Laitinen, R., & Lowther, D. (1997). The success of schools in implementing eight restructuring designs: A synthesis of first year evaluation outcomes. *School Effectiveness and School Improvement, 8*(1), 95-124.

Sergiovanni, T. J. (2000). *The lifeworld of leadership: Creating culture, community, and personal meaning in our schools.* San Francisco, CA: Jossey-Bass.

Stringfield, S., & Datnow, A. (1998). (Eds.). *Education and Urban Society, 30*(3).

Stringfield, S., Ross, S., & Smith, L. (1996). (Eds.) *Bold plans for school restructuring.* Mahwah, NJ: Erlbaum.

Task Force on the Principalship. (2000). *Leadership for student learning: Reinventing the principalship.* Columbus, OH: Institute for Educational Leadership.

Wong, K., & Meyer, S. (1998). Title I schoolwide programs: A synthesis of findings from recent evaluation. *Educational Evaluation and Policy Analysis, 20*(2), 115–136.

NOTES

1. A more detailed description of the history of the NAS initiative and the design teams appears in Berends, Bodilly, & Kirby, 2002; Bodilly, 1998; Glennan, 1998; and Stringfield, Ross, & Smith, 1996. See also Desimone, 2000; Datnow, 2000; Datnow & Castellano, 2000; Herman et al., 1999; Ball, Camburn, Cohen, & Rowan, 1998; Stringfield & Datnow, 1998; Datnow & Stringfield, 1997, 2000; Ross et al., 1997, 1998. For descriptions of NAS and the design teams on the Web, see http://www.newamericanschools.org/, which has links to each design team's Web site.

2. NARE's development into America's Choice reflected a major change in the design, from NARE's emphasis on changing the school system (e.g., organization, governance, and assessments) to America's Choice additional emphasis on curriculum, instruction, and professional development changes within classrooms and schools. Despite this change, the school principals in the sample analyzed in our study continued to report that they were implementing the principles of the NARE design.

3. At the beginning of the scale-up phase, Maryland and San Diego were not far enough along in their implementation to warrant inclusion in RAND's planned data collection efforts. Since then, several of the design teams reported experiences implementing in Maryland and San Diego.

4. See Berends, 1999, 2000; Berends, Bodilly, & Kirby, 2002; Berends, Chun, Schuyler, Stockly, & Riggs, 2002; Berends, Kirby, Naftel, & McKelvey, 2001; Kirby, Berends, & Naftel; 2001; Bodilly, 1996, 1998, 2001; Glennan, 1998; Bodilly, Purnell, Ramsey, & Smith 1995; Mitchell, 1996.

5. This information is based on interviews with district staff and some design teams after the superintendent's departure as well as on reports in the *San Antonio Express-News*.

6. This information is from an article in *The Commercial Appeal* article by Aimee Edmonson entitled "Watson Kills All Reform Models for City Schools" (June 19, 2001). See also NAS's response in a press release of June 28, 2001—"New American Schools' Statement on Memphis Superintendent's Decision to Drop Comprehensive School Reform." (Retrieved June 21, 2002, from http://www. newamericanschools.com/press/062801.phtml).

7. In San Antonio, the RW design was never fully implemented. The schools we studied were interested only in the Success for All reading portion of the RW design.

PART III

Annenberg Challenge Initiatives

CHAPTER SEVEN

The Chicago Annenberg Challenge

Lessons on Leadership for School Development[1]

MARK A. SMYLIE, STACY A. WENZEL, AND CAROL R. FENDT

In January 1995, the Chicago Annenberg Challenge launched a six-year initiative to improve Chicago's public schools. It set out a broad vision for change, calling for the "enhancement of learning for all students through dramatically improved classroom practice and strengthened community relationships" (Hallert, Chapman, & Ayers, 1995). In order to achieve its vision, the Challenge funded networks of schools and external partners to develop and implement activities to promote local school development. Between 1995 and 2001, more than 200 schools organized into 45 networks received Annenberg support. Their efforts focused on many areas of school development, including strengthening curriculum and instruction, enhancing student learning climate and social services, promoting teacher and leadership development, and building parent and community support.

In 1996, a group of researchers at the Consortium on Chicago School Research was commissioned by the Chicago Challenge to study the Challenge and its work. This research project, which extended through the life of the Challenge, had two main purposes. The first was to document and assess the activities and accomplishments of the Challenge as a major school development initiative in Chicago. Because the Challenge provided a unique opportunity—a "window"—to investigate over an extended period of time more general issues of urban school development, the second purpose of this study was to explore processes of school development and to identify factors that appeared to support or constrain them.

This chapter does not focus on the work of the Challenge *per se*. The Chicago Annenberg Research Project, as our study was called, has chronicled the activities and accomplishments of the Challenge in its various technical reports (see Smylie et al., 1998; Wenzel et al., 2001; Smylie et al., 2002).[2] Instead, this chapter presents several findings about school development from a longitudinal field-based study of 12 Annenberg schools and discusses the lessons they suggest for school-level leadership. Our findings also have implications for district or system-level leadership, but these implications are beyond the scope of this chapter.

Our findings about school development and lessons for leadership were derived in the context of a particular large-scale reform initiative—the Chicago Annenberg Challenge—and in a particular historical and political policy context—Chicago school reform. Because these contexts form the "window" through which we viewed school development, we begin by describing the Chicago Annenberg Challenge and, in broad brush strokes, school reform in Chicago. Our findings and lessons also pertain to a particular conceptual framework of school development. We present this framework—the Model of Essential Supports for Student Learning—following our descriptions of the Chicago Challenge and Chicago school reform. In the final part of our introduction, we summarize the methods we used to conduct our study.

THE CHICAGO ANNENBERG CHALLENGE

The Chicago Annenberg Challenge promoted local school development through networks of schools and their external partners. It followed a logic that schools that work together with an external partner will find more direction and support for development than if they acted alone. The Challenge operated much like a foundation (Shipps, Sconzert, & Swyers, 1999b). It distributed its resources through planning and implementation grants to networks and external partners and provided some technical assistance to grant recipients. The Challenge articulated only general goals for school development; it did not specify any particular activities or processes for schools to follow. It called for teachers, parents, and communities to rethink and restructure the basic elements of schooling. Rather than specify programs schools should adopt, the Challenge believed that educators, parents, and community members should identify their own ways to solve local problems and address local needs.

Initially, the Challenge encouraged schools and external partners to focus on three basic problems of school organization that were seen as obstacles to development: (a) the lack of time for effective teaching, student learning, and teacher professional development; (b) the large size of school enrollment and instructional groups that hinders the development of personalized, supportive adult-student relationships; and (c) the isolation of schools from parents and communities. The problem of isolation came to include teachers' isolation from one another, which was thought to limit opportunities for teacher learning, innovation, and professional accountability. After making its first network grants, the Challenge encouraged schools and external partners to focus more specifically on teaching and learning, teacher professional development, and whole school change, not just change among groups of teachers within schools. Schools and external partners that had already received funding were asked to demonstrate a relationship between their Annenberg-supported activity and improvements in student learning.

By design, the scope of the Challenge was broad. Between 1995 and 2001, the Chicago Challenge made grants to 43 networks. Through these networks, it provided funds to between 200 and 220 schools, or 35% to 40% of all schools in the system. An average-size network consisted of six schools. The Chicago Challenge supported a wide range of development activity. About 55% of the networks focused primarily on curricular and instructional development. About 16% worked to develop student learning climate and social services for students and families. Another 13% were concerned primarily with parent and community support and development. The remaining 16% of Annenberg networks adopted more comprehensive foci, working to achieve development in a number of areas including curriculum and instruction, leadership development, student learning climate, and parent and community support. Within these general categories were a number of specific initiatives including parent education programs, literacy programs, the integration of arts and technology into the curriculum, health/science education, the creation of small schools, middle school restructuring, principal and teacher leadership development, and the strengthening of school-community ties.

The Challenge fostered working relationships among schools and a diverse group of external partners (Newmann & Sconzert, 2000). Of the 43 external partners working with Annenberg schools, about 35% were Chicago-area colleges and universities. Another 23% were arts and cultural institutions, and 28% were education reform and advocacy groups. The remaining 14% of the Challenge's external partners were neighborhood organizations, business groups, regional education organizations, teacher organizations, and foundations.

Grants made to schools and networks were relatively modest. On average, in 1999 at the peak of network funding Annenberg schools received about $47,000 a year from the Chicago Challenge in money or resources provided by external partners through Annenberg grants (Newmann & Sconzert, 2000). This was about 1% of an average school's annual operating budget, not including other grants that the school might obtain. On average, external partners received about $160,000 per year to work with their networks. While external partners spent their Annenberg funds in a number of ways, in practical terms the money was about enough to support two professional staff members to work, on average, with six schools.

Overall, Annenberg schools' demographic characteristics resembled closely those of the system. Schools that first received Annenberg funds differed somewhat from the system in that a slightly larger proportion had predominantly low-income enrollments and a slightly larger proportion had enrollments of more than 85% African American or mixed African American and Latino students. Moreover, a slightly larger proportion of Annenberg schools had large student enrollments and a greater percentage of low-achieving students. By the 1998–1999 school year, after more schools joined the Challenge, these differences had all but disappeared. As shown in Table 7.1, the racial composition, percentage of low-income students, and size of enrollment in Annenberg schools and across the system were virtually identical. So, too, were the percentage of students enrolled in bilingual education programs and the percentage of students scoring at or above national norms on the reading and math portions of the Iowa Tests of Basic Skills (ITBS).

Chicago School Reform

One cannot fully understand the Chicago Annenberg Challenge without also understanding the broader context in which it operated.[3] The Chicago Challenge was established with a grant from the Annenberg Foundation in January 1995. It was grounded in the principles of democratic localism and grassroots action inherent in Chicago's 1988 decentralization reform. The Challenge sought to extend the 1988 reform from governance to other areas of school development. Six months after the Challenge was established, the Illinois legislature passed the 1995 school reform bill. This bill added a new dimension to school reform—restructuring the central administration through the creation of a corporate-style management team that included a chief executive officer (CEO) to replace the superintendent and a five-member Reform Board of Trustees appointed by the mayor. The law established greater accountability within the system by clarifying and extending the authority of the CEO to intervene in nonimproving schools.

As the Chicago Challenge began awarding its first network grants, the new central administration introduced two major initiatives to bring centralized, high-stakes accountability into the system. The administration placed schools with less than 15% of students scoring at or above national norms on the ITBS on academic probation and assigned to each a probation

Table 7.1 Demographic Characteristics of Schools, 1999

	All Chicago Elementary Schools	Annenberg Elementary Schools	Study Schools
Average student enrollment	696	706	900
Racial/ethnic composition of student enrollment			
Percentage African American	53%	54%	49%
Percentage Latino	33%	34%	41%
Percentage White	10%	9%	8%
Percentage of low-income students	85%	85%	89%
Percentage of students scoring at or above national norms on the ITBS reading	36%	35%	40%
Percentage of students scoring at or above national norms on the ITBS mathematics	43%	42%	41%

SOURCE: Chicago Public Schools.

NOTE. Percentage of low-income students is the percentage of students who are eligible for free and reduced-price lunch.

manager to direct school improvement efforts. Schools on probation that failed to improve their test scores over a period of time could be reconstituted. The administration also developed a new policy to end social promotion. Students in third, sixth, and eighth grade were required to meet specified cut-off scores on the ITBS in order to advance to the next grade level. If they failed to meet these benchmarks, they had to attend summer school and, if they failed again at the end of the summer, they were retained.

A year later, the administration developed new system-wide goals and standards for student learning. It created lesson plans keyed to these standards across grade levels and curriculum-specific examinations for high school graduation. It also began a major capital improvement initiative to construct new schools, repair and renovate existing facilities, and alleviate overcrowding in many buildings. It established the Lighthouse program to provide after-school academic and recreational opportunities for students. It also began to place more emphasis on early childhood education.

Against this backdrop of centralized initiatives and test-driven accountability, the Challenge made grants to support local school development initiatives. As noted earlier, it first emphasized the organizational issues of time, size, and isolation. Later, it intensified its focus on teaching, learning, and whole school change. In particular, the Challenge began to promote intellectually challenging instruction and teacher professional development. It encouraged teachers to analyze their students' classroom work to stimulate instructional improvement.

There were several areas where the school system's initiatives and Annenberg efforts to promote school development were consistent and mutually supportive. For example, at some schools in our study the system's capital development efforts were instrumental in developing learning climates that were more conducive to teaching and learning. On the other hand, the Challenge promoted a reform agenda that sometimes collided with specific system policies, creating tensions and dilemmas for principals and teachers at the school and classroom levels. Nowhere were the tensions and dilemmas between the Challenge and the system more sharply pronounced than in the interaction between high-stakes standardized testing and efforts to improve instruction. Our research found that at the school level, high-stakes testing, coupled with the system's probation and student retention policies, became a double-edged sword (Wenzel et al., 2001). In a number of schools, it created a much-needed press for accountability and a perceived need for change. In some schools, high-stakes testing pushed teachers and principals to focus on the quickest means of administrative compliance—test preparation—and abandon, or push aside at least for a while, efforts to achieve more ambitious, long-term instructional improvement.

It was in these reform contexts that Annenberg schools worked to get better, and it was in these contexts that we studied school development. Our research is bound to the particular context in which it was conducted, however, throughout this chapter we show how our findings relate to other research on leadership and school change. Certainly, more work needs to be done to explore and test out the findings and lessons we present. At this point, they should be considered propositional and provisional. At the same time, the consistency of our findings with the findings of other studies gives our work credibility and, in Yin's (1995) terms, an amount of "analytic generalizability" (p. 30).

Defining School Development

To say that a school has developed means that it has moved in a positive direction—some aspects of its organization or practices have changed in a specific way to help achieve a valued goal. It is important, therefore, to understand our definition of school development, for our study was focused on how development by that definition can be promoted. School development has many valued goals. In our study of the Chicago Challenge, we were particularly concerned with student academic learning that not only includes but goes beyond the acquisition of basic knowledge and skills to encompass a deep understanding of subject matter. This type of learning develops cognitive capacities that allow students to work with existing knowledge in order to create new knowledge to analyze and solve real-world problems, to manage their personal affairs, and to become economically productive and responsible members of society (Newmann, Bryk, & Lopez, 1998). In defining school development, we needed to identify those aspects of school organization and practice that, when strengthened, helped to promote such academic learning among students.

We used the Model of Essential Supports for Student Learning to frame our study of school development. This model identifies seven areas of school organization and practice that support the type of ambitious academic learning described above: (a) school leadership; (b) teacher professional community; (c) parent and community support; (d) student-centered learning climate; (e) high-quality instruction; (f) social trust, and (g) instructional program coherence.

We selected this model for several reasons. First, it has strong support in the empirical literature on academically effective schools and school improvement and is being successfully validated by ongoing analyses at the Consortium on Chicago School Research (see Bryk et al., in press; Designs for Change, 1993; Newmann, Bryk, & Lopez, 1998; Newmann, Bryk, & Nagaoka, 2001; Wenzel et al., 2001). Second, the model was developed in Chicago and has become well-established in the Chicago Public Schools (CPS). It had guided local school improvement planning for several years prior to the Challenge and had been adopted as a model for principal leadership development. Third, and perhaps most importantly for our study, the model was consistent with the types of development sought by the Chicago Annenberg Challenge (Chicago Annenberg Challenge, 2000; Hallert, Chapman, & Ayers, 1995).

Specific indicators of high and low states of development on each of the seven supports and the research from which they were derived are described in detail in our technical reports (e.g., Wenzel et al., 2001). For this chapter, it is sufficient to present a summary of these indicators in Table 7.2. When we speak about schools that have developed, we are referring to schools that moved from lower to higher states on one or more of the essential supports. When we speak about schools that failed to develop, we are referring to schools that made no progress from lower to higher states of development. Finally, when we speak about schools that regressed, we mean schools that dropped from higher to lower states of development.

Our Study Methods

Our study of school development was divided into two related areas of work. The first area involved documenting changes in the essential supports for student learning that occurred in Chicago Annenberg schools. The second area focused on documenting and analyzing school development processes and factors that may contribute to or constrain development.

Table 7.2   Summary of Indicators of High and Low States of Development of the Essential Supports for Student Learning

Essential Support	Low State	High State
School Leadership	Principal is exclusive leader. Decision-making is authoritarian. Teachers do not plan improvements. Leadership does not work to protect school from disruptions. Principal fails to articulate, communicate plans and goals for school. Leadership lacks focus or focus is not on instruction. Lack of accountability. Principal fails to support teachers in their development. School is chaotic and poorly managed.	Leadership is broad-based and includes principal, teachers, and others. Decision-making is democratic and shared. Teachers plan improvements regularly. Leadership buffers school from disruptions. Principal articulates, communicates plans and goals for school. Leadership focuses on instruction. Principal and teachers take responsibility. Principal promotes teacher development. Management is effective and efficient.
Teacher Professional Community	Teachers' vision and goals are ambiguous or not shared. Lack of common language. Fragmented subcultures. Teachers are isolated from one another and do not share reflective dialog or inquiry and do not engage in joint work. Teachers feel responsibility and accountability only to themselves. Limited communication channels. Limited opportunities for collaboration. Disruptive, counterproductive political and intellectual tensions.	Teachers share clear vision and goals. Common language. Normative coherence among social groups and subcultures. Teachers collaborate through reflective dialog, inquiry, and joint work. Teachers feel shared responsibility and accountability. Expansive communication channels. Sufficient opportunities for collaboration. Productive political and intellectual tensions.
Parent and Community Involvement	Lack of parent support for student learning at home. School fails to draw on community resources and institutions. Little outreach to parents as resources.	Strong parent support of student learning at home. School actively draws on community resources and institutions. Active outreach to parents as resources.

Student-Centered Learning Climate	School is disorderly with many disruptions. Students feel physical and/or psychological risk/danger. Impersonality and alienation describe teacher-student relations. Teachers hold low academic expectations for students. Little peer support for academic learning.	School is orderly and students feel physically and psychologically safe. Personalism and belonging describe teacher-student relations. Teachers hold high academic expectations for students. Strong peer support for academic learning.
Quality Instruction	Curriculum is paced slowly with a great deal of review and repetition. Instruction aimed only at mastery of basic skills. High-quality instructional materials not available or not used. Instruction frequently disrupted.	Curriculum is well-paced and coordinated across classrooms and grade levels. Instruction is aimed at the production of challenging intellectual work as well as mastery of basic skills. High-quality instructional materials are used. Instructional time is protected from interruption.
Social Trust	Distrust and cynicism characterize relations between teachers and principal, teachers and students, teachers and parents, and among teachers themselves.	Trust and optimism characterize relations between teachers and principal, teachers and students, teachers and parents, and among teachers themselves.
School Instructional Program Coherence	Instructional programs have different and sometimes divergent goals. So many programs that teachers cannot keep track of them. Student support services, teacher professional development, etc., not aligned to support instructional program.	Instructional programs share common focus and direction. Small enough number of programs that teachers can keep track of them. Student support services, teacher professional development, etc., aligned to support instructional program.

The foundation of this study was longitudinal school-level field research.[4] We studied a small purposive sample of Annenberg schools for five years to understand reasons for more or less successful development. Sample selection began at the network level. We identified 10 networks stratified by development focus (e.g., curricular and instructional development, improving parent and community support), type of external partner (e.g., university, community organization, cultural institution), and history (i.e., whether the network was newly formed or had been formed before the Annenberg Challenge). Then, we selected two or three schools as research sites from each of these networks. One or two schools were chosen because of their promise for working well with their external partner and succeeding in their efforts to develop. Another school was chosen because of indications that it might struggle to succeed. Our selections were informed by external partner assessments and by school-level data previously collected by the Consortium. We sampled networks and schools in two stages, according to their year of entry to the Challenge.

We focused our analysis on 12 elementary schools that participated fully in the research from the 1996–1997 or 1997–1998 school years—depending on their year of entry—through the 2000–2001 school year. Although we did not intend to select a demographically representative group of schools to study, the schools in our sample were typical in many ways of all Annenberg elementary schools and of elementary schools system-wide (see Table 7.1). On average, however, our field research schools served greater proportions of Latino students and smaller proportions of African American students. They were, on average, somewhat larger than other schools.

A team consisting of a senior researcher and one or two research assistants was assigned to each school. These teams made a series of visits to their assigned schools throughout the five-year study period. During these visits teams documented the development of their schools on each of the essential supports. They also documented activities that their schools engaged in to get better and factors that appeared to support or constrain development. Each year the research teams conducted an average of 22 interviews of administrators, teachers, external partners, and other key informants in each school. They made observations at the school and classroom levels and collected documents and other relevant artifacts. From these data, the teams wrote structured case reports of the status of their schools' development at three points during the project: (a) the end of the 1996–1997 or 1997–1998 school year (the school's year of entry); (b) the end of the 1998–1999 school year, and (c) the end of the 2000–2001 school year. For the remainder of the chapter, we will refer to these three points as 1997, 1999, and 2001. Each team also wrote descriptions of their schools' development activities in each of these three years and in the two years in between.

Case reports for the 12 schools were independently read and analyzed by three qualitative analysts. Discrepancies were discussed and reconciled by consensus. Where necessary, the case reports where checked against the original field data. Each school was classified as "developing" or "not developing" according to indicators of the essential supports, and each was categorized by specific areas of development. In addition, the case reports, documentation of specific development activities, and reports of factors that support or constrain development were analyzed to identify themes and patterns across developing and nondeveloping schools. From these themes and patterns, we deduced our findings concerning the promotion of school development and the lessons they suggest for school leadership. Our findings were presented to and verified by the field researchers. The specific examples we identified to illustrate our findings were also verified by the field researchers.

PROMOTING SCHOOL DEVELOPMENT

We identified four patterns of school development across the five years of our study. These patterns are illustrated in Figure 7.1. This figure is a heuristic. The lines represent general directions of development. They do not indicate actual magnitudes of change nor relative differences in starting or ending points among schools. The first pattern is illustrated by two schools—Group 1—that were relatively high on our indicators of essential supports in 1997 and did not change in any appreciable way during the study period. The second pattern is illustrated by another two schools—Group 2—that made net gains in development on one or more of the essential supports between 1997 and 2001. The third pattern is illustrated by four schools—Group 3—that developed positively on one or more of the essential supports between 1997 and 1999 but then regressed between 1999 and 2001. The fourth pattern is illustrated by four schools—Group 4—that were quite low on our indicators of the essential supports in 1997 and failed to make any progress.

When we examined efforts these schools made to develop, when we compared those that were relatively high on indicators of the essential supports to those that were relatively low, and when we compared those schools that made progress to those that did not, four general findings emerged. First, school development was associated with coordinated or concerted attention to multiple essential supports. Second, school development was associated with the use of multiple, reinforcing strategies for change. Third, school development was associated with a strong base of external resources aligned with the school's development agenda. Finally, school development was associated with strong, broad-based, distributed leadership. As shown in Table 7.3, whether these findings were true about a school was, with few exceptions, associated with that school's group classification and pattern of development. In general, these four findings were consistently true or more true than false of more highly developed schools

Figure 7.1 Patterns of Development in Study Schools, 1997 to 2001

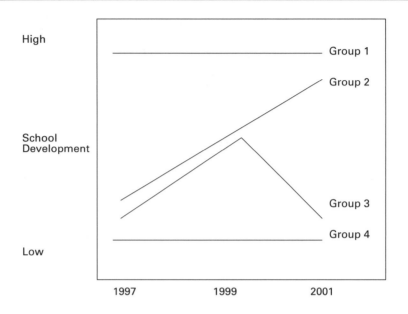

and schools that developed stronger essential supports during our study. These four findings were consistently not true of schools that were relatively weak in the essential supports in 1997 and subsequently failed to develop. For schools that developed between 1997 and 1999 but regressed between 1999 and 2001, these findings were true in 1999 but two or more were not true in 2001. This suggests that the different aspects of a school development process represented by these findings work in conjunction, and that if one or two fall away, school development may be compromised.

Targeting Multiple Essential Supports

The first finding we drew from our field research is that school development is associated with a coordinated focus on multiple essential supports. Recall that these supports include school leadership, teacher professional community, parent and community involvement, student-centered learning climate, high-quality instruction, social trust, and instructional program coherence. In our most highly developed schools and in schools where we found the most development, change initiatives focused on development of several related essential supports (Groups 1 and 2). We found that attention to multiple-related supports created synergy to promote or sustain overall school development. When schools focused on single supports, or when they focused on multiple supports in an uncoordinated manner, we found little overall development (Group 4). When schools shifted from focusing on multiple supports to focusing on

Table 7.3 Relationships Between Patterns of School Development and Findings on School Development Processes

Findings	Group 1 Higher Initial State; No Development	Group 2 Ongoing Development	Group 3 Initial Development Then Regress	Group 4 Low Initial State; No Development
School targets multiple essential supports in a concerted or coordinated manner.	School A + + School B – +	School C + + School D + +	School E + + School F + + School G + – School H + –	School I – – School J – – School K – – School L + –
School uses multiple, complementary change strategies.	School A + + School B + +	School C + + School D – +	School E + + School F + – School G + – School H + –	School I – – School J – – School K – – School L + –
School has strong, aligned base of external resources.	School A + + School B – +	School C + + School D + +	School E + – School F + – School G + – School H + –	School I – – School J – – School K – – School L + –
School develops strong distributive leadership.	School A + + School B + +	School C + + School D + +	School E + – School F + – School G + – School H + –	School I – – School J – – School K – – School L + –

Note: A "+" symbol means a finding is true or more true than false about the school. A "–" symbol means a finding is not true about the school. The right-hand symbol represents status of a finding in 1999. The left-hand symbol represents status of the finding in 2001.

single supports, or when their efforts to address multiple supports lost momentum or coordination, they regressed (Group 3).

Why would a school be more likely to develop by targeting multiple supports? As other Consortium research argues, the essential supports are not discrete, independent elements (Bryk et al., in press). Rather, they operate as related parts of a system. The supports that represent key organizational capacities—school leadership, professional community, and parent and community support—are crucial for developing and supporting school practices—student learning climate and quality instruction—that in turn are instrumental for promoting student learning. This logic is consistent with other literature that contends that school development requires long, steady work that is not focused solely on the implementation of specific programs and policies, but on the broader coherent development of school organization and practices (e.g., Elmore & McLaughlin, 1997; Fullan, 2001; Louis & Miles, 1990).

Our field research suggests that the success of efforts to develop learning climate and instruction is contingent on previous or concurrent development of school organizational capacity (Wenzel et al., 2001). For example, strong leadership is necessary to create and sustain a well-paced, challenging, coherent instructional program (see Newmann, Smith, Allensworth, & Bryk, 2001). There must be a strong professional community of teachers who work together to coordinate the curriculum, achieve consistency in expectations for student learning, develop intellectually rigorous tasks, and engage students in those tasks. It is unlikely that such a professional community can thrive over time if school leadership does not help develop it and provide enough time and resources to get its work done. Overall then, focusing on one essential support may promote development of that particular support, but that development is likely to be limited and difficult to sustain if there are weaknesses in others.

Two examples from our study illustrate these points. School J's efforts to develop its instructional program were undermined by its failure to develop other essential supports. When this school began working with its Annenberg partner in 1997, it focused on raising the quality of reading instruction. Even though initial efforts were promising, weak school leadership and teacher professional community soon compromised them. School H made a concerted effort to develop multiple essential supports, albeit without much coordination or a clear overarching vision for the school. Its Annenberg external partner organized a group of teachers to develop professional community, promote professional development, and improve student learning climate and instruction. At the same time, the principal focused his energy on increasing student test scores, improving student discipline and safety, and promoting small group instruction. Although the Annenberg teachers and the principal focused on different areas of school development, their work converged around the promotion of small group instruction. These efforts helped School H develop between 1997 and 1999, but between 1999 and 2001 initial progress began to fall apart. The school regressed because its development efforts began to diverge and conflict. Teachers working to promote more small group instruction faced a principal who began to assert student discipline as the school's first priority. The principal quashed teacher efforts to develop smaller more flexible instructional groups because those efforts required students to move among self-contained classrooms. The principal believed that such movement posed too great a chance for disruption and student misconduct.

As Table 7.3 indicates, School H's turn-around was also related to a shift toward reliance on one change mechanism. Initially working to achieve change through teacher professional development and student test score accountability, School H came to rely primarily on test score accountability to promote change. In addition, School H lost a key resource to support its development efforts; its Annenberg external partner began to withdraw from the school. Finally, where once teachers shared in leadership for school development, the principal began to consolidate his control over school decisions. These matters are the subjects of our other findings.

Employing Multiple, Reinforcing Strategies

Our field research findings are consistent with the literature on educational change that tells us there are no "quick fixes" or "cookbook solutions" for school development (e.g., Fullan, 2001; Maeher & Midgley, 1996). As with the literature, our research shows that successful school development is achieved not just from the "top down" or "bottom up," but also from the "inside out" through a combination of strategies that most effectively develop teachers' "will" and "skill" (Newmann & Wehlage, 1995; Sarason, 1990; Tyack & Cuban, 1995). There was no single program or initiative that provided any of our sample schools with everything it needed to develop. Our analyses revealed that school development was associated with employing idiosyncratic combinations of complementary, mutually reinforcing strategies instead of a reliance on any single one (see Firestone & Corbett, 1988).

Literature on education reform identifies three types of mechanisms by which change may be promoted at the school and classroom levels (Hannaway, 1993; Smylie & Perry, 1998). The first consists of bureaucratic and normative controls and sanctions that seek to compel individuals and schools to take specific actions. The second consists of incentives to prompt voluntary action. The third consists of learning opportunities that develop new knowledge and skills and, from that development, evoke new action.

We found many examples of incentives, learning opportunities, and controls introduced to promote development in our study schools. Some principals and external partners offered teachers incentives to adopt and develop commitment to new teaching practices. These came in the form of monetary stipends, public praise and encouragement, time to work with colleagues or pursue professional development, consultations with experts, increased classroom autonomy, and opportunities to exercise greater influence in decision making. Numerous opportunities for learning and development were available to teachers, principals, and other school staff in our study schools. These included workshops and conferences, collaborative planning and work groups, networking with teachers from other schools, working with in-house curriculum coordinators, new mentoring relationships, access to professional journals, and increased opportunities for collegial interaction. There were also a number of controls at work. In most of our study schools, Chicago Public Schools (CPS) retention and probation policies were highly influential sources of accountability and control for principals and teachers. There were a number of principals who created additional monitoring and accountability systems. Several developed and enforced their own set of expectations for staff and student performance. At one school, the Annenberg external partner instituted a formal review process that made staff members publicly accountable to the partner and to each other. In several schools, the growth of teamwork and collaboration, along with the expansion of teachers' leadership, reinforced collegial accountability and control.

The literature indicates that none of these mechanisms alone is likely to promote and sustain school development over an extended period of time (e.g., Smylie & Perry, 1998). Indeed, in our study, developing schools and schools that were initially strong and steady in their development (Groups 1 and 2) were more likely than nondeveloping schools (Group 4) to use a variety of strategies to trigger development, but they did not use them in any common combination or order. Different mechanisms were instrumental in sparking development activity in each of the schools. Some were motivated to act by the threat of administrative sanction; others were prompted by the adoption of a promising new approach to teaching. In no instance were the mechanisms that initiated the action adequate to sustain development over an extended period of time without the introduction of others. For example, School D accelerated its development between 1999 and 2001 in large part because it introduced a broader range of change mechanisms. On the other hand, loss of progress among all but one school in Group 3 was associated with movement away from a coordinated combination of change mechanisms and increased reliance on one—bureaucratic accountability through high stakes student testing.

Although we were not able to detect any patterns in the strategies developing schools used to change, it is likely that a school's particular situation may call for specific combinations, or for certain ones to be used before others (Firestone & Corbett, 1988). For some schools, the most effective means to initiate change might be the introduction of a new accountability system or the replacement of the principal or members of the teaching staff. For other schools, this strategy could be completely ineffective. Likewise, professional development might motivate teachers at one school to adopt new practices, but be largely ignored at another. The apparent context-specific, idiosyncratic nature of effective strategies requires additional investigation. For now, it seems that evocation of effective combinations of strategies depends on understanding the strengths and weaknesses of the particular school and the needs and interests of the people who work there (Evans, 1996).

Securing External Resources

Many different types of resources are needed for school development. These include people, time, money, and materials. They also include ideas and expertise, leadership, political support, beliefs and values, and social trust. Which new external resources a school may need are dependent upon the areas it seeks to develop, the strength of its internal resources, and the external resources it has already accumulated.

External resources for school development may come from a variety of places—the central administration, external partners, community organizations, and parents. Underresourced and underdeveloped schools may depend a great deal on external resources to promote development. Indeed, failure to secure adequate external resources may thwart development efforts (Fullan, 2001).

Our study schools drew from several different sources of support. Many had multiple external partners and other service providers, however, the CPS system and the Chicago Annenberg Challenge stood out as the most predominant sources of external support. Beyond supporting basic school operations, CPS provided several of our study schools budget directors, instructional consultants, and probation managers. The central administration's capital improvement initiative funded badly needed repairs, renovations, and new construction at several schools.

The Annenberg Challenge linked schools with new human and intellectual resources and provided modest financial support for school development. Annenberg external partners brought ideas and expertise, focus, and impetus to promote school development (Newmann & Sconzert, 2001). Through networks, partners expanded the intellectual and social resources available to schools by linking them with other schools engaged in similar development activity. Annenberg grants, while averaging no more than 1% of a school's operating budget, were used to purchase important resources for school development such as in-house curriculum coordinators, teacher professional development, classroom libraries, and new instructional materials. The Challenge also provided some technical assistance in the form of workshops, conferences, and consultations with Challenge staff. Finally, participation in the Challenge helped schools leverage additional resources. Such was the case among several schools that were working with their Annenberg external partners to increase parent involvement and cultivate stronger, more supportive relationships with organizations in their communities.

While CPS and the Annenberg Challenge made new external resources available to schools, our research points to a more complicated story about the relationship between securing additional resources and school development. We found that developing schools and more highly developed schools (Groups 1 and 2) were generally more effective than nondeveloping schools (Group 4) at searching for, securing, and taking full advantage of external resources. At the same time, what distinguished more highly developed and developing schools from nondeveloping schools was not simply entrepreneurial ability. Some nondeveloping schools were very good at obtaining external resources. Rather, what distinguished them was the ability to secure resources aligned with a particular agenda for development and the ability to employ these resources in an efficient and strategic manner. These points are well illustrated by the four schools in Group 3, whose loss and fragmentation of key resources were associated with regress.

Several of the nondeveloping schools in Group 4 had relatively few resources, and it was apparent that the lack of resources constrained their efforts to develop. There were also several nondeveloping schools in that group that had substantial resources, but they were acquired in an indiscriminant manner and were not coordinated with the schools' development agendas. These schools did not always use their resources to their full potential.

Distributing Leadership for School Development

Our first three findings focused on aims, strategies, and resources for school development. Our fourth finding focused on the different figures who led development efforts. When we looked closely at our field study schools, we saw that the strength and breadth of leadership distinguished more highly developed and developing schools (Groups 1 and 2) from nondeveloping ones (Group 4). Schools that made the greatest progress were those that had cultivated strong, distributive leadership. Poorly developed and nondeveloping schools were likely to have a single source of consolidated leadership or simply have weak overall leadership (Group 4). In schools where we saw losses in development (Group 3), we found that leadership that was once strong and distributed had weakened or had become more authoritarian and consolidated in one role, usually that of the principal. These findings are consistent with other studies of distributive leadership and the implementation and institutionalization of complex educational change (e.g., Heller & Firestone, 1995; Mayrowetz & Weinstein, 1999; Spillane, Halverson, & Diamond, 2001).

In each of the schools we studied, development was more likely to occur when key leadership tasks were performed in a coordinated manner by multiple actors in a school community, including the principal, teachers, external partners, coordinators, and parents. These tasks included: (a) creating and sustaining a vision for school development across multiple essential supports; (b) engaging others in school development initiatives; (c) promoting coherence among those initiatives; (d) providing incentives and opportunities to develop staff knowledge and skills; (e) developing curriculum and student assessments; (f) monitoring, providing encouragement, and holding staff members accountable for progress made toward school development; (g) obtaining external resources to support the school's development agenda; and (h) managing external influences on the school in ways that support development. Most of these tasks are inherent in our first three findings.

While our study points to the importance of the distributive performance of such tasks to school development, it also highlights the "make-or-break" role that principals play in school development. By virtue of the authority associated with their position and their access to and control of key resources, principals played a special role in promoting school development. In our study schools, they were often at the heart of successful development activity. We found that the most effective principals performed a number of common leadership tasks. They may not have performed them alone, but they performed them nonetheless. They articulated a clear, coherent vision of strong instructional practice and effective school organization. They communicated high expectations for teachers as both instructors and leaders of development, and they pressed teachers to meet those expectations. These principals persistently promoted the development of professional competence and leadership capacity among staff members and could be counted on to provide the resources to support that development. Principals at our developing schools distributed leadership among others and managed their "leadership work." At the same time, these principals could be forceful and directive to ensure that the school stayed focused and that the work got done.

Principals in more highly developed and developing schools effectively managed their schools' external resources. They obtained the human, intellectual, and material resources needed to support their schools' development efforts. They established strong, productive relationships with their Annenberg external partners and with central administrative staff. These principals effectively protected their schools from external distractions and interference. When distraction and interference did intrude, they worked to minimize any disruptive effect. Principals were also among the first in the school community to feel the sparks of external pressure and opportunities for school development. This put them in a unique position to initiate development. Because they had the opportunity to marshal external support, principals could couple the initiation of development activity with new resources to fuel it. Finally, because of their position of authority within the school and between the school and its environment, these principals could bring coherence among school development goals, strategies, and internal and external resources.

We found further that when working with their principals, teacher leaders could be powerful change agents for school development. In our developing schools, teachers contributed additional expertise, skills, and perspective. They helped to create and sustain a vision for school development, and their assistance was crucial in promoting and engaging other teachers in development initiatives. Teacher leaders facilitated professional development, monitored and held other staff accountable for developing their practices, and helped the school obtain external resources.

One particularly notable way that leadership was distributed to teachers in our study schools was the creation of full-time in-house coordinator positions. These new positions focused primarily on the development of classroom curriculum and instruction. Half of the schools in our study sample had at least one in-house coordinator. These coordinators were usually teachers at the school who had been released from their classroom duties to help other teachers develop classroom practice. Selected because of their excellence in teaching and their ability to work well with colleagues, these teachers were usually trained by Annenberg external partners to use promising professional development and mentoring strategies to promote the partners' curricular and instructional programs and practices at the classroom level.

The specific work these in-house coordinators performed varied among our study schools. Creating these positions usually led to a growth in overall school leadership. Coordinators led workshops, worked individually with teachers, observed classroom practice, and obtained new curricular and instructional materials. These teacher leaders became focal points for professional development. Teachers in some schools began to turn more often to them than to their principals for instructional expertise and assistance. Coordinators often served as liaisons between teachers and principals, and they facilitated communication with Annenberg external partners and other schools in Annenberg networks. We found these roles performed particularly well in several of our more highly developed and developing schools. Indeed, in several schools the loss of effective in-house coordinators was a central reason for their regress.

LESSONS FOR SCHOOL-LEVEL LEADERSHIP

Our study of Chicago Annenberg Challenge schools says a great deal about leadership for school development. As we argued at the beginning of the chapter that the lessons we draw, while propositional and provisional, are quite consistent with other research on leadership and educational change.

First, our study strongly indicates that principal leadership matters in promoting school development and it matters a lot. Even though it is very important that other members of a school community perform leadership tasks, the principal occupies a unique position in school organization to initiate, manage, and sustain school development. The principal is crucial in developing leadership capacity among others and in distributing and managing the performance of leadership tasks by others. While strong principal leadership alone may not be sufficient to promote and sustain school development over time, it is clearly necessary. There is some debate in the literature about the importance of the principal in the context of distributed leadership for implementing and institutionalizing complex innovation (e.g., Heller & Firestone, 1995; Mayrowetz & Weinstein, 1999). In our study of Chicago Annenberg schools, there is really no debate. Principals played a "make or break" role in promoting and achieving school development.

Second, our findings point to the need for leadership to think systemically about schools and their development. The most successful schools in our study were those that targeted for development multiple, mutually reinforcing aspects of school organization and practice. In order to set and pursue such an agenda for development, leadership must see school organizations in terms of their dynamic, interdependent parts (see Bolman & Deal, 1997; Bryk et al., in press). Leadership must understand how these parts work and change together and how they can support each other in promoting effective teaching and student learning. Leadership must understand the dynamic quality of school organizations and how change in one aspect can affect the other aspects positively or negatively.

Third, our study points to the importance of organizing development efforts around strong theories of change. These theories should identify and target multiple, mutually influential elements of school organization and practice. In addition, they should evoke a complementary array of strategically chosen change mechanisms, tailored to the particular organizational strengths and weaknesses of the school, the school's development goals, and the needs and interests of the people who are part of the school's community. Strategies to develop individual and collective capacity—the "will" and the "skill"—for leadership, for organizational development, and for improved classroom practice appear vital to successful development efforts. Our findings indicate, however, that strategies to develop capacity may not be sufficient to promote development over time without complementary incentives and systems of accountability that reinforce efforts to develop and enact new capacity. Likewise, our findings suggest that leadership would be ill-advised to rely exclusively on accountability mechanisms to achieve much school development. While in some schools, development may need a "kick-start" from a high-stakes accountability system, it is unlikely that such a system will take the school very far without the introduction of strategies to develop new knowledge and skills and incentives to develop new commitments.

Fourth, this chapter points to the importance of coherence in efforts to promote school development. It also points to the importance of leadership in achieving coherence. Leadership, particularly principal leadership, is crucial to align development goals, strategies, and internal and external resources around a strong, robust vision of a good school, good teaching, a learned student, and a sound theory of change. As we mentioned earlier in the chapter, by virtue of the authority of their roles and their access to and control of resources, principals are in a unique position in the school organization to promote coherence. The alternative is fragmentation that, according to our study and other research (see Fullan, 2001; Newmann et al., 2001), can become a serious impediment to school development.

Finally, our five-year study should remind school leaders that school development takes time and requires long steady work. It should remind school leaders that progress is fragile and that initial gains can be easily lost. Our findings suggest that beyond patience and persistence, sustainable school development requires ongoing monitoring and assessment of development goals, progress toward achieving those goals, and the effectiveness (or lack thereof) of development strategies. Development may also require flexibility and adjustment of goals, strategies, and resources as conditions inside and outside the school change. These demands of school development point to the importance of organizational learning. As others have argued (see Fullan, 2001), re-forming schools as professional communities to support organizational learning may be a crucial step in promoting and sustaining overall school development. Itself a difficult and complex change to achieve, developing this crucial organizational capacity may provide a foundation necessary to develop and support what is perhaps the most difficult aspect of schools to penetrate and change—classroom teaching and student learning.

REFERENCES

Bolman, L. G., & Deal, T. E. (1997). *Reframing organizations: Artistry, choice, and leadership* (2nd ed.). San Francisco: Jossey-Bass.

Bryk, A. S., Sebring, P. B., Kerbow, D., Rollow, S. G., & Easton, J. Q. (1998). *Charting Chicago school reform: Democratic localism as a lever for change.* Boulder, CO: Westview Press.

Bryk, A. S., Sebring, P. B., Allensworth, E., Luppescu, S., Easton, J. Q., & Gladden, M. (In Press.). *Long term academic gains in Chicago elementary schools: A theory of essential supports.*

Chicago Annenberg Challenge (2000). *How to grow healthy schools: A guide to improving public education.* Chicago: Chicago Annenberg Challenge.

Designs for Change (1993). *All our kids can learn to read.* Chicago: Designs for Change.

Elmore R. F., & McLaughlin, M. W. (1997). *Steady work: Policy, practice, and the reform of American education* (R-3574-NIE/RC). Santa Monica, CA: RAND.

Evans, R. (1996). *The human side of school change.* San Francisco: Jossey-Bass.

Firestone, W. A., & Corbett, H. D. (1988). Planned organizational change. In N. Boyan (Ed.), *Handbook of research on educational administration* (pp. 321–340). New York: Longman.

Fullan, M. (2001). *The new meaning of educational change* (3rd ed.). New York: Teachers College Press.

Hallert, A., Chapman, W., & Ayers, W. (1995). *The Annenberg Challenge: Good schools for a great city.* Unpublished paper.

Hannaway, J. (1993). Decentralization in two school districts: Challenging the standard paradigm. In J. Hannaway & M. Carnoy (Eds.), *Decentralization and school improvement* (pp. 135–162). San Francisco: Jossey-Bass.

Heller, M. F., & Firestone, W. A. (1995). Who's in charge here? Sources of leadership for change in eight schools. *Elementary School Journal, 96,* 65–86.

Hess, A. G., Jr. (1991). *School restructuring Chicago style.* Thousand Oaks, CA: Corwin Press.

Hess, A. G., Jr. (1993, April). *Buying or aiding teachers? The reallocation of funds under Chicago school reform.* Paper presented at the annual meeting of the American Educational Research Association, Atlanta.

Louis, K. S., & Miles, M. (1990). *Improving the urban high school: What works and why.* New York: Teachers College Press.

Maeher, M. L., & Midgley, C. (1996). *Transforming school cultures.* Boulder, CO: Westview Press.

Mayrowetz, D., & Weinstein, C. S. (1999). Sources of leadership for inclusive education: Creating schools for all children. *Educational Administration Quarterly, 35,* 423–449.

Newmann, F. M., Bryk, A. S., & Lopez, G. (1998). *The quality of intellectual work in Chicago schools: A baseline report.* Chicago: Consortium on Chicago School Research.

Newmann, F. M., Bryk, A. S., & Nagaoka, J. K. (2001). *Authentic intellectual work and standardized tests: Conflict or coexistence?* Chicago: Consortium on Chicago School Research.

Newmann, F. M., & Sconzert, K. (2000). *School improvement with external partners.* Chicago: Consortium on Chicago School Research.

Newmann, F. M., Smith, B. A., Allensworth, E., & Bryk, A. S. (2001). *School instructional program coherence: Benefits and challenges.* Chicago: Consortium on Chicago School Research.

Newmann, F. M., & Wehlage, G. G. (1995). *Successful school restructuring: A report to the public and educators.* Madison: University of Wisconsin, Center on Organization and Restructuring of Schools.

Sarason, S. (1990). *The predictable failure of educational reform.* San Francisco: Jossey-Bass.

Shipps, D., Kahne, J., & Smylie, M. A. (1999). The politics of urban school reform: Legitimacy, city growth, and school improvement in Chicago. *Educational Policy, 13,* 518–545.

Shipps, D., Sconzert, K., & Swyers, H. (1999). *The Chicago Annenberg Challenge: The first three years.* Chicago: Consortium on Chicago School Research.

Smylie, M. A., Bilcer, D. K., Kochanek, J., Sconzert, K., Shipps, D., & Swyers, H. (1998). *Getting started: A first look at Chicago Annenberg schools and networks.* Chicago: Consortium on Chicago School Research.

Smylie, M. A., & Perry, G. W., Jr. (1998). Restructuring schools for improving teaching. In A. Hargreaves, A. Lieberman, M. Fullan, & D. Hopkins (Eds.), *International handbook of educational change* (pp. 976–1005). Dordrecht, Netherlands: Kluwer.

Smylie, M. A., Wenzel, S. A., Fendt, C., Hallman, S., Luppescu, S., & Nagaoka, J. K. (2002*). Development of Chicago Annenberg schools: 1996–2001.* Chicago: Consortium on Chicago School Research.

Spillane, J. P., Halverson, R., & Diamond, J. B. (2001). Investigating school leadership practice: A distributed perspective. *Educational Researcher, 30*(3), 23–28.

Tyack, D., & Cuban, L. (1995). *Tinkering toward Utopia.* Cambridge, MA: Harvard University Press.

Wenzel, S. A., Smylie, M. A., Sebring, P. B., Allensworth, E., Gutierrez, T., Hallman, S., Luppescu, S., & Miller, S. R. (2001). *Development of Chicago Annenberg schools: 1996–1999.* Chicago: Consortium on Chicago School Research.

Yin, R. K. (1995). *Case study research* (2nd ed.). Thousand Oaks, CA: Sage Publications.

NOTES

1. The research described in this chapter was supported by a grant from the Chicago Annenberg Challenge. The chapter reflects the interpretations and conclusions of the authors alone and does not necessarily represent those of the Challenge, the Consortium, or the Consortium's Steering Committee members and their institutions. No endorsement of this chapter by any of these groups should be assumed.

2. These and other reports of the Chicago Annenberg Research Project are available from the Consortium on Chicago School Research at www.consortium-chicago.org.

3. For more information about school reform in Chicago, see Bryk et al. (1998), Hess (1991, 1993), and Shipps, Kahne, & Smylie (1999a). For a detailed analysis of the influence of Chicago school reform on the development of the Chicago Annenberg Challenge, see Shipps, Sconzert, & Swyers (1999).

4. Our full study of school development—our research samples, data sources, methods of analysis, and findings—is described in detail in Wenzel et al. (2001) and Smylie et al. (2002).

CHAPTER EIGHT

The Bay Area School Reform Collaborative

Building the Capacity to Lead

MICHAEL AARON COPLAND

> *If the capacity of teachers and principals to enrich rather than diminish each other's lives and work is to be realized—conditions must change. Somehow the school principal must assume more of the burden of protecting the best interests of teachers and liberating more of the constructive power of which teachers are capable. In addition, each teacher will have to assume more ownership for the best interests of the school—including other teachers, other teachers' pupils, and the principal.*
>
> (Barth, 1990, p. 28)

Imagine a school where Barth's vision of enriched capacity and shared ownership of continual improvement has come to fruition. What would it look like? Principals and teachers creating and sustaining widely distributed leadership systems, processes, and capacities. The work of improving teaching and learning is continuous and focused on students, high standards, equity, and best practices. The school organizes its continual reform work around actions that will make a difference to increase achievement for all. The school also manages its context to sustain the work, taking on a leadership role and sharing its progress and challenges in the district and broader community. A grand vision? Indeed. Yet the challenges of developing a school where leadership is broadly distributed, and the work of reform is ongoing and sustainable, are significant.

Not the least of these challenges is the fact that the leadership functions necessary for improving schools have been disproportionally heaped on one formal role in the system—the principal. Clearly more so than any other, the principal's role in leading school improvement is widely recognized as central, and the expectations associated with the role are scrutinized from many angles in the literature. As the formal leader in the school, the principal has been the target of researchers attempting to understand the various functions associated with leadership in schools. In doing so, research and scholarship has perpetuated a myth of principal as everything to everyone.

Conceptions of *instructional leadership*, for example, allocate authority and influence to the principal's role, assuming as well considerable influence through expert knowledge on the part of those occupying such roles (Hallinger & Murphy, 1985; Hallinger & McCary, 1990). In pursuing *participative leadership*, principals are called on to provide leadership in various domains, while operating under a collaborative arrangement that actively seeks to involve various others from the school community in the decision-making process (Murphy & Beck, 1995). As *transformational leaders* (Burns, 1978), principals are called on to craft a vision, establish school goals, provide intellectual stimulation, offer individualized support, model best practices and important organizational values, demonstrate high-performance expectations, create productive school culture, and develop structures to foster participation in school decisions (c.f., Leithwood, Tomlinson, & Genge, 1996).

The principal's role has elsewhere been characterized as one of *manager* (Duke & Leithwood, 1994), *minister* or *steward* (Sergiovanni, 1996), *visionary* (Barth, 1990), *potter* or *poet* (Hart & Bredeson, 1996), *architect* or *commissar* (Hughes, 1999), and *moral leader* (Hodgkinson, 1991) to name but a few. These conceptions trickle down from academe to influence writing on the principalship that appears in well-respected and widely read mainstream educational publications such *Education Week* and *Phi Delta Kappan*. Professional practitioner journals such as the *NASSP Journal, Principal,* and *American School Board Journal* routinely feature pieces that center on understanding the principal's role.

What emerges from these various conceptions of the principalship is a portrait of a role that, even in theory, appears extremely difficult. This has prompted some to suggest that, in practice, the principalship encompasses leadership functions so numerous that it is no longer possible for one person to consistently live up to all that is expected in the role (Copland, 2001; Kimball & Sirotnik, 2000). Therefore, rethinking leadership in schools is a crucial first step in moving toward shared, ongoing, and sustainable school improvement.

RETHINKING SCHOOL LEADERSHIP

The sheer scope of expectations associated with principals' leadership has prompted rethinking already, particularly given the prevalent push for school improvement and reform. And, while a significant body of very recent work is developing on this topic, conceptual forays staking out new directions, away from role-based conceptions of leadership and toward functional or organizational views, are not all new.

A handful of notable scholars have been productively engaged in this thinking for nearly 20 years. In an early treatise, Sergiovanni (1984) argued that leadership is an artifact or product of organizational culture, and that the particular shape and style of leadership in an organization is not a function of individuals or of training programs; rather, it has to do with the mixture of organizational culture and the density of leadership competence among and within many actors. Sergiovanni posited a fundamental shift, discerning leadership less as a set of management techniques, and more as a set of norms, beliefs, and principles that emerge, and to which members give allegiance, in an effective organization. In a complementary vein, Murphy's (1988) comprehensive analysis of the first decade of instructional leadership literature devoted considerable attention to analyzing problems that emerged from a general failure in the scholarship on that topic to consider both the micro- and macro-level contextual issues of school leadership. Murphy criticized what he viewed as errantly placed attributions of causality in the literature; attributions that improvements in teaching and learning were because of the efficacy of actions performed by persons in formal roles of authority, rather than organizational conditions. Such early work underpins the recent emergence of broader considerations of leadership in schools.

Current efforts to reframe leadership in schools are rooted in notions of distribution. In an important contribution, Elmore (2000) sets out a framework for understanding the reconstruction of leadership roles and functions around the idea of distributed leadership in the service of large scale instructional improvement. This new way of seeing is rooted in principles of distributed expertise, mutual dependence, reciprocity of accountability and capacity, and the centrality of instructional practice. Elmore identifies five leadership domains—policy, professional, system, school, and practice—each encompassing multiple actors, and develops a robust understanding of leadership functions associated with each domain. In this way, Elmore pushes the field to relocate the authority and responsibility for improving teaching and learning, separating it from the sole control of those "up the chain" of the administrative hierarchy, and embedding that authority and responsibility in the daily work of all those connected to the enterprise of schooling.

Similarly, Spillane, Halverson, and Diamond (2000) suggest that school leadership is necessarily a distributed activity "stretched over" people in different roles rather than neatly divided among them, a dynamic interaction between multiple leaders (and followers) and their situational and social contexts. Lambert (1998) also understands leadership as broad concept, separated from person, role, and a discreet set of individual behaviors. Rather than being primarily centered on the principal, the capacity for leadership resides within and among all members of the larger school community, administrators, teachers, parents, and students, suggesting shared responsibility for a shared purpose, and requiring the redistribution of power and authority. Complementary to this understanding, others offer the view that leadership is an organizational quality, originating from many peoples' personal resources, and flowing through networks of roles (Pounder, Ogawa, & Adams, 1995; Ogawa & Bossert, 1995).

Empirical evidence is also surfacing in support of the notion that, within successful school communities, the capacity to lead is not principal-centric by necessity, but rather embedded in various organizational contexts. McLaughlin & Talbert (2001), for example, examined organizational context effects on teacher community, teaching, and teachers' careers and found no instances of administrative leaders who created extraordinary contexts for teaching by virtue of their unique vision; nor did the study reveal any common patterns in strong principals' personal characteristics. Successful principals were men and women with varied professional backgrounds who worked in collaboration with teacher leaders and in respect of teaching culture. They found various ways to support teachers in getting the job done. The leadership of these principals was not superhuman; rather, it grew from a strong and simple commitment to making the school work for their students, and to building teachers' commitment and capacity to pursue this collective goal. Perhaps most importantly, the responsibility for sustaining school improvement was shared among a much broader group of school community members, rather than owned primarily by a solitary leader at the top of the organizational chart.

There remains much to explore and learn about the process of moving from a hierarchical conception of leadership within schools to one that distributes the functions of leadership more broadly. The balance of this chapter reports on an ongoing study of school leadership in the context of a large-scale, regionwide school reform initiative in the San Francisco Bay Area that specifically intends to promote broadly shared leadership within schools, with the goal of fostering and supporting schools as learning organizations. The research has explored several questions to date:

- Within schools identified as "leaders" in building leadership capacity, what evidence can be found to suggest that sharing or broadening of leadership is occurring? What does shared leadership look like, and how did it evolve?
- What are key leverage points or strategies for promoting and building broadly shared leadership capacity within a school community?

- What, if anything, happens to leadership functions typically associated with the principal's role within schools intentionally attempting to broaden and share responsibility for leadership? What functions remain crucial to a successful principalship?
- What are the challenges to promoting shared leadership?
- How, if at all, does the sharing of leadership within a school community impact student learning?

The balance of this chapter presents a synthesis of the research to date in exploring these questions.

Policy for Building Leadership Capacity

The Bay Area School Reform Collaborative (BASRC), a five-year reform effort involving schools throughout the 118 district Bay Area region supported by the Hewlett-Annenberg Challenge, seeks to "reculture" schools in ways that support whole school change.[1] BASRC aims to change the way schools do business. BASRC's design for reform understands that school improvement necessarily requires cultural change and posits a missing element in schools' cultures as evidence-based decision making centered on a focused reform effort.

BASRC's theory of action holds that the important work of reforming schools must be done primarily by schools themselves. The theory suggests a model for leadership less dependent on the actions of singular visionary individuals, but rather one that views leadership as a set of functions or qualities shared across a much broader segment of the school community that encompasses principal, teachers, and other professionals both internal and external to the school. BASRC's overall strategy for promoting leadership uses a school-based cycle of inquiry to inform school reform efforts, and marshals diverse forms of knowledge to support teachers' learning and change.

The cycle of inquiry required of BASRC schools is intended to help schools pose, investigate, and respond to questions about policies and practices and has six steps (see Figure 8.1). The first two steps have to do with selecting and narrowing a question for investigation. The next step is to identify measurable goals. This step recognizes that setting specified targets is a measure for success that is critical in determining the success or failure of an action. The fourth and fifth steps include creating and implementing a particular action—connecting knowing and doing. The sixth step is to collect and analyze results from data generated by the action taken.

Finally, the cycle connects back to the first step as the problem statement is refined in light of new evidence. Simply stated, BASRC's cycle of inquiry strategy aims to inform schools about the degree to which they are actually accomplishing what they think they should be in terms of a focused reform effort and consequences for students.

Figure 8.1   BASRC Cycle of Inquiry

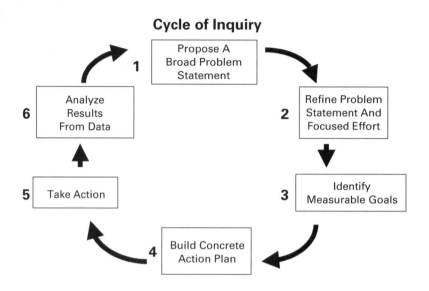

The initiative also attends to the learning skills teachers will need in order to carry out a cycle of inquiry. In an effort to foster teachers' capacity and comfort in generating knowledge of practice, teachers receive training in asking probing questions, in developing an accountability framework to guide their school's cycle of inquiry, and in constructing standards against which to measure their school's progress in their focused reform effort. They practice these skills in many BASRC events. For example, regional meetings of hundreds of Bay Area teachers, administrators, parents, support providers, and funders were convened to score schools' portfolio applications for BASRC Leadership School status. Subsequently, regional preparation and review of Leadership Schools' Reports of Progress immersed teachers in the use of rubrics to evaluate progress on five dimensions of whole school change: equity and achieving high standards, depth, breadth, leadership, and coherence.

SAMPLE AND METHOD

The research reported here incorporates findings from a spring 1999 survey of principals conducted across all BASRC Leadership Schools, as well as a 1999–2000 survey of a sample of Leadership School teachers. Data from observations of BASRC-sponsored regional principal gatherings were collected and analyzed, as were various school documents related to the reform work. In addition, 16 identified leadership schools were targeted for closer study of leadership issues. Schools within this purposive sample were either recommended by BASRC personnel or identified by members of the research team as potentially rich examples of schools with broadly shared leadership capacity. The sample included four high schools, eleven elementary schools, and one K-8 school. With one exception, all schools were members of the first or second BASRC cohorts of leadership schools.[2] The schools varied broadly in terms of socioeconomic status, ethnicity of student population, and school size. The focused research effort within the identified schools involved analysis of a series of interviews conducted with principals and teacher leaders serving in formal, compensated roles as building-level BASRC reform coordinators, and observations conducted by the research team at the school sites. Finally, standardized test data focused on academic performance was collected and included in the analysis.

FINDINGS

Evidence of Shared Leadership

Findings from two different surveys, one conducted in the spring of 1999 with BASRC Leadership School principals, and the other conducted during the 1999–2000 school year with a sample of Leadership School teachers, suggest some common themes with regard to the emergence of shared leadership across Leadership Schools.

Principal Survey Results

A survey of principals within BASRC Leadership Schools attributed positive changes in the development of teachers' leadership capacity to schools' involvement with BASRC (N = 63 principals). The principal survey revealed that 91% of the Leadership School principals agreed or strongly agreed that their school's BASRC involvement was instrumental in a change in teacher leadership, while 97% noted agreement that BASRC involvement promoted teachers' consensus on needed areas for whole school change (see Table 8.1). Ninety-two percent of surveyed principals suggested that the use of data for decision-making had moderately or substantially increased as a result of the school's involvement with BASRC. Sixty-five percent agreed or strongly agreed that their teachers are engaged in systematic analysis of student performance data. Fully 95% of surveyed principals indicated either agreement or strong agreement that their school's BASRC involvement has promoted staff discussions of teaching and learning, and 71% indicated that BASRC work has promoted teachers' voice in school decision-making.

Leadership school principals also are positive in their assessment of BASRC's role in promoting broader sharing of leadership among other stakeholders in the school community. Seventy percent of principals

Table 8.1   Principal Survey Responses on Development of Leadership
Capacity (N = 63)

Q: Indicate your level of agreement that BASRC involvement has changed the following at your school	Strongly Disagree	Disagree	Neutral	Agree	Strongly Agree
• Teacher's voice in school decisions	0	0	29%	53%	18%
• Parent's voice in school decisions	0	0	30%	55%	15%
• Teacher's consensus on desired learning outcomes	0	0	10%	53%	37%
• Teacher's consensus on needed areas for whole school change	0	0	3%	52%	45%
• Teacher leadership	0	0	9%	47%	44%
• Staff discussion of teaching and learning	0	0	5%	49%	46%
• Interaction between different stakeholder groups	0	0	30%	57%	13%

Q: How has BASRC involvement changed your school's use of data as basis for decision-making?	Big Decrease	Some Decrease	No Change	Some Increase	Big Increase
	0	0	8%	50%	42%

surveyed agree or strongly agree that their school's involvement with BASRC has promoted parent voice in school decisions. Seventy percent also indicate agreement that BASRC involvement has promoted interaction between different stakeholder groups (e.g., classified staff, teachers, parents, community, and district administration).

Teacher Survey Results

In a similar vein, a surveyed sample of teachers in BASRC Leadership Schools (N = 27) centered in part on aspects of shared leadership in schools, and the development of leadership capacity. These questions focused on the use of the cycle of inquiry, presence of a schoolwide vision, broad encouragement of reform work, use of data in making school decisions, and the responsiveness of the school as a whole to making changes intended to address student needs.

Table 8.2   Correlation of Teacher and Principal Responses on Questions of Leadership Capacity

		Principal Questions (N = 63)	
	Correlation **=.05 alpha* ***=.01 alpha*	*Are Teachers* *Engaged in* *Analysis of* *Student Data?*	*Do Teachers* *Regularly* *Examine School* *Performance?*
Teacher Questions (N = 27)	Use of data for decisions?	.258	.541*
	Use of cycle of inquiry?	.534*	.633**
	School has a vision for reform?	.597**	.595**
	School encourages inquiry?	.531**	.596**
	Progress is examined?	.603**	.508*
	Teachers collect data?	.519*	.623**
	School makes changes for student needs?	.566**	.629**

Teacher responses were significantly correlated with responses made by principals to questions of teacher engagement in data analysis and in the general examination of school performance (see Table 8.2). Teachers' responses about the use of the cycle of inquiry, use of data in decision-making, presence of a shared schoolwide vision of reform, schoolwide encouragement of inquiry, and school responsiveness to making changes based on student needs were all strongly positively correlated with principal responses to a question regarding the extent of teachers' regular examination of school performance. Teachers' responses about their level of involvement in data collection, the examination of progress at the school, the school's encouragement of inquiry, and the presence of a schoolwide vision of reform all correlated strongly and positively with principal responses to a question about the level of teachers' engagement in analysis of student data.

Strong corresponding evidence pointing to the development and existence of shared leadership across the leadership schools surfaced throughout qualitative data obtained via interviews and observations on site. Sharing the work of leadership in the context of whole school reform is viewed as a necessity, as illustrated by this comment from an elementary principal:

Every (staff) person has some form of leadership role because there's not enough time in the world to do all the leadership things that need to be done. So . . . we have grade-level leaders, and during our grade-level meetings, these people take a leadership role in making sure that the agendas are organized and that the work that needs to be done in a grade level is maintained. And then we have content leaders in science, technology, mathematics, as well as literacy and social science. There are many different leadership roles that function across the school. How do they come about? Well, basically, out of need and. . . . It's just kind of the culture now. (Principals know) we can't be involved in all the decisions because there's not enough time, so we really have to disaggregate the jobs and kind of fit them where they go.

Leadership Leverage Points and Strategies

The following section presents findings about leverage points and strategies for building leadership capacity within the sample of 16 leadership schools, summarizes key understandings, and characterizes BASRC's role in building leadership capacity at these sites. Findings suggest that formal leaders (principals and teacher leaders serving as reform coordinators) often provide the catalyst for change early in a school's reform work. Second, data suggest that the BASRC Cycle of Inquiry is a powerful strategy for developing a shared vision, and broadening involvement in ongoing reform work. Third, across the sample of sixteen BASRC Leadership Schools, new leadership structures have emerged that promote broader involvement in the work of reform. These structures are most secure within schools with greater longevity in reform work. Finally, leadership transitions remain difficult for schools, but these can be successfully negotiated with preparation.

Leaders in Formal Roles Provide a Catalyst for Change Early in Reform Work

Among the 16 schools in the leadership sample, strong formal leadership, vested in the role of the principal or BASRC reform coordinator, initially puts reform on the school's agenda so it cannot be ignored. Formal leadership is highly important in this sense, providing a catalyst for the work, and serving notice that the reform effort is not another change fad that will quickly pass. For example, one principal from the sample noted:

> There's no substitute for the principal of a school showing that this is what matters. . . . I think in the absence of that, people just kind of tend to brush it off as one more thing on their too-full plate.

Of crucial importance within most of these schools is the presence of the reform coordinator. In virtually all cases, BASRC Leadership Schools use a portion of grant funds to hire a coordinator whose primary responsibility focuses on the reform effort. This person is most often a classroom teacher freed from teaching responsibilities, and in fewer cases a classified employee or hired member of the community (a parent, for example), who oversees the reform work and acts as a liaison with BASRC. Schools decide how to use this resource; some reform coordinators function in the role full-time, others have teaching or administrative responsibilities assigned part of their workday. Early on in the process, the work of reform often brings a huge new workload; without the reform coordinator to handle this extra work, much of it would logically fall on the principal, a role already overtaxed in most schools. However, negotiating this new role creates a set of challenges for the persons who occupy it. For example, one reform coordinator commented on the difficulty of figuring out her place in the organization that as yet lacked structures and supports for sharing leadership:

> The change process can be a very painful thing. I think in my first year of doing (the job of reform coordinator) there were a lot of growing pains of figuring out how to take the negative feedback about all the work, and all the time, and all this stuff, and to figure out my role in it . . . being both a teacher and then in this other role that is seen I think, at times, as quasi-administrative. So, walking that line is definitely a challenge.

BASRC's Cycle of Inquiry

Findings suggest that the cycle of inquiry is a critical component to developing vision, giving credence to shared leadership structures, and constructing a culture of data that de-centers visioning, planning, decision-making, and accountability away from individuals in traditional leadership roles (e.g., school administrators) and seeks to involve and incorporate the broader school community (e.g., teachers, parents, and at the secondary level, students). The use of an inquiry-based approach builds a common vocabulary, enables articulation of the one or two key issues that the school aims to address, and is a key vehicle for building the leadership capacity. To illustrate, a comment from a teacher serving as reform coordinator in one of the sixteen sampled schools tied the shared vision for the school directly to their reform work this way:

> Our vision of the school is to lower the equity gap, the achievement around equity in our school. . . . I think we don't want to give up; I think we want to make learning meaningful for our kids in our school—make them want to be there, and while we're doing that, give them important skills and ideas and thoughts to carry on in their lives. Along with making sure that it happens for everybody and not just our white kids.

Among the sample of 16 leadership schools, we see that the use of the Cycle of Inquiry provides support and encouragement for reform work. In these schools, the Cycle of Inquiry has begun to mature into an accepted, iterative process of data collection, analysis, reflection, and change. These schools function as learning communities, and themselves constitute teachers' essential site and source of learning. These schools appear to be recultured in the way BASRC's theory of change envisioned. The whole school is both the site of inquiry and the focus for change; the community of explanation incorporates most of the faculty, not just a smaller group of reformers. Discourse about students' standards-based achievement and expectations about evidence are commonplace rather than exceptional. Leadership for change comes from within the school, growing out of the inquiry process.

Knowledge of best practice is both sought and filtered through knowledge of student outcomes and evidence of links to practice. Teachers' new knowledge about how students do across groups and across grades enables them to see ways in which they need to improve, and the kinds of resources they need to begin making those improvements. One teacher commented, for example, that the links between the staff's focused effort on literacy and their students' work has allowed them to see connections they had not observed before. Likewise, after examining their students' poor performance on writing subtests, an elementary school faculty discontinued the use of a popular reading program and moved to a literacy effort that features writing. Teachers in such schools have become particular and demanding in terms of what their school needs by way of knowledge resources from the outside, and in what form they should be provided. Knowledge of their practice has made them more powerful as consumers.

It is also apparent that school-level inquiry adds meaning to classroom-based inquiry. One school experienced with action research before involvement with BASRC quickly saw how this classroom-based research needed to be situated in school-level inquiry if it were to add up to coherent knowledge for school decision making. The principal points directly to the strategic relationship between these two forms of evidence:

> Whatever's happening in the classroom that a teacher is doing in terms of action research . . . has to be linked to overall school goals. Because one of the dangers of doing action research is you can have a whole bunch of teachers doing that kind of work and it will look classroom-by-classroom real specific. However, if they don't have any relationship to each other and there's no relationship to overall school goals, the value of it will have very different kinds of results. And also what we find is that for action research you need some people to be involved in some common problem-solving issues [part of the cycle of inquiry]. If there's no one doing something in common, there's nobody to help you debrief and talk deeply about what you might be doing.

Emerging New Leadership Structures

Across Leadership Schools, a number of new leadership structures have developed or been reinforced through BASRC work. Examples include organizational schemes featuring: a rotating lead teacher instead of a principal; two coprincipals; principal/reform coordinator partnerships; and inter-school leadership structures and strategies. Findings suggest that these new leadership structures are linked with developing school culture that supports reform work.

One new structure that emerged in this research is the rotating lead teacher. The lead teacher assumes most leadership functions typically associated with the principalship but stays in the position only for a predetermined term. In a K-8 school included in the sample, the lead teacher holds this formal position for a period of up to three years and then rotates back into a faculty teaching position, while another member of the faculty steps in to assume the role of "leader." Sharing service in a formal role enables many teachers on the faculty to develop a system view of the school, including the interface of the school's change efforts with the district, and sustaining the school's valued, shared, ongoing work of reform. Such an arrangement builds capacity within the faculty and works in favor of sustaining reform. A teacher who formerly served in the role of lead teacher spoke about the perceived merits of this leadership structure at the school:

> Usually (the lead) teachers come up through the leadership organization in the school. People have already recognized that person as a leader and as a person who knows the direction of the school, has some wisdom, and we have confidence in. And, beyond that, is a leader in the school. Almost always that person has been part of the leadership team for three years or more, and so has taken part in professional development, and we've already called on their expertise. So I think they go in first as being valued from the staff as a leader.

Another novel leadership structure features two coprincipals. Coprincipals spread the responsibility for leadership functions across two individuals rather than centering all the work on one person's shoulders. This structure appears to allow the formal leaders greater flexibility in focusing and coordinating their available time, together with other personnel resources in the school, on the work of reform. Two coprincipals, Sam and Sally, discuss leadership at their school this way:

Sally: Sam and I really share the principalship in that we're both experienced principals, so either one of us can do anything here at the school, it's just a matter of what comes up on the calendar. We've divided up the (supervision of) new teachers, and grade levels. We both deal with discipline, we both (work with) school site council.

In terms of professional development, we both work with the leadership team. We have a reform coordinator that is a classified (noncertificated) position, and (that person) coordinates all our reports and all our technical kinds of things. (The reform coordinator) makes all the contacts and does all the nitty-gritty stuff. We just do head stuff.

Sam: We have a leadership team that is representative across the grade levels. All of the conversations (around) planning, (about) work on the (BASRC) review of progress, happen with those people on release days, working with us. In addition, we have different inquiry studies happening throughout the school with groups of teachers all focusing on literacy and reading, each with different questions related to our data and things we want to find out.

Sally and Sam's exchange also highlights the crucial importance of principal-reform coordinator partnerships, which are among the most common new leadership structures in BASRC Leadership schools. As noted earlier, enriched funding provided schools with the opportunity to hire reform-coordinators who function in support of reform work, providing leadership through oversight, planning, organization, and hands-on work with teachers in classrooms focused on goals for schoolwide change. In the best of cases, these reform-coordinators function in concert with the building principal, bearing the brunt of much of the "grunt work" inherent in school reform, while also playing a key role in supporting and sustaining the work.

Some emerging interschool leadership structures and strategies for promoting the development of professional community within, and between, schools are evident in our data. One particularly interesting strategy, called the "design studio," is a process whereby a host school immersed in the development of some best practice, or set of practices, invites other schools to visit, and opens its work up for scrutiny and sharing. Visiting schools use their visit as an opportunity to learn and design for their own school based on what they observe, and to ask questions of those at the hosting site. A high school reform coordinator in a school employing the design studio concept expresses the benefits of this leadership structure:

The key principle that most (visiting) people keep leaving with is that school is a professional community. The Design Studio really models what it's like to be a professional learning community; people get a sense of what it's like to be part of one right in a school. (The Design Studio) is facilitated by teachers, not by administrators and principals. They're part of it, but they're not the main show. And it's apparent there's a lot of ownership in the school (among) the people who work there. Design Studio says, "There are some things we're really proud of, we want to show you, we think it can be helpful for you. (And) there are also lots of things we're working on, you can help us think through too."

Findings suggest that broad-based leadership structures are linked with a school culture that supports reform work. To illustrate, one school emphasizes that constantly getting new people involved in leadership roles and attending conferences has helped them to gain a shared feeling that the reform work is "integral" to everything they do. One principal expressed that she felt those norms had developed in her school:

> What we've created in the work is the kind of passion for the work that pushes people rather than the (teacher union) contract pushing the work. . . . And so because that's systemically there, they're going to think differently about how they lead, how they teach, what responsibilities they're willing to take.

Schools With Greater Longevity in Reform Tend to Exhibit Greater Sharing of Leadership Within the School Community

Schools exhibiting the deepest and broadest sharing of leadership functions tend to be those with the longest sustained history of reform work, in many cases predating their involvement with BASRC. These also tend to be schools that are engaged in multiple reform agendas in addition to their participation in BASRC. In these schools, the leadership is evolving to include new faces who tackle new functions, and work from different vantage points in the school.

In schools with longer reform trajectories, individual classroom teachers assume greater leadership for reform by communicating the school's focused effort routinely and directly to parents. As the most trusted professional in the school from the parents' perspective, the classroom teacher operates from a unique vantage point in terms of the ability to communicate schoolwide goals to parents, and to translate those goals into meaningful language connected to classroom work done by students. These conversations occur in a variety of formats that range from individual one-on-one discussions between teachers and parents, to a series of public accountability events required as part of BASRC membership, where evidence about student achievement is presented to the parent community. Regarding this process, one teacher said:

> The accountability events have really been fabulous for us. I mean, I think we've had four of them now, and each one has been really insightful. And I think parents have truly enjoyed and learned a lot (from these events). We've shared the hard data with them. We've shown them we're doing a great job for some kids and not for

others. . . . We're not doing as well for narrowing the gap for our African-American kids and Latino students, and we've been very clear about it and asking (parents) how they think they can help, both for their own students and then for other students.

An elementary principal in a school with a lengthy reform history articulated the key leadership role played by classroom teachers this way:

It all comes back to the fact that teachers have such a commitment to developing relationship with their (students') parents. There's a lot of trust. And we also do a pretty good job about letting people know what we don't know, too. Through our conversations. Again, what happens, is . . . its not what the SCHOOL says or does. . . . The power is in the relationship between the teacher and the parent. And if the teachers are on board and really understand, then that is communicated in every drop and drip of conversation.

Many BASRC schools have leadership teams in place that include administrators, teachers, classified staff members, parents and, in some cases, at the secondary level, students. An evolution can be observed for teams within schools with longer histories of reform. Early on in reform efforts, teams typically function as sounding boards for the principal, but evidence suggests that this conception changes with extended time and effort. To illustrate, in one school within the sample of sixteen, the leadership team has become a group primarily concerned with framing problems and delegating problem solving to other groups within the school:

The leadership team has changed now to be instead of a problem-solving team, it's more of a team that sorts issues and . . . helps expedite what's the best way to deal with an issue.

In another school, the reform coordinator shared how a systems approach to accountability has helped keep their focused effort in view, saying,

(The work will) sustain as long as there's this sort of system in place; that there's a leadership team that's interested in all the committees, creating goals, reflecting on those goals, and always asking themselves at a broader level, "Is this committee's work tied to our focused effort?"

In schools with greater longevity in the work of reform, evidence exists of principals and teachers sharing a support function—encouraging, nourishing, bolstering, and reminding others within the school community of the shared vision and values that serve as motivation for the work of reform. In these schools the provision of support and encouragement takes place beyond formal role-bound rituals; day-to-day work is imbued with a spirit of support and encouragement of progress that is shared broadly within the professional community. One principal commented on the relational benefits of engaging in reform work:

> I think the biggest benefit is in the area of relationships. Relational situations tend to make your work either good or bad. Bottom line. And I think that for my staff as well as myself, the relationships that we have developed have been nothing but beneficial.

Preparation for Leadership Transition

Key leadership transition or turnover creates a challenge for schools engaged in reform work. However, schools in which personnel have a shared vision work to sustain the reform by preparing for the transition, and by hiring people into leadership positions who share that vision. In one school, the leadership team, in conjunction with several teacher-led teams focused on particular issues, led the selection process of their new principal. They were careful to ensure that the applicant's vision matched their own, and as a result, their work continued forward. A principal, new to a high school entering its third year of reform, pointed out the importance of staff involvement in the selection process:

> I think the interview process probably was very helpful in ensuring they (the staff) had a candidate. . . . they had selected someone who matched the school. And so I think already there was an awareness on my part and the staff's part that I was in alignment with what the school was doing. And I know there was concern about "Who are we going to get? And what if they're not on board?" I think the staff did a very good job of that, and I was aware that (the reform effort) was a big issue.

It should be noted, however, that an understanding of the importance of preparing for leadership transition remains more the exception than the rule within the identified schools. Attention to this issue endures as a key challenge for schools attempting to sustain the work of reform.

The Principal's Role

The role of the principal remains crucially important in the work of reform. Several strong themes emerged from the data in this regard. Principals who have been successful in promoting shared leadership perform key functions that protect the vision for the school's reform work, and in some cases, act as a buffer between district and school. In addition, principals in schools where shared leadership has taken hold appear to exert less role-based authority, opting instead to frame questions and provide support. For many principals this involves a process of renegotiating their "old" authority, and allowing others to step forward to handle important leadership duties. This is not to suggest that principals in successfully reforming schools instantaneously let go of large chunks of responsibility, and that others magically step in to fill the void. Rather, the process of expanding and sharing leadership evolves within reforming schools.

Principals Perform Key Personnel Functions That Protect the Vision for Reform

Principals have the authority to hire and fire staff to protect the vision of a core group for broadening and deepening leadership without an "antireform" group becoming a barrier. They also play a necessary role as buffer between district and school, protecting the work initiated at the school site, particularly in cases where the work conflicts with other priorities. One elementary principal within the sample of sixteen illustrated:

> We have had some teachers join our staff who didn't share our vision after the fact. And I'm telling you the staffing is what makes or breaks anything. So we had some rigmarole around personnel and I have dismissed (teachers), or people would say coerced . . . talked into leaving. Other people are asked to leave.

A high school principal pointed to his responsibility for personnel, and specifically, for hiring the right people, as a tremendously important contribution to sustaining the effort:

> I think that my biggest contributions are the people that we've brought in the last two years. Because those are the people that really stir it up in a positive way—because there are people who stir it up negatively—but they stir it up positively. And so I think that as they empower themselves it's going to continue to be a positive force.

Principals Asking Questions Versus Telling

Principals in the 16 sampled schools appear to be moving away from leadership that rests on formal role authority in the district hierarchy, to practice that can be characterized as leadership of inquiry. Principals who are successful in broadening leadership typically are not those who exercise authority by telling others what to do. Rather, these principals are engaged in asking questions, exploring data, and engaging faculty and the broader community in questions that can move the school forward. In some cases, this means principals have to be willing to let go of leadership functions traditionally associated with the role. To illustrate, one elementary principal noted that the leadership team at the school "organized and completed the Review of Progress (ROP) process virtually without (the principal's) participation" and went on to extol the shared commitment to the process exhibited by her staff.

Where the principal relinquishes control, teachers move beyond typical advisory roles by necessity. To illustrate, in one high school, an ad hoc team of teachers has come together to prepare a schedule of presentations of best practices by teachers and staff for their colleagues. In a middle school, teachers are leading the community selection process of their next principal. And, in another high school, department heads are leading the way in curriculum, working to change their own practices as a group and their ability to articulate what their goals are and why they are important before dialoguing with the rest of their staff.

However, in some cases, turnover in key positions has pushed some teachers into unfamiliar roles. One teacher shared her experience of, "trying to help the people we're working with, but at the same time we don't have all the answers." We see that there is a paradigm shift that accompanies teachers hearing their own voice within reform work. This shift moves from the traditional view that it is not the teacher's role to get the big picture, placing the responsibility for crafting and sustaining a vision with the administration, to a norm where teachers are expected to be leaders, and work through their own cycles of inquiry within the classroom to inform the broader whole school cycle. This is not an easy shift to make while engaged in the work. Some schools still point to their site administrators as the key persons "in charge of" reform and call upon them to "lead the effort."

Reframing the Principalship Doesn't Mean Letting Go of Everything.

The opening section of this chapter focused on conceptions of the principal's role, and this research effort has not led us to conclude that the principal's role is doomed to extinction at any point in the near future. On the contrary, many of the key functions outlined in literature and played out in practice still are part of what the principal must accomplish, even in a system where leadership is shared more broadly. Within the sample of 16 Leadership Schools, principals continue to play prominent roles as catalysts for change, protectors of vision, and leaders of inquiry. These elements specifically relate back to functions of leadership embedded in conceptions of principal as instructional leader, participative leader, and transformational leader noted earlier. Yet the process of engendering shared leadership does require principals to let go in new and important ways. One principal, who joined a reforming high school quite far along in its work, put it this way:

The planning team here is a strong leadership group compared to what I was used to in other schools. I mean, I'm used to having strong leaders, but usually it's not a cadre, it's not a large group. It may be isolated individuals working within their own area, but I think this is schoolwide. (That affects the principal's leadership role in that) you have to give up ego and power and any illusion that you can say anything about anything. And that's okay.

Important as well is the notion that principal leadership can and should evolve over time. Through this work, the nature of a principal's leadership can be understood as much more situational or context dependent than a static definition will allow. For schools well along in developing shared leadership capacity, such as those included in the sample of sixteen, principals can become one important member of a "community of leaders" as Barth (1990) suggests. In such a situation, a principal attempting to exercise an authoritarian, hierarchical kind of leadership would, in all likelihood, not be tolerated by the rest of the community; a principal persisting in this manner would ruin the work of reform. However, for schools at the beginning of the process, principals may need to be much more active in catalyzing the work, establishing the vision, and developing strategies for building leadership capacity within others.

Student Achievement:
Promising Indicators of Cultural Change

BASRC's vision ultimately translates into enhanced student learning. A recultured school with broadly shared leadership, fully engaged in an ongoing process of evidence-based reform using the cycle of inquiry, should produce youngsters that learn more. Data that would allow a broader evaluation of any connection between sustainable shared leadership within schools and student achievement in our schools are still being generated and collected. At present, one can report only on some promising indicators. Table 8.3 provides data collected on academic performance within the sampled schools over the past two years.

As noted earlier, the schools within the small sample, with one exception, were granted BASRC membership in either the first cohort (1996) or second cohort (1997) of schools. In the 2000 BASRC review of progress, which assesses school improvement on several rubrics, all the sampled schools were noted to be either at a "systematic" or "sustainable" level on the leadership rubric, the two highest rankings on a four-point scale. The schools are a fairly representative cross-section of Bay Area Schools, with free and reduced lunch counts that range from 0% to 80%, and widely ranging demographics.

Standardized test scores for students across the identified schools were collected and analyzed for the school years 1998 and 1999. With one exception, all schools within the sample of sixteen identified for study showed

Table 8.3   Academic Performance Indicators Within the 16 Sampled Schools

School	BASRC Cohort	2000 ROP Leadership Rank	% F/RL 1999	SAT9 Difference 99-98	API 1999	API 2000 (Diff 99-00)
Elementary A	1	Sustainable	54%	+14.33	646	677 (+31)*ᵏⁱ
Elementary B	2	Systematic	59%	+.47	653	719 (+66)*
Elementary C	2	Sustainable	42%	+10.30	640	672 (+32)*
Elementary D	2	Systematic	16%	+6.87	720	762 (+42)*
Elementary E	2	Systematic	39%	+26.67	631	669 (+38)*
Elementary F	1	Systematic	0%	+18.63	897	927 (+30)*
Elementary G	2	Systematic	23%	+11.90	756	805 (+49)*
Elementary H	1	Sustainable	0%	+12.37	908	934 (+26)*
Elementary J	1	Systematic	65%	+28.55	550	609 (+59)*
Elementary K	1	Systematic	80%	+11.40	379	468 (+90)*
Elementary L	1	Sustainable	0%	+11.60	918	933 (+15)*
K-8 School A	1	Systematic	57%	+15.37	682	727 (+45)**ᵏⁱⁱ
High School A	3	Systematic	12%	+1.10	627	643 (+16)*
High School B	2	Systematic	12%	(−.17)	692	715 (+23)*
High School C	2	Systematic	7%	+16.33	713	684 (−29)
High School D	2	Sustainable	3%	+.80	754	816 (+62)*

1 The Academic Performance Index (API) is a school ranking system devised by the State of California, primarily based upon performance on the Stanford 9 Achievement Test. Prior to 1999, the SAT 9 was the standardized assessment employed by the State. Schools are accountable to meet a target score for schoolwide improvement each year, and are also ranked against comparable schools.

* Indicates that the school met target established by state for schoolwide improvement on the API, as well as target established for comparable improvement relative to other schools with similar demographics.

** Indicates that the school met target established by the state for schoolwide improvement on the API index, but not the comparable improvement target.

increases in overall SAT9[3] aggregate mean scores between 1998 and 1999. This translated into a schoolwide 13.7-point average gain in the SAT9.

With the beginning of the 1999 school year, the State of California implemented an assessment and accountability strategy known as the Academic Performance Index (API). Although the intention is to enrich the measure over time, for the first two years (1999, 2000) the API was calculated primarily on the SAT9 scores for school. Using the 1999 measure as a baseline, the state calculates a growth target for each school, and schools reaching or exceeding the growth target are eligible for enhanced funding awards. With one exception, all schools in the leadership sample exceeded the growth target established by the state for academic performance in the school year 1999–2000. In addition, 14 of the schools exceeded the target established for comparable improvement relative to other schools with similar demographics.

Although these data are too limited to allow any general statement regarding the influence of shared leadership on student learning, it appears that standard measures of student achievement are trending to the positive within the 16 identified schools.

Challenges in Developing Leadership Capacity

While there are some notable successes for BASRC in developing leadership capacity within schools, and some emerging evidence of how this capacity develops within a group of 16 identified schools, challenges remain for schools engaged in the reform effort. These challenges include the recognition that structural change alone is not sufficient to broaden leadership, and that structures require people with skills to carry out the work. Thus, thoughtful preparation for turnover in important leadership positions is crucial. Yet, this occurs in only a limited number of schools, and the lack of preparation makes sustainability of the reform difficult. We have also learned that external stresses create barriers to the development of broader leadership.

Structural Changes Alone Are Not Enough

Creating new structures to support changes at school can provide a means for building leadership capacity, but the ability to keep key people in those structures is equally important. Turnover of key leaders, both principals and teachers, make sustainability difficult, and preparation for leadership turnover receives limited attention. Of all the challenges involved in reform work, schools point to leadership turnover as the most disabling factor in the support and encouragement of reform. One reform coordinator we spoke with talked about the tension of getting handed different functions by the new principal. She noted, "We're not sustainable, we have (had) four new principals. I used to (handle) curriculum instruction, (and) I'm not ready to hand this off yet." When some teachers or administrators are asked what would happen if key leaders left the school, they react with worry that reform as it now exists will not continue. In one example, when a principal was asked what would happen if he and the reform coordinator left, he said:

> We have a couple (teachers) who would try to keep it going, but there would not be a big push, and then it would stop. . . . But my honest thing is if (the reform coordinator) and I did not come back on January 3, by March if you came in you probably wouldn't

know what the focused effort was. It would be.... If you asked them [teachers], "Well, we used to do that when they were here."

Too Many Stresses Lead Teachers to Prioritize Reform Work, Focus Inward

The weight and breadth of whole school reform can be considerable, and one middle school teacher described the move by teachers to focus inward as "paring back" and "pruning."

Added on top of the BASRC effort, an elementary school reform coordinator noted the multitude of new initiatives at the school as a major contextual challenge:

> We had class size reduction, we had new standards, we had the SAT9, we had the API (Academic Performance Index) and it has just turned up the heat . . . managing the feelings of stress and overwhelmedness that teachers experience I think is one of the biggest challenges of this work. . . . It is hard for teachers to hold onto their successes and so we are working hard this year to make it more explicit and visible to teachers that our data is showing a trend toward improving student performance. But it is hard for teachers to hold on to that because they are in the trenches thinking about "What am I going to teach tomorrow?" (In addition) the state took away our staff development days and so you are dealing with "Learn more and learn it faster—with no time." That leads to a real sense of crush for people, I think.

With so many competing interests and stresses, many teachers and schools shift their attention to address anxieties they can resolve. To illustrate, in one year-round school, reflection and the tracking of progress are challenged by irregular breaks. A teacher noted,

> It's this anxiety about 'Are we moving fast enough? Are we doing things fast enough'? So having so much time between meetings when we can dialogue as a staff and actually do those group decision-making activities is a frustration to me.

Many teachers' attention remains largely focused on their work within the classroom as they seek to understand their particular role within reform before engaging in inquiry around the broader focused efforts at their sites.

CONCLUSION

Findings from this ongoing study of San Francisco Bay Area schools engaged in reform point out the efficacy of a policy strategy that provides a new focus for school leadership. Key within that strategy is the notion that the distribution and sharing of leadership should be the focus of reform policy, moving beyond narrow role-based strategies of that have defined school leadership for decades. Within the identified subset of BASRC schools studied here, findings suggest that the distribution of leadership functions across a school, given adequate time and personnel to handle the tasks, can provide the capacity, coherence, and ownership necessary to sustain and deepen reforms. Perhaps most significantly, this research provides initial evidence of the power of inquiry as the engine to enable the distribution of leadership, and the glue that binds a school community together in common work. Finally, given that role-based leadership strategies have been essentially unable to meet the complex challenges associated with school change, the research reported herein suggests we look anew at the role of the principal as one to engender and sustain the functions of leadership distributed across the broader school community.

REFERENCES

Barth, R. (1990). *Improving schools from within*. San Francisco: Jossey-Bass.

Burns, J. M. (1978). *Leadership*. New York: Harper & Row.

Copland, M. A. (2001). The myth of the superprincipal. *Phi Delta Kappan, 82*(7), 528–533.

Duke, D., & Leithwood, K. (1994). *Management and leadership: A comprehensive view of principals' functions*. Toronto: Ontario Institute for Studies in Education, mimeo.

Elmore, R. F. (2000). *Building a new structure for school leadership*. Washington, DC: Albert Shanker Institute.

Hallinger, P., & McCary, C. (1990). Developing the strategic thinking of instructional leaders. *Elementary School Journal, 91*(2), 89–107.

Hallinger, P., & Murphy, J. (1985). Assessing the instructional management behavior of principals. *Elementary School Journal, 86*(2), 217–247.

Hart, A. W., & Bredeson, P. V. (1996). *The principalship: A theory of professional learning and practice*. New York: McGraw-Hill.

Hodgkinson, C. (1991). *Educational leadership: The moral art*. Albany: SUNY Press.

Hughes, L. W. (1999). The leader: Artist? Architect? Commissar? In L. W. Hughes (Ed.), *Principal as leader*. Upper Saddle River, NJ: Prentice-Hall.

Kimball, K., & Sirotnik, K. (2000). The urban school principalship: Take this job and . . . ! *Education and Urban Society, 32*(4), 535–543.

Lambert, L. (1998). *Building leadership capacity in schools*. San Francisco: Jossey-Bass.

Leithwood, K., Tomlinson, D., & Genge, M. (1996). Transformational school leadership. In K. Leithwood et al. (Eds.), *The international handbook of educational leadership and administration* (pp. 785–840). Dordrecht, Netherlands: Kluwer.

McLaughlin, M. W., & Talbert, J. E. (2001). *Professional communities and the work of high school teaching*. Chicago: Chicago University Press.

Murphy, J. (1988). Methodological, measurement, and conceptual problems in the study of instructional leadership. *Educational Evaluation and Policy Analysis, 10*(2), 117–139.

Murphy, J., & Beck, L. (1995). *School-based management as school reform.* Thousand Oaks, CA: Corwin Press.

Ogawa, R., & Bossert, S. (1995). Leadership as an organizational quality. *Educational Administration Quarterly, 31*(2), 224–244.

Pounder, D., Ogawa, R., & Adams, E. (1995). Leadership as an organization-wide phenomena: Its impact on school performance. *Educational Administration Quarterly, 31*(4), 564–588.

Sergiovanni, T. J. (1984). Leadership as cultural expression. In T. J. Sergiovanni & J. E. Corbally (Eds.), *Leadership and organizational culture* (pp. 105–144). Urbana: University of Illinois Press.

Sergiovanni, T. J. (1996). *Leadership for the schoolhouse.* San Francisco: Jossey-Bass.

Spillane, J., Halverson, R., Diamond, J. B. (2000). Investigating school leadership practice: A distributed perspective. *Educational Researcher, 30*(3), 23–27.

NOTES

1. The Bay Area School Reform Collaborative (BASRC) formed in the spring of 1995 as part of the nationwide Annenberg Challenge. BASRC became the Hewlett-Annenberg Challenge, funded jointly by Hewlett and Annenberg, which provided $50 million to Bay Area public schools to be matched by public and private funds over a five-year period. The Collaborative established by BASRC currently includes 86 leadership schools, each of which receives grants of up to $150 per student for three to five years after completing a rigorous, evidence-based, peer-reviewed portfolio process. Leadership schools use these grants to fund support services, time for school inquiry and professional development, and other resources in support of their focused reform effort.

2. Cohort 1 schools have completed their fifth year as Leadership Schools in BASRC; Cohort 2 schools have completed their fourth year.

3. The SAT9 is the California version of the Stanford Achievement Test, a standardized instrument used to assess student achievement.

PART IV

Other National Comprehensive School Reform Designs

Chapter Nine

Success for All

District and School Leadership

Amanda Datnow and Marisa Castellano

It is axiomatic that strong leadership is critical for successful whole school reform. But what type of leadership is required from different types of reform initiatives? And from whom? In this chapter, we explore leadership in Success for All (SFA) schools. SFA is a research-based whole-school reform model that organizes resources to ensure that students succeed in reading throughout the elementary grades (Slavin et al., 1996). SFA is used as a case in point as it, like many other reforms, views leadership as critical to reform success. Using qualitative data gathered in six SFA schools located in three districts, we will focus on three "levels" of leadership—the district administration, the principal, and the teacher leader (the SFA in-school facilitator)—and how they interact in their local contexts and with the SFA design team to shape the adoption, implementation, and sustainability of SFA.

DISTRICTS, PRINCIPALS, AND TEACHER LEADERS IN SCHOOL REFORM: A REVIEW OF THE LITERATURE

The District and School Reform

Building supportive conditions at the district level is important to successful implementation and sustainability of school-level reforms, particularly when reforms move from one school to many (Anderson & Stiegelbauer, 1994; Bodilly, 1998). Fullan (2001b) states, "it is impossible to get large scale reform without a dramatic improvement in the infrastructure—the policies, practices, and structure at the district and state levels" (p. 16).

Fullan argues that for such reform to be successful, districts need to focus on instruction, accountability (e.g., standards of performance, consequences), capacity building (e.g., resources, time, rewards), and fostering lateral exchanges across schools. These changes often require reshaping the culture of school districts, as many are not yet oriented in these directions. Instead, districts tend to be overburdened with multiple and sometimes competing reforms (Fullan, 1991; Spillane & Thompson, 1997), as well as a host of political and fiscal issues that can make it difficult for them to support schools effectively.

Sustaining high-quality leadership at the district level is essential to creating supportive conditions for reform. Superintendents need to be active—and ongoing—participants in the change process, providing both support and pressure (Fullan, 2001a). District administrators can influence the pace, quality, and form of school reform through their own stability or instability (Bodilly, 1998; Desimone, 2000). Yet, stability among district administrators is sometimes quite elusive. The turnover of superintendents in urban districts is very high (Fullan, 2001a). Leaders move on and along with them goes the commitment to reform.

Prior studies of the role of district support in schools or jurisdictions implementing comprehensive school reform models have found district leadership stability, among other factors, to be essential to the implementation of reforms (Bodilly, 1998; Berends, Kirby, Naftel, & McKelvey, 2001; Datnow, 2001). For example, in describing why the New American Schools (NAS) designs lasted in Memphis schools longer than most other places, Bodilly (1998) points to leadership stability, a focus on (a) NAS reform as a top priority, (b) professional development, and (c) achievement results, as well as the absence of a serious crisis in the district during the period of reform. As we can see, these supportive characteristics overlap with those noted by Fullan (2001b) above.

Principals and School Reform

The role of the principal as an active and ongoing supporter of reform is critical to the success of a schoolwide change effort (Muncey & McQuillan, 1996). For principals to be effective at guiding change, they need to do many things, including play an instructional leadership role: "A good administrator . . . supports improvement that is responsive to the classroom context" and provides support for classroom teachers (Fraatz, 1989, p. 19). Principals must also create and maintain a sense of trust in the school, use positive micro-politics to negotiate between managerial, technical, and institutional arenas, and create a professional community and networks for communication within the school (Murphy & Louis, 1999). They must also maintain a momentum of continuous growth (Goldring & Rallis, 1993).

Engaging in school change requires principals to move from being managers of the status quo to facilitators of reform (Frederick, 1992). In doing so, principals often have to develop skills of collaboration and learn to share power with teachers (Louis & Miles, 1990; Wasley, 1989). For principals, this involves a balancing act of knowing when to be directive and when to step back and allow teachers to direct reform efforts (Leithwood & Jantzi, 1990; Muncey & McQuillan, 1996). This is difficult for some principals, who may end up maintaining the status quo instead of empowering teachers (Anderson, 1991).

The newly defined roles that principals are asked to play in reform are accompanied by a series of other challenges. Reform is often accompanied by role ambiguity or overload and loss of a sense of identity for principals (Murphy, 1994; Prestine, 1993). Principals often must spend increased time promoting the school's image and working more closely with parents, school boards, and other external agents (Goldring & Rallis, 1993; Murphy, 1994). This is a role in which some principals are uncomfortable (Hallinger & Hausman, 1994; Murphy, 1994). Principals also face challenges in ensuring that teachers implement reforms at the classroom level, as teachers are accustomed to substantial professional autonomy and might resist encroachment (Fraatz, 1989). Even when principals are supportive of reform, their ability to provide effective leadership may be hampered by their own experience, training, or beliefs (Hallinger, Murphy, & Hausman, 1992; Murphy, 1994), or their lack of understanding of the reform itself (Neufeld, 1995).

The Teacher Leader in School Reform

The implementation of comprehensive school reform can also dramatically affect the professional lives of teachers. In our prior research, we analyzed classroom teachers' responses to SFA (Datnow & Castellano, 2000a). In this chapter, our concern is the teachers who occupy positions of leadership in SFA schools—the facilitators. There is a plethora of research describing the development of teacher leadership, as this is generally thought to be a precondition for school improvement (Smylie, 1997; Wasley, 1989). Opportunities for teacher leadership have also recently arisen from policies that designate master teachers to direct school improvement (Smylie, 1997). However, the role of teachers who are out of the classroom, occupying the position of full-time reform facilitator or coordinator, has gone relatively unexplored. The few studies that do exist suggest that the facilitator role is important for reform efforts and involves a tricky balance of multiple, sometimes conflicting, activities (Muncey & McQuillan, 1996; Neufeld, 1995; Nunnery et al., 1997; Smylie & Brownlee-Conyers, 1992; Smylie & Denny, 1990; Wasley, 1989).

For example, teacher leaders are sometimes reluctant to challenge the norms that characterize the professional lives of teachers for fear of separating themselves from their colleagues (Smylie & Brownlee-Conyers, 1992; Smylie & Denny, 1990). Wasley (1989) reached similar conclusions about the constraints provided by teacher leaders' own conceptions of their roles, as well as the role conceptions held by their administrators.

Similarly, Muncey and McQuillan's (1996) ethnography of the Coalition of Essential Schools revealed that reform coordinators found it difficult to be educational leaders, because of uncertainty in how aggressively they could or should promote change. Teachers also saw coordinators as occupying an ill-defined role that constituted a "no-man's land" between teacher and administrator (p. 59). As some of the aforementioned studies point out, power relations and status issues come into play in the changing leadership roles of teachers and administrators (Evans, 1996).

Overall, the studies reported here illuminate some of the issues that district administrators, principals, and teacher leaders might encounter in SFA schools. However, much of the research is discussed in terms of more general school improvement initiatives (e.g., site-based management, standards-based reform) or school restructuring. There has been a dearth of research on how the new generation of externally developed school reform models, including SFA and others, affect the nature of leadership. With specified curriculum and implementation plans, some of these reform models raise a new set issues for leaders, who must learn to manage and guide the use of new instructional models and learn to interface with external reform "design teams." In sum, despite a growing research base on districts, principals, and teacher leaders in reform, there are still questions about how these school leaders actually work together to achieve school improvement.

Why Study Leadership in Success for All Schools?

In this chapter, we seek to fill some gaps in the literature as we examine the role of district administrators, principals, and facilitators in leading SFA schools. SFA and other externally developed reform models, some of which redefine teaching and administration, are shaping the next wave of school reform in the United States. In 2001, there were more than 1,800 elementary schools implementing SFA and the numbers continue to grow, particularly since the passage of the Comprehensive School Reform Demonstration Program in the U.S. Congress in 1997.

SFA was developed by Robert Slavin, Nancy Madden, and a team at Johns Hopkins University and is now based at the Success for All Foundation in Baltimore. SFA is known for its specificity, its popularity in urban schools, and its strong record of achievement effects (see Herman et al., 1999). SFA is primarily focused on improving students' literacy skills. Major components of SFA include a 90-minute reading period, the regrouping of students into smaller, homogeneous groups for reading instruction, eight-week assessments, cooperative learning, one-to-one tutoring, and the institution of school-based management and family support teams. The SFA reading curriculum is comprised of an Early Learning program for prekindergarten and kindergarten students; Reading Roots, a beginning reading program; and Reading Wings, its upper-elementary counterpart (Slavin, Madden, Karweit, Dolan, & Wasik, 1992). There are both English and Spanish versions of the program; the Spanish version of SFA is called *Exito Para Todos*.

SFA is a reform model that takes an aggressive approach to changing teaching and learning. As a result, the program is highly specified and comprehensive with respect to implementation guidelines and materials for students and teachers. Almost all materials for students are provided, including reading booklets for the primary grades, materials to accompany various textbook series and novels for the upper grades, as well as workbooks, activity sheets, and assessments for all grade levels. Teachers are expected to closely follow SFA lesson plans, which involve an active pacing of multiple activities during the 90-minute reading period (Madden, Livingston, & Cummings, 1998).

The SFA Foundation (SFAF) requires that a school staff interested in the model attend an SFA Awareness Presentation. At least 80% of a school's teaching staff must vote to adopt the program before the SFAF will provide the materials and technical assistance. The SFAF also asks that schools employ a full-time SFA facilitator, organize a Family Support Team, and organize biweekly meetings among Roots and Wings teachers. Implementation of the program is supported through ongoing professional development from SFA trainers and through local and national networks of SFA schools (Slavin & Madden, 1996). Teachers receive three days of training in SFA before implementation begins, and facilitators and principals receive five days of training.

Numerous studies of SFA have found consistent positive effects on student reading achievement, as well as reductions in special education placements and grade retention (e.g., Nunnery et al., 1997; Slavin et al., 1996; Slavin & Madden, 1999). SFA has among the strongest quantitative research bases of any of the current school reform models (Herman et al., 1999). The qualitative research base on SFA is much smaller, however (see Cooper, Slavin, & Madden, 1997; Datnow & Castellano, 2000a, 2000b; Stringfield et al., 1997, for exceptions). This study adds to the qualitative research base through an in-depth investigation of leadership in SFA schools. SFA is a reform that focuses squarely on the details of teaching and learning and thus provides an interesting opportunity to assess how leadership works to improve these aspects of schooling.

However, it should be noted that SFA does not call for a fundamental restructuring of principal and teacher roles in terms of creating shared leadership. Though SFA does ask that schools establish school-based management teams (if they do not already have them), the reading curriculum and the organization that accompanies it are the major elements of the reform. Moreover, teachers are simply implementers of the SFA curriculum, not designers of the innovation. Even though SFA does not seek to radically transform leadership structures, it does introduce a new set of demands on leaders, and as a result it changes the context for leadership.

METHODS

The chapter draws on qualitative data gathered in case studies of six elementary schools that implemented SFA. Data were collected over a series of four site visits to each school that took place from 1997 to 1999. Three of the schools are located in different districts in California (CA), and three schools are located in one district in a state in the Southeast (SE).[1] The schools in California were part of a larger study of implementation and teaching and learning in SFA schools (see Datnow & Castellano, 2000a; 2000b), and the schools in the Southeast were part of a longitudinal study of school restructuring in a linguistically and culturally diverse school district (see Datnow, Stringfield, Borman, Rachuba, & Castellano, 2001; Stringfield, Datnow, Ross, & Snively, 1998; Yonezawa & Datnow, 1999). Both studies were funded by the U.S. Department of Education (see "Acknowledgments" for details) and were based at Johns Hopkins University; however, neither of the authors had an affiliation with the SFA program.

All of the schools we studied serve primarily low-income student populations (at least 70% free- or reduced-price lunch), and four schools are located in urban areas. Three of the schools serve a majority of Latino students, and three serve a majority of African American students. Four of the six schools serve large numbers of Limited English Proficient (LEP) students (e.g., 40% or more); in three schools, these students are native Spanish speakers and in one school, the LEP students speak Haitian Creole. The principals of these schools were a mix of new and experienced administrators, men and women, and an even mix of white, Latino, and African American. The SFA facilitators in our study shared some common characteristics: all were former teachers with 15 to 20 or more years of experience, and all were women. Four were white, one was Latino, and one was African American. The district administrators we interviewed were experienced, a mix of men and women, and an even mix of white and Latino.

We conducted more than 100 interviews and focus groups with district administrators (including superintendents, assistant superintendents, and directors of curriculum and instruction), principals, facilitators, and teachers. For the purposes of confidentiality, the identities of schools, their exact locations, and the names of the personnel within them are concealed. Interviews with principals, district staff, and facilitators tended to last one hour or longer. Each interview with the teachers took approximately 45 minutes. In the three schools in the Southeast, interviews with teachers were conducted in small groups of two to four teachers at each grade level. In California, teachers were interviewed individually. All interviews were guided by semi-structured protocols and were taped and transcribed verbatim. Informal interviews with school staff were also conducted.

According to the case study methods of Yin (1989) and the grounded theory approach of Strauss and Corbin (1990), our data analysis proceeded following the theoretical propositions that led to the study. Leadership had emerged as a theme in the process of writing case reports on each school, and thus we chose to pursue it in more depth after reviewing literature on the topic. We coded interview transcripts according to the methods of Strauss and Corbin (1990), who argue that coding is the central process by which theories are built from data. Not surprisingly, during this process we found it necessary to consult additional literature on leadership and school reform, as issues and themes emerged in the data that were not addressed or were inadequately covered in our initial framework. The process of writing theoretical notes as accompaniments to the data allowed us to engage in a continuous dialogue between theory and data.

THE ROLE OF THE PRINCIPAL AND DISTRICT ADMINISTRATORS IN THE ADOPTION OF SFA

Most often, the strong pressure from the district level to improve test scores motivated principals to push their staffs to adopt SFA and to secure resources for the reform. However, across the six schools, we also found that the principal was an independent proponent for the adoption of SFA. In the three schools in the Southeast, SFA was first introduced by way of a district "fair" showcasing various reform models, which was attended by principals and groups of teachers. In each case, the principals returned from the fair very impressed with SFA and presented the model to the rest of the staff. For principals, attractive features of the program included the fact that the district was promoting it, SFA's history in raising students' test scores in reading, and the staff development that accompanied SFA. One principal explained that he was "won over" by SFA and said, "As principal, I told them [the teachers] where I thought we ought to be going."

Events unfolded similarly in the other two schools in the Southeast, where teachers were ostensibly given the opportunity to vote on whether or not to adopt SFA, but principals' strong support influenced decisions. In all three schools, more than 80% of the teachers voted in favor. Subsequently, however, some of the teachers in these schools revealed that they did not have enough information about SFA before voting to adopt the program. As one teacher described, "This was pretty much forced on us. I mean, it was a vote, but we voted until they got their way."

The circumstances were similar at one of the schools in California, where a district administrator strongly encouraged the school and nine other low-performing schools in the district to adopt SFA. The district offered to pay fully for the first three years of SFA implementation at all 10 schools; however, if they chose not to adopt SFA, they would need to develop their own literacy programs and achieve comparable gains, without support from the district. After attending an SFA Awareness Presentation, the principal encouraged the staff to adopt SFA, arguing that the program fit in well with the school's existing efforts to improve student literacy. Most of the newer teachers were in favor of adoption for similar reasons, but some veteran teachers were vehemently against SFA. What finally led them to vote unanimously in favor was the staff's realization that it would be difficult to develop a program of their own in lieu of SFA.

At the other two schools in California, the principals introduced SFA to their staffs and were strong proponents of adopting the program. In both cases, they were concerned about low student achievement and family literacy skills. At one site, a teacher remarked that most teachers thought SFA would be "dry and boring. . . . But then when we looked at our test scores and we realized . . . it couldn't have gotten much worse. It's worth trying something." SFA was the only program that the principal could find that had "statistics behind it," which was a requirement of the Title VII grant the school was pursuing to fund its literacy efforts. At the other school, the principal first heard about the program at the county office of education and was said to have declared, "That's the program we're going to get." After hearing the SFA Awareness Presentation, 80% of the teachers voted in favor of SFA, but according to a teacher, "Some of the [teachers] felt railroaded," because the principal was so enthusiastic about the program. Another teacher disagreed, saying, "It was a fairly collaborative process." While district administrators supported the adoption of SFA at these two schools, in neither case did they place pressure on the schools to adopt SFA.

In sum, in four schools the impetus for SFA came from the district level, but principals convinced staff to adopt SFA thereafter. At two schools, it was the principals alone who encouraged staff to vote to adopt SFA. In all cases, the principals achieved a positive vote for SFA among the majority of their staff, but genuine buy-in among all teachers was not apparent. Relations of power influenced actions at all levels—from the districts to the principals and from the principals to the teachers.

It is important to note that in the case of two schools, there was a turnover in principalship that occurred just after the adoption of SFA (because of district changes, not because of the reform). The new principals described themselves as strong supporters of the program, but in one case, teachers questioned whether the principal was rather an unfortunate heir who "does what he can" to make the program work.

THE ROLE OF THE DISTRICT IN SUPPORTING SFA

During the period of our research, there were no SFA manuals nor training specifically geared toward district administrators, though there were for principals and facilitators and these were made available to central office staff as well. The principal and facilitator's manual available during the period of our study (and since updated) suggests what type of district support for SFA would be beneficial:

> In districts with many SFA schools, there is often a district coordinator for the SFA program. This person often convenes and usually attends regular meetings [among SFA schools], and uses this opportunity to learn what is going well, to find out what problems the schools may be having, to make the participating schools aware of changes in district policies and opportunities for funding, and so on. The district coordinator can help maintain communication between the central office and the SFA schools, make sure that the needs of these schools are taken into account in district-policymaking, and help the schools take advantage of district resources to support their SFA programs. (Madden, Livingston, & Cummings, 1998; p. Networking-2)

Our interviews with district administrators revealed that the SFA design team worked closely with personnel from the districts of a number of schools implementing SFA in order to ensure support. Such guidance was customized according to the district's needs and circumstances. Recently, the SFA Foundation has begun to offer a comprehensive leadership academy involving both district and school administrators, and such training is also customized to local needs.[2]

At all three districts in California, district administrators were supportive of SFA. Strong district support for SFA was most obvious at the site where the district pushed the school to adopt the program. The assistant superintendent had thoroughly researched the program, and argued it was based on "common horse-sense" good practices and that it would not "leave much room for error on people's parts." She explained: "I've done my homework. SFA is the only model that does anything." District administrators were applauded for visiting schools in the first year of implementation to hear teachers' reactions to the program and answer questions. The assistant superintendent also met with the SFA facilitators in the district. The facilitator explained: "She left us all with the opinion that the district is behind this program, which is what we needed to hear as facilitators."

While perhaps not as active, district support for SFA was readily apparent in the other two CA sites. One district administrator explained: "Our district is really committed to SFA, and we see it as something that has made a difference for kids' learning." While the district had not provided funds to assist in implementation initially (as the school had a federal Title VII grant), they had since provided funding for SFA tutors through a community foundation grant and supported several summer school classes for SFA. In another CA district, the school was given a small amount of funding to support implementation initially (though most costs for SFA were paid through the school's Title I budget). Here, an assistant superintendent remarked, "I'm a cheerleader," and explained that, "The district's standpoint is that SFA certainly has a lot to offer. . . . However, we're not pushing it down anybody's throats." In both of these districts, district administrators were familiar with SFA and the research behind it. They were supportive of SFA, but it is important to note that it was not at the top of their own agendas.

When our study began in the SE district in 1995–1996, the then-superintendent was much in favor of promoting the use of comprehensive school reform designs, including SFA. He supported the reform fair described above. In schools that voted to implement a reform design, the district agreed to pay for teacher training, materials, and a full-time reform facilitator. The district created an Office of Instructional Leadership to support the implementation of a variety of reform designs, including SFA. Regional directors in this office provided information, practical assistance, and encouragement to the restructuring schools. "We help them, we support, and we give them technical assistance in reviewing the plan with them, and then identify what kind of support they need," explained one regional director. Support for SFA was particularly strong, and after seeing positive results in some SFA schools, the district mandated that more than 40 of its lowest-performing schools adopt SFA. (None of the schools we studied were part of this group.)

However, in late 1996, the district leadership changed and agendas began to shift. The Office of Instructional Leadership was dismantled, and comprehensive school reform designs were no longer as well-supported; funding was withdrawn. Marking a significant shift away from SFA, in 1998 the district developed its own reading program, which became the default "choice" for most schools not already implementing SFA.

One of the major issues that affected the level of support for and longevity of SFA in all districts was the intensified focus on state-level testing and standards in both states during the period of our study. This focus meant that districts paid much more attention to test score data, particularly as a measure of the success of SFA. In the CA district that encouraged schools to adopt SFA, raising students' reading achievement to grade-level standards was a goal for the administration, and indeed, they saw SFA as a vehicle to that end. However, schools that adopted SFA were given some time to show improvement, as one district administrator explained: "Because they went with the model, they're going to be given at least two to three years, I'm not going say, 'we're going to dump you.'"

Districts measured the success of SFA according to achievement gains, and they continued to support SFA in places where those gains were apparent and removed their support in places where gains were not being made. The comments of administrators in a district in CA and in the SE serve as a useful illustration:

> CA district: Both [SFA] schools gave a board report this spring and really were able to show student growth based on where they were at the beginning level from year to year . . . the evidence and the data was really very compelling, and the school board was very excited about it.

> SE district: The board doesn't want to know about climate survey or soft data. They want to know about test scores.

In the SE district, the board asked the district to conduct evaluations on the reforms being undertaken in order to determine whether support for external programs should continue and at what level. At the time, SFA was the most widely used reform in the district. "After we see what works, we'll put budget enhancements in place to support models," explained one high-level administrator. The results of the SFA evaluation, which some argued was flawed, were nevertheless not favorable.

In all cases, district administrators realized that providing a supportive climate was critical to the success of SFA. The changes in the SE district resulted in a difficult climate in which to sustain reform. As one district administrator stated, "It's very difficult to sustain . . . when there are shifts at the district level as well as at the school level." An administrator in a CA district agreed, although the climate for support differed sharply there: "I think if you don't have the leadership you're not going to have the implementation. And right now I see it as a major dedication from all the leadership in the district."

HOW PRINCIPALS' LEADERSHIP STYLES MESHED WITH SFA

The principal and facilitator's training manual for SFA (Madden, Livingston, & Cummings, 1998, p. Role-1) states that the job of the principal is to be the "keeper of the vision." In doing so, the principal must (a) ensure that the resources are available to support SFA (e.g., to pay for materials, training, tutors, etc.), (b) keep staff focused on essential goals of SFA, (c) arrange the schedule and rules so that reading occurs for 90 uninterrupted minutes each day, (d) ensure that the facilitator has the support needed to perform her or his job effectively, and (e) monitor and celebrate progress. The guidelines for principals are quite detailed in the manual. A separate guide specifically on how to provide quality leadership is now also available, but was not during the period of our study.[3]

By establishing these guidelines, the SFA Foundation defined the role of the principal as having the responsibility for major decisions in very specific areas (e.g., finances, hiring, scheduling) often dealt with by principals. Indeed, the principals in the six schools we studied fulfilled their functions of securing resources and arranging the 90-minute reading schedule, albeit with some occasional struggles along the way. While these two functions are fairly concrete, the functions of the principal as "keeper of the vision," as helping staff focus on the essential goals of SFA, and as supporting the facilitator are much more open to interpretation. As a result, the principals' ideologies and leadership styles shaped how they interacted with teachers and facilitators with respect to SFA and also influenced implementation.

The principals varied in the flexibility they allowed teachers with respect to the SFA curriculum, with some requiring more stringent fidelity to the model and others approaching it with a more lax attitude. One principal approached SFA in a rather strict manner, particularly in the first two years of implementation. This fit with his leadership style. He described himself as "a strong, military-type" principal. The teachers confirmed this, explaining that complaints about the lack of flexibility in SFA were simply not tolerated by the administration. Teacher support for the program was not strong in this school at the outset and did not improve over time. As a result, the principal eventually attempted to loosen the reigns a bit. "I sort of have to listen a little bit more, and sometimes lose a battle," he admitted.

Most other principals tended to be willing to allow for at least some flexibility in how teachers implemented the SFA curriculum. For example, one principal felt he was as strict as he could be with regard to implementation, considering his own leadership style: "People come back from . . . these school visits, you know, these fascist regime SFA schools, which I would never—, I'm not going to ever have them. It wouldn't be me." He also felt that flexibility was required to engage teacher support for SFA: "There's always the possibility that all the teachers can say, 'We don't like this thing. We're not going to do it.' You have to make it palatable." However, the facilitator at this school thought that the principal "tries to accommodate teachers—almost too much."

Another principal, who had inherited the program from his predecessor, found SFA to be too rigid. As a result, he encouraged teachers to "deviate slightly, not out in left field, but if you do take advantage of that opportunity or enhance that lesson, nobody is going to raise a red flag and crucify you on the spot." This fit with his leadership style, which involved a strong trust in the teachers and their professional opinions. He also admitted that while he supported SFA, he had some personal reservations about it.

The principals also developed varied strategies for dealing with teachers who were resistant to SFA. One principal approached the issue this way:

"I like to let teachers vent and say whatever they want to say . . . [but] this is our program and this is the way we have to go." On the other hand, some principals were far less tolerant of teacher resistance to SFA, encouraging teachers who did not support the program to leave the school. They were not willing to listen to teachers' complaints about the program, believing that if they voted it in, they needed to support its implementation. One principal explained what he said to resistant teachers: "What I said was, 'Look, there are no hard feelings. I will encourage you and assist you to get to a place [where you can be happier].'" Reinforcing her role as the leader, another principal remarked: "The principal here says you're going to do it. . . . They can implement Success for All or you're bye-bye."

Not only did principals shape reform implementation, but the reform itself also reshaped the role of the principal. Some of the principals reported that the implementation of SFA increased their involvement in reading instruction. Previously, teachers used eclectic methods to teach reading. As one teacher explained, "we had no language arts program really . . . it was kind of like 'do whatever you can do.'" Since the implementation of SFA, principals were more knowledgeable about the methods and curriculum teachers were using in reading and could assume a greater leadership role. For some principals, the implementation of SFA also meant much more involvement in classrooms than in the past. It was during classroom observations that principals performed their monitoring function set forth by SFA. One principal explained: "I check lesson plans. I observe teachers teaching. I observe students reading to me. . . . I have stickers and things I give to students when I go out and I hear them reading." She added: "My role is to make it comfortable, enjoyable, a learning environment for my students to learn and my teachers to teach."

While SFA brought about positive and clear role changes in terms of the principal's involvement in curriculum and instruction, learning to deal with the SFA design team brought about role ambiguities for some principals. During these biannual "implementation visits," SFA trainers monitor the progress of implementation, help schools solve problems, and provide feedback. One principal found the rubric that the trainers used in their implementation checks to be discouraging: "It makes us feel like we've barely done anything, and we're doing terribly, and yet we know we've done so much and worked so hard." As a result, she chose not to share the results with the staff after the first few times.

At two schools, the principals and facilitators complained that the implementation visits should involve more direct, verbal feedback from the trainers to the teachers, instead of a reliance on the principal or facilitator to communicate the (sometimes discouraging) results of the implementation checks. As one principal explained: "You can't leave it that they're doing a great job and then we're going to be coming in and saying [they're] not. That's not kosher." The way these particular implementation visits were conducted appeared to divide the teachers and the administration in this school, instead of connecting them (Murphy, 1999).

THE ROLE OF THE SFA FACILITATOR

The leadership of the SFA facilitator is also critical for successful implementation, arguably more critical than that of the principal. The principal's and facilitator's training manual for SFA explains that the facilitator's responsibilities are to: (a) know the progress of each teacher in implementing the program and to provide support accordingly, (b) know the progress of each student and ensure that no student falls through the cracks, and (c) manage assessments and regrouping efficiently. The manual further states that "the facilitator must be a mentor, and not an evaluator," and that the relationship between the facilitators and teachers should be "respectful and supportive" (Madden, Livingston, & Cummings, 1998, p. Role-3).

As these responsibilities suggest, the facilitator's leadership role in SFA is much more specific than that of the principal, particularly when it comes to monitoring the implementation of the program at the classroom level for both teachers and students. Not only is the facilitator's job wide-ranging, it also requires someone with good interpersonal skills. All of the educators we interviewed agreed that this position required a special type of person. The principal at one school reiterated: "It's going to take someone who is going to be here day and night. . . . It takes time, personal time, you know, time away from their family and all. . . . Someone with the right personality who can relate to everyone, who can be accepted by everyone, who doesn't intimidate, you know . . . and very organized."

Each of the facilitators was invited to take the position by the principals at their schools. Four of the facilitators had been teachers or coordinators at their schools before taking the position, often for long periods of time. All of the facilitators in this study worked full-time, except for one, who worked a four-day week because of funding constraints. The facilitator's job was expansive and on any given day involved issuing and organizing materials, observing in classrooms, monitoring tutors, meeting with teachers, meeting with the principal, attending a family support team meeting, training teachers, calling the SFA trainers, and assessing and regrouping students. One facilitator explained her mission as she saw it: "You have to make this program work as easily as possible for the classroom teachers because they have so many other responsibilities."

By and large, teachers believed that the facilitator really did make their teaching of SFA easier. About her school's facilitator, one teacher said: "She runs everything off for us. . . . We don't have to do anything. We go up there, we get our materials, we come back, and we teach it. That's half the reason it [the planning] takes ten minutes." Most principals, teachers, and the facilitators themselves recognized just how critical the facilitator role was for the success of the reform. Oftentimes it was not just having someone in the facilitator position that was critical, but also the particular person and the unique qualities and commitment that they brought to the job. As one facilitator remarked, "If I walked out, it would fall apart." The principal agreed: "I don't think it would cut it without [the facilitator]." A teacher stated: "I could see if you had a poor facilitator, it would kill this program." In fact, one school where the facilitator was clearly not as strong as those in the other five schools struggled with implementation.

Facilitators and their colleagues described facilitators variously as "taxed," "overburdened," and "swamped." Yet, despite these hardships, most of the facilitators remained very committed to their jobs and felt that the success of the reform hinged to a large degree on their efforts. They felt needed. Still, one facilitator admitted that she would return to being a classroom teacher immediately, if she had the opportunity. Two facilitators stated that the experience had taught them that they would never want to be administrators.

To be sure, being the SFA facilitator did allow a teacher to assume a spot in the limelight and to work closely with the principal. It is also a position that provided new challenges for an experienced teacher who had mastered her craft. In some cases, being chosen as the facilitator was akin to being nominated as a mentor teacher, and thus it was perceived as an honor. However, while the position of SFA facilitator brought with it a leadership role and added responsibility, no extra money was provided. This is unlike some other teacher leadership opportunities, such as mentor teaching or career ladders, which are accompanied by additional financial rewards (Hart, 1995).

One of the key roles of the SFA facilitator is to closely monitor teachers' implementation of the curriculum. Unlike the principals, who fell back on their own leadership styles in decisions about how much flexibility to allow teachers, the facilitators' actions reflected their need to maintain the collegiality of the teachers and, at the same time, satisfy SFA program demands. Whereas principals had their institutional position of power to rely on in their dealings with teachers, facilitators had to establish themselves as a trusted authority. For example, one facilitator explained that because she was new to the school, she felt the need to be flexible with teachers: "I felt that I was at a little bit of a disadvantage coming in as an outsider and never having taught Success for All. . . . So that was a little hard, and I really tried not to be that hard on teachers."

At another school, the SFA facilitator tried to maintain a good balance between program fidelity and flexibility by telling teachers that small adaptations to the program were acceptable, as long as there were not too many, and as long they asked permission first. Her approach generally worked well but caused conflict with a few teachers who described her as a rigid enforcer of the SFA model. As one teacher remarked: "What I hear from the SFA Boss is that, no, you can't do anything but what's in these planners." He added: ". . . and [the principal] backs her up on that." The facilitator found such attitudes from her long-time teacher colleagues upsetting: "It's kind of hurtful when teachers say, 'Oh, you're Mrs. SFA. Better do it your way.'" Despite the fact that facilitators may have been seen as the "boss" of the reform, most were still able to maintain a good rapport with many teachers and serve as mediators of the reform. The facilitators in two schools had more difficulty in their relations with staff, in part because some teachers used them as scapegoats for their problems with SFA.

Not only did the quasi-administrative status of facilitators raise questions about their authority in dealing with teachers, it also led to ambiguities in their relationships with principals. We found variation in how closely principals and facilitators worked together. The nature of their relationship was influenced by how each person conceived of the boundaries of his or her role and the context for leadership in each school. Again, relations of power came into play as principals and facilitators negotiated ways to jointly lead reform.

In two schools, the principal and facilitator worked in very close partnership with each other, sharing the leadership responsibilities for the reform. One principal described: "[The facilitator] and I have worked out a real nice system where she's the good guy and I'm the bad guy." She felt that her position as principal allowed her to enforce the implementation of SFA with more power than the facilitator had. Also, whereas the facilitator's relationship with teachers was somewhat fragile, the principal could bear the brunt of teachers' criticism without losing institutional power.

Some principals expected the facilitator to adopt a position of power with respect to implementation enforcement. However, the constraints of the facilitators' own definitions of their roles and school structures created tensions for some facilitators. In one school, the facilitator worried that if she were to adopt a role that assumed more power in enforcement of implementation, the strong teachers' union, of which she was, ironically, a member, might intervene. She said: "If I start going out on a limb and saying, 'This is what we'll do,' then it starts looking like I'm the administrator. . . . So I've got to be very careful." She described a difficult situation that arose when a teacher was formally reprimanded (in writing) for not complying with the SFA curriculum. "It's sort of like you're tattle-taling," said the facilitator. This placed her in the tricky position of evaluator, a role in which she was not comfortable.

CONCLUSION

This study of how district administrators, principals, and facilitators defined their leadership roles with respect to the SFA reform design yielded several findings. First, in the schools' initial adoption of SFA, district administrators and principals figured strongly. The principals in all of the schools we studied were strong proponents of SFA, even in cases where district administrators also encouraged adoption. Although the principals sought teacher buy-in to the decision to adopt SFA, in reality a fair number of teachers felt pressured to adopt the reform. This is not surprising, as prior research reveals that the principal's vision for the school often has a major influence on the direction of decision-making about reform (Louis & Miles, 1990).

District administrators supported or hindered SFA implementation and sustainability through their decisions regarding the provision of support and resources, and how they measured reform success. For the most part, district administrators were supportive, though some did not see SFA as the linchpin of their reform agendas. Turnover of key supporters of SFA at the district level had detrimental effects on the sustainability of the reform in the Southeast district we studied.

Once the SFA reform was in place, it shaped principals' roles, and the principals' leadership styles in turn shaped the implementation of the reform. The SFA Foundation set forth very specific, mostly managerial functions for principals such as ensuring resources for the reform, arranging the schedule, and monitoring progress. Although some aspects of reform management were fairly straightforward, we found variation in how principals' leadership styles meshed with the monitoring aspect of the reform—with some expecting more stringent fidelity to the SFA model and others approaching it with more flexibility.

Principals grappled with how much accommodation to allow on the part of teachers, and what the consequences of their decisions might be for teachers' interest in continuing with the reform. As others have suggested (Fraatz, 1989; Leithwood & Jantzi, 1990; Muncey & McQuillan, 1996), this involved a delicate balancing act—which was made trickier in this case because of the principal's accountability to the SFA trainers. Communicating the results of the SFA trainers' implementation checks caused some discomfort for principals who did not want to be seen as the "heavy" and preferred that the trainers occupy this role. While other studies have found that principals find it risky to relinquish some of their control (Anderson, 1991; Prestine, 1993), in this study some principals worried about exerting too much control. The major role change for principals that was brought about by the implementation of SFA was a sharper focus on teaching and learning. SFA created an opportunity for principals to be involved in and knowledgeable about classroom instruction, which is often seen as critical for successful school change (Fraatz, 1989; Murphy & Louis, 1999).

An examination of the role of facilitators in SFA schools revealed a teacher leadership position that is critically important to the successful implementation of SFA. Again, functions of the facilitator were well specified by the SFA Foundation and ranged from monitoring implementation, teacher and student progress, and tutoring, to training teachers and assessing students. In this regard, the SFA facilitator role was different from the more amorphous teacher leader roles described elsewhere (e.g., Muncey & McQuillan, 1992; Smylie & Brownlee-Conyers, 1992), wherein such individuals are often uncertain about exactly what their job involves. The SFA facilitator role, on the other hand, was an expansive one that required extensive time, effort, and the juggling of multiple, well-defined functions.

Ironically, in spite of this specificity, the SFA facilitator position was characterized by role ambiguity. The SFA facilitators found that they occupied a netherworld that was neither that of the administrator nor that of the teacher. These findings about the tensions in the teacher-leader role are consistent with prior studies (e.g., Muncey & McQuillan, 1996; Smylie & Denny, 1990; Wasley, 1989), yet illuminate how a very explicit comprehensive school reform model—which specifies the functions of the principal, facilitator, and the teachers—contributes to this dynamic.

This study contributes new insight into the possibilities and challenges of leadership in the case of highly specified, comprehensive school reform models. The success of this reform hinges on facilitators and principals who make certain that teachers teach the curriculum as it is designed and ensure uniformity of the taught curriculum across the school. To some degree, this places these leaders in an evaluative role and the teachers in a compliance role, leaving perhaps limited opportunities to share leadership and jointly negotiate aspects of how the reform operates at the classroom level.

This chapter advances the knowledge of leadership in school improvement by illuminating the issues that arise for district administrators, principals, and teacher leaders when schools implement comprehensive school reform models. This study also expands the research base on the role of teacher as full-time reform facilitator. Differing reform model goals and characteristics (e.g., centralized versus decentralized, comprehensive versus unspecified curriculum, strong relationship with the design team versus weak) and the corresponding expectations for district personnel, principals, facilitators, and teachers may influence leadership in varied ways. The growing popularity of comprehensive reform models such as SFA makes it imperative to continue to examine their effects on school and district leadership in a variety of contexts.

ACKNOWLEDGMENTS

Portions of this chapter derive from Datnow and Castellano (2001). The work reported herein was supported by a grant from the Office of Educational Research and Improvement, U.S. Department of Education, to the Center for Research on the Education of Students Placed At Risk (Grant No. R-117D-40005) and a grant to the Center for Research on Education, Diversity, and Excellence under the Educational Research and

Development Centers Program, PR/Award Number R306A60001. However, any opinions expressed are the authors' own and do not represent the policies or positions of the U.S. Department of Education. We wish to thank the participants in the schools and districts who gave so freely of their time for the purposes of this study. We also wish to thank Bob Slavin, Kathleen Stringfield, and the staff of the Success for All Foundation for their assistance.

REFERENCES

Allen, J. D., Halbreich, R., Kozlovsky, J., Morgan, R. D., Payton, F. R., & Rolewski, M. (1999). *Quality leadership for SFA schools: Suggestions for school leaders* (1st ed.). Baltimore, MD: Success for All Foundation.

Anderson, G. (1991). Cognitive politics of principals and teachers: Ideological control in an elementary school. In J. Blase (Ed.), *The politics of life in schools: Power, conflict, and cooperation.* Thousand Oaks, CA: Sage Publications.

Anderson, S., & Stiegelbauer, S. (1994). Institutionalization and renewal in a restructured secondary school. *School Organization, 14*(3), 279–293.

Berends, M., Kirby, S. J., Naftel, S., & McKelvey, C. (2001). *Implementation and performance in New American Schools: Three years into scale-up.* Santa Monica, CA: RAND.

Bodilly, S. (1998). *Lessons from New American Schools' scale up phase.* Santa Monica, CA: RAND.

Carlin, P. (1992). The principal's role in urban school reform. *Education and Urban Society, 25*(1), 45–56.

Cooper, R., Slavin, R. E., & Madden, N. A. (1997). *Success for All: Exploring the technical, normative, political, and socio-cultural dimensions of scaling up* (Report No. 16). Baltimore, MD: Center for Research on the Education of Students Placed at Risk, Johns Hopkins University.

Datnow, A. (2001). *The sustainability of externally developed reforms in changing district and state contexts.* Paper presented at the annual meeting of the American Educational Research Association, Seattle, WA.

Datnow, A., & Castellano, M. (2000a). Teachers' responses to Success for All: How beliefs, experiences, and adaptations shape implementation. *American Educational Research Journal, 37*(3), 775–799.

Datnow, A., & Castellano, M. (2000b). *An "inside look" at Success for All: A qualitative study of implementation and teaching and learning.* Report No. 45. Baltimore, MD: Center for Research on the Education of Students Placed at Risk, Johns Hopkins University.

Datnow, A., & Castellano, M., (2001). Managing and guiding school reform: Leadership in Success for All Schools. *Educational Administration Quarterly, 37*(2), 219–249.

Datnow, A., Stringfield, S., Borman, G., Rachuba, L., & Castellano, M. (2001). *Comprehensive school reform in culturally and linguistically diverse contexts: Implementation and outcomes from a 4-year study.* Report submitted to the Center for Research on Education, Diversity, & Excellence, Santa Cruz, CA.

Desimone, L. (2000). *Making comprehensive school reform work.* New York: ERIC Clearinghouse on Urban Education.

Evans, R. (1996). *The human side of school change: Reform, resistance, and the real-life problems of innovations.* San Francisco: Jossey-Bass.

Fraatz, J. M. B. (1989). Political principals: Efficiency, effectiveness, and the political dynamics of school administration. *Qualitative Studies in Education, 2*(1), 3–24.

Frederick, J. (1992). Ongoing principal development: The route to restructuring urban schools. *Education and Urban Society, 25*(1), 57–70.

Fullan, M. (1991). *The new meaning of educational change,* 2nd ed. New York: Teachers College Press.

Fullan, M. (2001a). *The new meaning of educational change,* 3rd ed. New York: Teachers College Press.

Fullan, M. (2001b). *Whole school reform: Problems and promises.* Paper commissioned by the Chicago Community Trust. Toronto: Ontario Institute for Studies in Education.

Goldring, E., & Rallis, S. F. (1993). *Principals of dynamic schools: Taking charge of change.* Thousand Oaks, CA: Corwin Press.

Hallinger, P., & Hausman, C. (1994). From Attila the Hun to Mary had a Little Lamb: Principal role ambiguity in restructured schools. In J. Murphy & K. S. Louis (Eds.), *Reshaping the principalship: Insights from transformational reform efforts* (pp. 154–176). Thousand Oaks, CA: Corwin Press.

Hallinger, P., Murphy, J., & Hausman, C. (1992). Restructuring schools: Principals' perceptions of fundamental educational reform. *Educational Administration Quarterly, 28*(3), 330–349.

Hart, A. W. (1995). Reconceiving school leadership: Emerging views. *Elementary School Journal, 96*(1), 9–28.

Herman, R., Aladjem, D., McMahon, P., Masem, E., Mulligan, I., O'Malley, A., Quinones, S., Reeve, A., & Woodruff, D. (1999). *An educators' guide to schoolwide reform.* Washington, DC: American Institutes for Research.

Leithwood, K., & Jantzi, D. (1990). Transformational leadership: How principals can help reform school cultures. *School Effectiveness and School Improvement, 1,* 249–280.

Louis, K. S., & Miles, M. (1990). *Improving the urban high school.* New York: Teachers College Press.

Madden, N., Livingston, M., & Cummings, N. (1998). *Success for All/Roots and Wings principal's and facilitator's manual.* Baltimore, MD: Johns Hopkins University.

Muncey, D., & McQuillan, P. (1996). *Reform and resistance in schools and classrooms.* New Haven, CT: Yale University Press.

Murphy, J. (1994). Transformational change and the evolving role of the principal: Early empirical evidence. In J. Murphy & K. S. Louis (Eds.), *Reshaping the principalship: Insights from transformational reform efforts* (pp. 20–53). Thousand Oaks, CA: Corwin Press.

Murphy, J. (1999). *Reconnecting teaching and school administration: A call for a united profession.* Paper presented at the annual meeting of the American Educational Research Association, Montreal, Canada.

Murphy, J., & Louis, K. S. (1999). Introduction: Framing the project. In J. Murphy, & K. S. Louis (Eds.), *Handbook of educational administration,* 2nd ed. (pp. xxi–xvii). San Francisco: Jossey Bass.

Neufeld, B. (1995). *Learning in the context of SDP: What are the opportunities? What is the context?* Paper presented at the annual meeting of the American Educational Research Association, San Francisco.

Nunnery, J., Slavin, R. E., Madden, N. A., Ross, S. M., Smith, L. J., Hunter, P., & Stubbs, J. (1997). *Effects of full and partial implementation of Success for All on student reading achievement in English and Spanish.* Paper presented at the annual meeting of the American Educational Research Association, Chicago.

Prestine, N. (1993). Shared decision making in a restructuring Essential Schools: The role of the principal. *Planning and Changing, 22*(3–4), 160–177.

Slavin, R. E., & Madden, N. A. (1996). *Scaling up: Lessons learned in the dissemination of Success for All.* Report No. 6. Baltimore, MD: Center for Research on the Education of Students Placed at Risk.

Slavin, R. E., & Madden, N. A. (1999). Effects of bilingual and second language adaptations of Success for All on the reading achievement of students acquiring English. *Journal of Education for Students Placed at Risk, 4*(1), 393–416.

Slavin, R. E., Madden, N. A., Dolan, L. J., Wasik, B. A., Ross, S. M., Smith, L., & Dianda, M. (1996). Success for All: A summary of research. *Journal of Education for Students Placed at Risk, 1*(1), 41–76.

Slavin, R. E., Madden, N. A., Karweit, N., Dolan, L., & Wasik, B. (1992). *Success for All: A relentless approach to prevention and early intervention in elementary schools.* Arlington, VA: Educational Research Service.

Smylie, M. A. (1997). Research on teacher leadership: Assessing the state of the art. In B. Biddle, T. Goode, & I. Goodson (Eds.), *International handbook of teachers and teaching,* Vol. I (pp. 521–592). Boston: Kluwer.

Smylie, M. A., & Brownlee-Conyers, J. (1992). Teacher leaders and their principals: Exploring the development of new working relationships. *Educational Administration Quarterly, 28*(2), 150–184.

Smylie, M. A., & Denny, J. W. (1990). Teacher leadership: Tensions and ambiguities in organizational perspective. *Educational Administration Quarterly, 26*(3), 235–259.

Spillane, J. P., & Thompson, C. L. (1997). Reconstruction conceptions of local capacity: The local educational agency's capacity for ambitious instructional reform. *Educational Evaluation and Policy Analysis, 19*(2), 185–203.

Strauss, A., & Corbin, J. (1990). *Basics of qualitative research: Grounded theory procedures and techniques.* Thousand Oaks, CA: Sage.

Stringfield, S., Datnow, A., Ross, S. M., & Snively, F. (1998). Scaling up school restructuring in multicultural, multilingual contexts: Early observations from Sunland County. *Education and Urban Society, 30*(3), 326–357.

Stringfield, S., Millsap, M., Herman, R., Yoder, N., Brigham, N., Nesselrodt, P., Schaffer, E., Karweit, N., Levin, M., & Stevens, R. (1997). *Special strategies studies final report.* Washington, DC: U.S. Department of Education.

Wasley, P. (1989). *Lead teachers and teachers who lead: Reform rhetoric and real practice.* Paper presented at the annual meeting of the American Educational Research Association, San Francisco. (ERIC Document Reproduction Services No. 311018).

Yin, R. (1989). *Case study research.* Beverly Hills, CA: Sage Publications.

Yonezawa, S., & Datnow, A. (1999). Supporting multiple reform designs in a culturally and linguistically diverse school district. *Journal of Education of Students Placed at Risk, 4*(1), 101–126.

NOTES

1. Our confidentiality agreement with the district that we studied in the Southeast necessitates that we do not reveal the name of the state in which the district is located.

2. The announcement for the Success for All Foundation Leadership Academy states the following: "The Leadership Academy is designed to build the capacity of district and school administrators, as well as school-based facilitators, to support a high quality of implementation of the Success for All program in order to improve student achievement." There are three one-day trainings offered for district administrators on the topics of leading SFA schools, data and resource management, and summarizing progress and future planning. The principal and facilitator training is eight days long.

3. This detailed guide for principals is entitled, "Quality Leadership for SFA Schools: Suggestions for School Leaders" (Allen et al., 1999), which was written by SFA school leaders for other SFA school leaders. The handbook is currently in revision.

CHAPTER TEN

The Coalition of Essential Schools

Leadership for Putting the
Common Principles Into Practice

PETER M. HALL AND PEGGY L. PLACIER

The Coalition of Essential Schools (CES) plays out a prevalent, ongoing tension in U.S. society and schools between ideas about heroic individual leaders and democratic, inclusive, collective leadership. While CES is identified with national charismatic figures such as Ted Sizer and Deborah Meier, its texts speak to "bold leadership" from a broad array of constituents, define a wide variety of behaviors as leadership, advocate active student involvement, and use democracy and equity as guiding principles (Coalition of Essential Schools, 2000). This chapter examines CES intentions for school leadership and descriptions of leadership practices from studies of CES schools. We propose a conceptual framework for understanding leadership in the CES process and then report our findings on CES leadership practices at the national, state, and school levels. In the process of our analysis, we came to view CES as a leadership development process, as well as a school reform "model."

CES AND LEADERSHIP

Because of its commitment to change initiated by people in schools, dependent on variable, contextualized interpretations of very broad principles, CES has been difficult to define as a reform "model" or "program"

(McDonald et al., 1999). CES is a national network of schools and regional centers committed to whole school reform based on 10 Common Principles (see Table 10.1). From its inception, CES has supported shared leadership. It was devised as a coalition of schools tied together by a consensual belief in a set of principles and by ongoing conversations about the multiple ways to translate those principles into practice. Rather than providing a structured "model" for a school to replicate, the purpose is to "inspire a school community to examine its priorities" in four interrelated areas: school design, classroom practice, leadership, and community connections (Coalition of Essential Schools, n.d.). The first step for a school exploring CES participation is to hold schoolwide conversations about the Common Principles in order to construct their meanings and implications in the local context. School staff attend CES meetings and conferences, for example, an intensive summer institute or "Trek." The three-year exploration process may culminate in CES membership, which means that a strong majority of faculty vote to join, the school submits an application, and there is a site visit of a team representing member schools or a CES center involving classroom observations and conversations with teachers and others in the school.

Early CES texts depicted the teacher as the central actor in school reform and stressed the necessity of teacher participation and influence in the affairs of the school (Sizer, 1984, 1992). CES schools have "coordinator" positions that blend teaching and administration. CES has also encouraged inclusion of students in school change through student leadership programs, and CES schools welcome parents and community members into their conversations and policy making processes. In 1997, with adoption of the tenth Common Principle (Democracy and Equity), CES expressly endorsed these practices.

From an original core of 12 schools, by the late 1980s the network of schools engaged in the CES conversation had grown substantially. CES began a period of demonstrating and documenting what was happening in those schools. Qualitative case studies identified leadership as an important theme in the data. From this inductive approach, recommendations for leadership practices in CES schools emerged. Researchers Wasley (1994), Wagner (1994), Muncey & McQuillan (1996), and McDonald (1996) came to these conclusions about leadership practices required to accomplish lasting CES reform:

- Facilitating development of a working consensus on values and goals, coping with resistance, disagreement, and "us-them" dynamics.
- Sharing power among teachers and principals, and overcoming traditional political and cultural norms of the school bureaucracy.
- Learning new skills and roles (teachers, as leaders, critical friends, decision-makers, collaborators; principals, as facilitators, delegators, advocates, motivators, empowerers).

Table 10.1 CES Principles and Leadership Benchmark Indicators[1]

Common Principles (abbreviated)	**Leadership Indicators** (abbreviated)
1. Use Minds Well. "... helping young people learn to use their minds well. Schools should not be 'comprehensive'... at the expense of the school's central intellectual purpose."	*work collaboratively* with stakeholders re: vision (and revision) *support* continued *intellectual focus* of staff and students *model intellectual curiosity*
2. Less Is More. "... student masters a limited number of essential skills and areas of knowledge.... shaped by intellectual and imaginative powers and competencies that students need, rather than by 'subjects.'..."	*coach, support, and encourage* teachers re: competencies for each student in each course *demonstrate* role as learner/teacher through *modeling and being present* in classroom *articulate and advocate* for "less is more" outside school
3. All Students. "... goals should apply to all students, while the means to these goals will vary as those students themselves vary."	*support teachers* in implementation of inclusion *model and promote* idea that all students can learn to use minds well
4. Personalization. "Teaching and learning personalized.... no teacher have direct responsibility for greater than 80 students at the high school or middle school and greater than 20 in elementary."	*model* personalization by knowing teachers, parents, and students well use *decision-making process* that *supports/promotes* personalization at student and teacher levels
5. Student-as-Worker. "... rather than ... teacher-as-deliverer-of-instructional-services ... coaching, provoke students learn how to learn and to teach themselves."	*make variety of resources available* *engage* wider community in educational discourse *model* metaphor of coach, authentic teacher, and learner
6. Authentic Assessment. "Learning documented and assessed with tools based on student performance of real tasks....	*educate* larger community about exhibitions for mastery *invite feedback* on process and content of exhibitions

(Continued)

Table 101 Continued

Common Principles (abbreviated)	*Leadership Indicators* (abbreviated)
Multiple forms of evidence . . . to better understand the learner's strengths and needs . . . no strict age grading or 'credits earned' by 'time spent' in class."	*negotiate* relationship between exhibition requirements and state and local standards *participate* in and *encourage conversations* in community and district re: grading and promotion
7. Tone of School. ". . . explicitly, self-consciously stress values of unanxious expectation, trust, decency. . . . Parents should be key collaborators, vital members of school community."	*model* respectful behavior *develop* clear norms, policies about "how we do things" *model tolerance, respect for diversity* with staff and students *structure staff policies* for more than one chance to succeed
8. Generalists, Multiple Obligations. ". . . principal and teachers [are] generalists first and specialists second . . . expect multiple obligations, commitment to entire school."	*share* leadership with others *interact* meaningfully with students inside and outside classroom *participate actively* in learning community
9. Resources. ". . . budget targets include, in addition to student loads, time for collective planning, competitive salaries, per pupil cost not to exceed traditional schools by greater than 10% . . . plans may have to show reduction or elimination of some services. . . ."	*display savvy* and *secure resources* to support work *clearly articulate* school's needs, strengths and weaknesses re: CES vision *make decisions* based on student needs and authentic teaching and learning
10. Diversity and Equity. ". . . demonstrate non-discriminatory and inclusive policies, practices and pedagogies . . . model democratic practices that involve all who are directly affected . . . honor diversity and build on the strengths of its communities . . . challenging all forms of inequity."	*build* a community of learners from within and without *model* open-mindedness seek diverse staff *model* practices/*create* policies that *develop a culture honoring diversity* *disaggregate student data* by race, ethnicity, gender, class, etc. to address and understand inequities in achievement

[1] For full text of common principles and leadership indicators, see Coalition of Essential Schools, 2000.

- Keeping goals and actions tightly coupled with teaching and learning.
- Drawing on outside resources, such as the CES network, to support professional development and add legitimacy.

While all four studies highlighted the importance of teacher leadership, "only in schools where the principal was an active and ongoing participant were the experiments of individual teachers incorporated into schoolwide change" (Muncey & McQuillan, 1996, p. 270). In three studies, administrative turnover was a major impediment to sustained change, even when a strong core of teachers were committed to continuing (Wasley, 1994; Muncey & McQuillan, 1996; McDonald, 1996). Therefore, although CES defines "leadership" broadly and inclusively, in a CES school the principal is a significant actor. Principals of some CES schools, such as Deborah Meier, have become national figures. Yet Meier defines her role as a facilitator of change whose work is dependent on the leadership of teachers and students (McDonald et al., 1999). Moreover, certain factors in the school context (size, history, faculty experience, teacher unions, community politics) can challenge even the most skilled and well-intentioned principal (Wasley, 1994; Wagner, 1994; Muncey & McQuillan, 1996; McDonald, 1996).

The CES newsletter *Horace* has disseminated many reports and reflections on school leadership. Articles combine school leaders' testimonies about "what works" (or does not) with advice from leadership experts such as Phillip Schlechty, Lee Bolman, Terence Deal, and Linda Lambert. The portrayal of leadership in *Horace* reflects the findings of studies of CES schools: Sharing power among administrators and teachers, as well as with students and parents; facilitating complex, time-consuming processes wisely and democratically; building a commitment to common values, especially student learning; modeling practices consistent with desired school changes; and mediating conflicts and being open to the perspectives of those who resist change (Cushman, 1998).

More recently, the national CES organization has expressed its intentions for leadership more explicitly. This statement reflects the perspectives of those at the national office:

leading a school well demands both high quality formal leadership and collaboration at every level. A key role of those in formal leadership positions is to support ongoing improvement in the instructional practices of the staff and to keep the school focused on its intellectual mission. The leadership structures and decision-making procedures should model democratic practices and should communicate a tone of high expectations, trust and decency. Teachers are key school leaders and should have substantial authority over their work and time to collaborate. (Coalition of Essential Schools, n.d.)

Interrelated programs on leadership guide professional development in CES networks and member schools, and "Leadership" is the theme of a strand of presentations at the CES national meeting, the Fall Forum. The Fall Forum itself exemplifies CES beliefs about leadership—it is interactive, collaborative, and inclusive (McDonald et al., 1999).

CES's most explicit statements on leadership are found in the Benchmarks and Indicators by which schools can assess their similarity to a "model" CES school. Creation of the Benchmarks involved a wide, diverse, experienced set of participants from CES schools, centers, and the national staff. Indicators were developed for each Common Principle in five domains—student achievement, classroom practice, organizational practice, leadership, and community connections. According to text accompanying the Benchmarks:

> Leadership is a critical component that cuts across all four domains . . . Student leaders, teacher leaders, administrative leaders, and community leaders all share responsibility for creating and sustaining a culture of inquiry which places students at the center of the educational experience. . . . (Coalition of Essential Schools, 2000, p. 2)

Analysis of the Leadership Indicators (see Table 10.1) shows that rather than abstract philosophical rhetoric, they express intentions for behavior. They have a general cast that can apply to all members of the school community, not just administrators. Even if one interprets them as applying to formal leaders, they call for behaviors such as creating conditions that facilitate others; modeling a democratic, equitable, intellectually focused learning community; actively interacting with others; and expressing values, spreading the word, and educating others outside the school. The leader is not a top-down, decision-making manager but a collaborative, engaged, symbolic leader, comfortable with facilitating, delegating, and providing resources to others.

Therefore, beginning with a set of principles derived from Sizer's studies, and observing what happens when people in schools attempt to put them into practice, CES gradually identified and now has formalized conceptions of leadership that are in many ways congruent with current leadership theories, especially "distributed leadership" (Spillane, Halverson, & Diamond, 2001).

Developing and assessing local leadership has become an important focus of CES as an organization. This chapter takes the work one step further by examining CES leadership on three levels—national, state and school—through the lens of the following conceptual framework.

THE TRANSFORMATION OF INTENTIONS AND DISTRIBUTED LEADERSHIP

Our study integrates an interactionist framework for analysis of educational reform processes (Hall, 1995; Hall & McGinty, 1997) with distributed leadership theory (Gronn, 2000; Neuman & Simmons, 2000; Spillane, Halverson, & Diamond, 2001). In a school restructuring process such as CES, actors in one time and place express intentions for the behaviors and attitudes of other actors in the future and in other places. Intentions are the purposes and goals that motivate people to act. In this case, national and state program advocates, policy makers, administrators, teacher leaders, and others have intentions for implementation of CES in local schools. Even with the highest levels of coordination and shared commitment, this would be a complicated process. There are distinct possibilities of resistance, contingencies, communication breakdowns, and multiple interpretations, because program initiators are dependent on others to fulfill their intentions. People in schools may rely on tradition, experience, or familiar, conventional strategies, or they may innovate and create new ways of "doing school" in their setting. The organizational structure is not deterministic; it both constrains and enables action, and may be altered in the process (Spillane, Halverson, & Diamond, 2001). The usual distribution of power may prevail, or those with less power may use resources or persuasive skills to redistribute power in unforeseen ways. This process transforms the intentions of the program initiators. The more different people, sites, and phases involved, the greater the possibility that their intentions will be transformed in unexpected ways.

This perspective has profound implications for leadership and implementation of reform "models." According to distributed leadership theory, power and influence are dispersed (Gronn, 2000) or "stretched across" multiple actors and situations (Spillane, Halverson, & Diamond, 2001) rather than concentrated in the hands of a single leader, such as a school principal. Implicit in technocratic/bureaucratic imagery of leadership is a mechanical process, in which the leader's intended plan is simply enacted as desired or written— implementers "follow the rules." The individualistic view of leadership grants agency only to leaders, not to "followers" (Gronn, 2000). However, as knowledge of school reform bears out, the process is more flexible. In addition to formal leaders, many others (teachers, other school staff, students, parents, community members) with their own intentions and interests enter into the process at different points in time. They negotiate, adapt, and adjust to each other within and across contexts. They further "produce" the program based on what they receive and what they believe is required in their school context. New or unrecognized intentions may emerge along the way. The transformation of intentions may even involve a subversive "double entendre," whereby some people resist and overturn the original intentions. Even those who do nothing influence the process (Gronn, 2000). The outcomes are always to some extent unforeseen.

CES leaders implicitly recognized some aspects of this perspective on school leadership from the start, discovered the rest through studies of CES schools, and have now formalized it in the Benchmarks and Indicators. Studies of CES schools have shown that the process is prone to competing interpretations, and unintended or surprising consequences are common (Wasley, 1994; Wagner, 1994; Muncey & McQuillan, 1996; McDonald, 1996). McDonald (1996) uses the term "serendipity" to describe the unpredictable complexity of the CES process and argues that it is more compatible with chaos theory than other reform schemes.

Spillane, Halverson, and Diamond (2001) argue that in order to understand school leadership, the focus of study should not be leaders, but leadership practices in situational contexts. In Table 10.1, we draw attention to practices by highlighting the verbs in the CES Leadership Indicators. However, the Indicators cannot show how these practices would manifest in particular situations. In this chapter, we will examine CES leadership practices at the national, state, and school levels in a particular social, historical, and political context.

DESIGN AND METHODS

The schools in this chapter are part of a larger, ongoing study begun in spring 2001, of 12 CES member schools in a midwestern state. All schools demonstrated commitment to and implementation of the Common Principles over a significant period of time, at least five years. Representatives of each school are being interviewed about involvement with CES, the change process, leadership perspectives and practices, contextual influences, and accomplishments. A narrative based on the interviews and documents is being constructed for each school.

Interviews have been conducted with representatives of six schools to date. After obtaining informed consent from the participants, the interviews were audiotaped and fully transcribed for qualitative analysis. The interviews were supplemented by documents from the schools and data on the national and state contexts of CES reform. To protect the participants' confidentiality, all names of individuals, schools, and districts were replaced with pseudonyms in this report. In addition, the analysis benefits from the experiences of the first author, who has a 10-year history of involvement with CES including serving as a member of the state department of education CES advisory committee, acting as a "critical friend" to several schools, being a delegate to the CES National Congress, and serving as a member and chair of the board of a regional CES center. In addition, an informant who has observed in many of the schools and is familiar with their history has added details and perspectives to the narratives. Another data source was a transcript of a session on leadership facilitated by the first author as part of a state CES conference. The session was attended by staff from schools in the study, as well as schools exploring CES membership. We focused our data analysis on identifying how leadership practices translated leaders' intentions into actions, comparing these practices with findings of previous CES studies and the Leadership Indicators.

The three schools in this chapter have been involved with CES for 9, 10, and 12 years respectively. They were selected because they represent different regions and school contexts, but their experiences mirror those of other schools in the study. Nothing we have found elsewhere contradicts these narratives, and they seem to dramatize "typical" aspects of the CES process. After we had selected the schools and begun to write the chapter we realized that the three leaders (two teachers, one administrator) whose voices are most prominently featured in the cases are female. Based on our other interviews so far, we do not claim that gender differentiates among leaders in CES schools, but it does seem notable that in these cases CES involvement facilitated the leadership development of three women, two of whom were teachers rather than administrators.

FINDINGS

National Leadership

CES began with a focus on "the teacher" as the unit of change, moved toward an emphasis on "whole school change" embracing the importance of leadership and community contexts, and then began to consider ways of "scaling up" consistent with its values (Coalition of Essential Schools, 1995). The original CES schools were geographically close enough for school leaders and CES staff to interact with some regularity. The assumption was that within networks or clusters, school people would talk with one another, learn from one another, and help one another—but never be "clones" of one another. The national leadership states that "No two Coalition schools are exactly alike, even when they are striving to fulfill all of the Common Principles—and this, in the Coalition's view, is as it should be" (Coalition of Essential Schools, n.d.).

Beginning in 1988, CES forged a partnership with the Education Commission of the States (ECS) called Re:Learning, based on the intention to link education reform "from the school house to the statehouse." The national CES office alone could not support expansion into states very distant from the national office, and ECS had the capacity to convince states to invest in CES under the new heading of "systemic reform." Re:Learning states were identified as those that devoted financial and professional development resources to CES school restructuring. A national faculty of teachers would be trained to serve as consultants to the schools.[1] Re:Learning encouraged rapid growth in the number of schools exploring CES membership, but the scaling-up process created a basic tension around injecting state power into what was meant to be a locally initiated change process. In addition, Re:Learning was subject to both the instability of state politics and the rigidity of state bureaucracies, and was forced to "compete" with other reform models in the marketplace of state policy (McDonald et al., 1999).

In 1994, CES marked its 10-year anniversary by forming a Futures Committee to envision its second decade. The committee's report (Coalition of Essential Schools, 1995) mentioned Re:Learning, but it was conspicuously missing as a priority for future organizational development. Rather, the most pressing concern the committee identified was to continue to build a coalition of *schools* that model the possibilities of schooling for a democratic society. The Organizational Principles in the report define CES as a "learning community, modeling the practices it expects in schools" and assert the values of "local wisdom" and decision-making, "flexibility to respond to local contexts," and democratic practices at all levels (pp. 7–8). Based on the report's recommendations, CES moved to decentralize, with semi-autonomous regional centers facilitating contact among member schools. Center representatives would attend a national congress that makes policy for the Coalition as a whole. At the same time, CES would stay involved in national and state conversations about moving policy in directions consistent with the Common Principles, and would emphasize accountability through public demonstrations of what could be accomplished through CES.

State Leadership

Before CES became linked with the education bureaucracy in the state in our study, two schools in one metropolitan area had already become CES member schools, on their own initiative. The beginnings of state involvement with CES can be traced to the late 1980s, when a large foundation and the Center for Policy Research in Education (CPRE) convened meetings including education leaders and state policy makers to move the state toward systemic reform. It was around this time that CES and ECS began the Re:Learning partnership, and the state pursued this direction. In 1992, the state legislature passed and the governor signed a bill establishing targeted incentive grants that schools could use to support CES restructuring.

The state department of education established a structure including regional coordinators and a state-level advisory group representing teacher organizations, foundations, legislators, and administrators. Several corporations donated funding to assist in hiring a state

Re:Learning Consultant, a central coordinator position. The number of schools exploring CES membership grew, supported by professional development opportunities at the state and national levels. Parallel to the national faculty, faculty could apply to become members of a state faculty network trained to facilitate, coach, and act as "critical friends" to educators in schools exploring CES. The advisory group evolved into a more active, hands-on Working Group—made up of teachers, administrators, regional coordinators, private sector representatives, and higher educators—that made important strategic planning and budgeting decisions for CES. Over time, teachers and principals of CES schools came to form the group's core membership. Therefore, CES was operating somewhat independently of, and differently from, the state education bureaucracy—modeling the democratic, inclusive leadership CES intended for schools.

After this promising beginning, the situation of CES in the state became more uncertain and ambiguous. Turnover in the Consultant position made it difficult to maintain continuity. In 1993 the legislature passed a comprehensive school reform act involving state standards and performance assessments, as well as funding for professional development and regional professional development centers. That is, the state established its own priorities for school reform, and addressing those priorities moved to the top of the state department's agenda. Among the major reform "models," Accelerated Schools had more support and stronger advocates within the department, as a more "structured" approach. When CES began its move toward regionalization, the state department and CES agreed that for two years the state would support CES's creation of two regional centers, one in each of two metropolitan areas. With some private foundation funding, in their second year the centers began an impressive effort, the Five Schools Project, designed to draw on the strengths of CES schools in five regions of the state. The schools made a three-year commitment to create project teams that would network among each other in order to align the new state standards with authentic pedagogy, develop professional communities, and prepare their faculties for rising expectations for student performance.

In the meantime, the CES national office was too financially stressed and organizationally stretched to offer the support needed by the growing number of CES schools created under Re:Learning (McDonald et al., 1999). The state was footing most of the bill for the CES centers, and this provided the department with a rationale for exerting increasing control over the CES effort. The cultural conflict between the state bureaucracy and the democratic localism of CES deepened, which was exhausting for the Working Group and the centers. Eventually, the state infrastructure that had provided training, networking, recruitment, planning, and other services to schools under Re:Learning collapsed. Many "exploring" schools gave up their exploration. In the face of uncertain state support and questions about leadership, foundation sponsors of the Five Schools Project pulled out. State funding for the centers ended after the two years of promised support, and one center closed. About two years later, because of shifting priorities, questions about effectiveness, and budgetary constraints, the state terminated the targeted incentive grants. The other center has survived because of a school district's commitment and, more recently, CSRD funds. Most CES schools located closer to the surviving center have maintained their membership, while many schools in the closed center's region have withdrawn. This, then, was the state political context surrounding the schools in our study.

School Leadership: Three CES Schools

The three high schools in this chapter benefited from state resources available under Re:Learning and made many positive changes through their affiliation with national CES. All became CES member schools for a significant number of years, although two are no longer involved. The schools are located in different geographic regions of the state and vary in terms of community contexts, size, student populations, and traditions. When they first encountered CES, the organization had not yet developed the Benchmarks or other explicit statements expressing intentions for leadership practices. In each school, we will highlight the leadership intentions, practices, and accomplishments of school leaders. These are stories in which school leaders used CES, and the resources available through Re:Learning, to fulfill their intentions for school reform. Whether or not the schools maintained their CES membership, the process resulted in many lasting structural and cultural changes. Perhaps just as important, while all of the leaders eventually left to work in other positions or schools, they carried the learning about leadership gained through CES with them into their new contexts. One can view CES not only as a school restructuring process, but as a leadership development process for teachers, principals, and students.

Green Fields High School

Located in a town of about 10,000 just outside a metropolitan area, this 800-student high school serves children of commuters as well as children of farm families. The district has a low tax base and a history of problems with community support. At the time this story began, in the early 1990s, Green Fields was a new school created by merging a 9th to 10th grade school with an 11th to 12th grade school. The two schools had had different cultures related to teachers of different generations (the 9th to 10th grade teachers were generally younger) with different philosophies and practices. A catalyst for CES involvement was mediation of differences between these groups of teachers. The district had also been implementing Outcomes Based Education (OBE), a model advocated by the state department of education. While the state abandoned OBE by 1993 because of political opposition, OBE had opened the door to rethinking teaching practices in order to improve student achievement.

School Leaders' Intentions for Reform. The principal of the new high school was a former teacher and assistant principal at the 9th to 10th grade school. His content intentions were to bring the achievement of the "bottom" group of students up to the "middle" and to reduce the dropout rate. He had been analyzing school data as part of his doctoral program in educational administration, looking for ways to turn the numbers around. His process intentions were to facilitate the merger of the two schools, initially working through a network of friends—teacher colleagues from the 9th to 10th grade school. The teacher leader we interviewed, Martie Johnson, described him as the "prime mover" in the CES process. However, he left to take a position in the central administration after just one year. A series of short-term principals with less interest in CES followed. In fact, a team of predominantly female teachers were the real "prime movers" of restructuring.

Johnson had grown up in the community and knew it well. She said she was known to other teachers as "outspoken," "nonjudgmental," "enthusiastic," a "cheerleader," and "supportive of trying new things." "Um, I guess I was a leader in the building . . ." she allowed, "because . . . I had a lot of fun teaching. I love my job, you know." Rising to department chair by age 28, she had also served as a coach, National Education Association (NEA) local president, and professional development committee member. She was an ally of the new principal and wanted him to do well, but she saw her "peers" (other teachers) as much more influential in her development than any administrator.

Her content intentions were that she wanted students to like learning and to be better "prepared for life" and "life-long learning" beyond high school. She wanted to work in a school with more positive relationships among teachers, as well as between teachers and students. The traditionalist 11th to 12th grade teachers referred to some students as "sweathogs" and had low expectations for many of them, contributing to discipline problems and the high dropout rate. To change this, she thought, would require higher teacher expectations; more collegiality; more active, performance-based, and hands-on instruction; and a new curriculum. Her process intentions were to use communication, training, and modeling to help other faculty change their teaching styles. She defined leadership as a process of taking risks and sharing power,

> taking chances with your friendships, as well as your professional collegiality with your peers. . . . Taking that chance and showing everyone that it's okay . . . you have to be willing to be involved yourself . . . but you also have to be able to delegate. . . .

She thought that a leader should "stand up for what the group wants." A leader should also include parents and students, to "trouble shoot questions and ideas they might have."

Why CES? For Green Fields, CES was the right restructuring model at the right time. The school was newly constituted. The faculty had been implementing OBE, which entailed creating a teacher advisory team and considering structural changes. The principal and an assistant superintendent saw CES as consistent with their ongoing efforts. "Plus," Johnson said, "the money [Re:Learning incentive grants] became available and we were a poor school. Wherever you can get money to train teachers and to look at the way you do things, to do them differently and better. . . . A windfall, if you will." But CES had unique attractions, related to the transformation of intentions and distributed leadership:

> We looked at two different [models], and that was the one we said we can live with it, we can adapt it. It was much more malleable, and much more freedom, in how you structure the change in your building . . . we could be ourselves and still be a coalition school.

Leadership Practices. Johnson described the restructuring process in some detail, using the term "we" to refer to the core group of teachers, mostly women, who "did all the grunt work." When the Re: Learning grant was awarded, a team of four teachers went to a summer Trek, where they thought about "what we wanted our ideal school to look like . . . where there was camaraderie, where it was safe, that all students could learn, and . . . education prepared students for their futures." They came back from the Trek "idealistic and ready to go" and then realized, "well, there are some people out there that don't think the same way we do." They developed a plan. First, each would recruit two other teachers, to form a core restructuring committee of 12 representing different departments. This group would then try to pull the remainder of the school's 65 teachers "on board." One member proposed that they assign themselves as "buddies" to resistant faculty, engaging in frequent, informal, positive communication with them about their teaching. There was an element of "subterfuge" in this strategy, because the team member might suggest innovative lessons, and then if the colleague liked the results, they would say, "Well, you know, that goes right along with what the coalition says. . . ." Some teachers joined the committee just "because they were antagonists," but in time became advocates. The restructuring committee "did a lot of training" with other teachers, trying to address their "angst about change, to tell them it's okay and that you're normal." They arranged for faculty to visit CES schools (a "turning point" for some skeptics). Some of the most resistant teachers also resigned, retired, or "just decided to shut up."

The teacher team invested untold hours on restructuring, over many years, with little principal support after the first year. Johnson believed that with more principal leadership the process might have been much shorter and less difficult. She served as an "informal" CES building coordinator, with no released time or compensation, because "you do the things you believe in and the things you believe are good for kids . . . you just find the time to do it."

What the School Accomplished. As a consequence of CES involvement and teacher leadership, many aspects of Green Fields were transformed. The core group won most of the faculty over to block scheduling, including common teacher planning times. Martie Johnson said that while this change was very difficult, "99.9%" of teachers would never return to 45-minute periods. Teachers revised the curriculum and implemented student exhibitions entailing integrative, cross-curricular teaching and learning. More students were attending college. They created a student leadership group, and counselors facilitated discussions on teenage problems. Working on the Tone of Decency principle, they reduced the number of disciplinary problems and constructed a relaxed climate in the school. They created a building advisory committee including parents and students.

State policy also propelled some of these changes. For example, new state standards and tests implemented in the late 1990s required curriculum revision around performance-based assessment. When the state created and funded its own school restructuring model demanding lower dropout rates and better preparation for postsecondary education (vocational or college) through more "applied" learning, Green Fields was one of a limited number of schools selected to participate. The team saw this program as complementary to, rather than competing with, CES. The school became affiliated with a corporate-funded urban learning center whose director was connected with CES. They adopted Character Education, which supported the Tone of Decency principle. They explored Tech Prep, a federal program to facilitate the transition between high school and technical training in community colleges. Under a new state accreditation policy, they were "accredited with distinction"—the first CES school in the state to merit this label. This was primarily because of improved test scores among the "bottom" group of students.

However, frequent turnover in the principal position somewhat limited the progress of restructuring. According to Johnson, a "vacuum" of principal leadership caused "turmoil and havoc in the building." She observed a return to teacher dissension and stagnation, a feeling that there was no longer a need to continue improving: "You can't be satisfied when your test scores go up and there are fewer discipline problems and all those things that you can show on paper." As older teachers left, new teachers required extensive orientation to the block structure and could become overwhelmed. Yet, supported by the close proximity of the remaining CES regional center, this school to date remains actively involved in CES. According to the teacher leader, "Coalition has truly made a difference in the school and the atmosphere in the students' lives." She recently moved to another district, where she is a CES building coordinator. Another lasting outcome of CES at Green Fields was her development as a leader.

Valley Vista High School

This large school (more than 1,500 students) is located in a suburban community of about 25,000 situated within the most populous metropolitan area in the state. While the community is predominantly white and middle class, Valley Vista has participated, along with many other suburban schools, in a voluntary busing program for desegregation that brings African American students (20% of the student body) into the school. Of the three schools profiled in this chapter, it is the only one with significant racial diversity.

School Leaders' Intentions for Reform. Administrators in this region have a tradition of networking; they tend to know what other districts are doing and to be aware of national and state reform trends. In the mid-1980s, when this account began, the district had a reform-oriented male superintendent who was very involved in state level efforts, and a male associate superintendent who encouraged the female school leader in our study, Barb Nebbits, to take the initiative in reform. At the time, she was an assistant principal in charge of school scheduling and other schoolwide planning. This gave her, she felt, an overview of the school as a whole—a position from which to consider structural change. She was also a former special education teacher who "knew about personalized education, 'cause that's how I designed my curriculum . . . it worked for a range of students. I also knew that when you have less class size, you can do that."

Her content intentions were to address what she saw as a pervasive problem in the school, "which is obviously what I saw every single day, where teachers were overloaded with work" because of large class sizes, and were consequently not assigning students very challenging work. "And I thought," she said, "no wonder teachers either leave, burn out, or become ineffective." Her process intentions were to use persuasion and positive "incentives" to convince faculty that investing time and effort in reform would make their work more satisfying and effective:

> I always believed that teachers were the key. . . . I'm a very logical thinker. If I work with a teacher, make their life better, then they're gonna make the kids' life better and they're gonna do what they need to do.

Why CES? In the mid-1980s, Nebbits read *Horace's Compromise*, which she saw as a vivid portrayal of teachers at Valley Vista. Two other schools in the metro area were early CES adopters, and Ted Sizer came to the city to speak at a CES forum, and she and others from the district attended. She said that she liked Sizer "immediately,"

> and I believed what he said because I had lived it and I knew exactly what he was talking about and I also knew from what I had witnessed, which was a very small microcosm . . . that secondary schools were not doing a very good job. They were too content driven and not looking at the whole picture.

However, Valley Vista would not pursue CES membership for 5 to 6 more years. As a first step, on her own initiative ("This was just me"), she proposed to change the schedule to create smaller class sizes. She took this idea to the department chairs, who "didn't want anything to do with it":

> They first of all didn't believe it, and second of all, did not want to give up their aides and their time off. . . . So I quickly realized that was not the way to go. I learned by trial and error. So I backed off.

It was not until a North Central Association (NCA) evaluation made it evident to others in the school and district that the school *did* have problems with large class sizes, contributing to teacher overload, lack of efficacy, and burnout, that the school began to consider restructuring. This outside perspective validated Nebbits' perspective and created an opening for CES.

Leadership Practices. The assistant superintendent promoted Nebbits to associate principal and formally charged her with working on educational reform at the school, "with the opportunity to see what I could do." She "invited" teachers, parents, and business and community leaders to join a 42-member Vision Committee to imagine what the school could become. With the assistant superintendent's help, she wrote grants for members to travel to other schools, including CES schools, as well as to meetings and conferences on school reform. The group studied the work of Goodlad, Sizer, and others. Barb Nebbits said, "I took them through a process . . . I met almost every night for three years." She also worked with individual teachers, "one person at a time."

Finally, the teachers themselves ("they") decided to focus on the CES Common Principles. Doing so much at once, however, seemed "overwhelming," and they started slowly. With the principal's urging (he had heard that other area schools were doing this), she enlisted four teachers to pilot a 9th grade team, to provide more personalization (Common Principle 4).

> I asked them to commit to me for at least two years. After that, if they didn't want to be a part, they were out. But I never made anyone do anything . . . but I never said anything that I wasn't gonna do and I was always there with them. . . . They started believing that I would really do what I said I would do.

Based on positive student and parent responses, as well as teacher evaluations, the pilot was very successful. The next year another team was added.

Teacher enthusiasm grew. "As the teachers saw things happening, they grabbed onto it. So that's how we did it, with the ripple effect." In 1989, Nebbits and a teacher (the future CES building coordinator) proposed to the faculty that Valley Vista should apply for CES membership. The proposal laid out several advantages: The Common Principles would provide a guide or framework for change; the school would become part of a national network of schools; CES staff would offer conferences and professional development; membership would afford advantages in obtaining grants; and CES would not prescribe a "fixed" path to restructuring—they could learn through experience. The last statement expresses the same awareness of the transformation of intentions and distributed leadership that we found at Green Fields. It was many months before a faculty vote was taken, and the 72% approval showed that some faculty were still resistant; but a revote the following year increased approval to 86%. Valley Vista became a CES member school and received one of the first state Re:Learning grants.

After CES membership, the pace of restructuring accelerated. Teachers were given the incentive of additional planning time if they tried something new. Nebbits said that she taught herself how to write grants and secured funding for professional development and travel from several sources, including local corporate foundations. She reflected that

> You give the teachers the opportunity and let them go and it's unbelievable . . . so I was the manager, I was the resource, I was the one that tried to make things happen for people. . . . It was just all of us learning how to do things together. . . . You just did the next logical thing that you should do to reach out to the network, 'cause that was the other thing I liked about Coalition was the networking and teachers weren't in isolation. . . . That's what I love about critical friends. So all of these things just kind of happened because teachers were allowed, and more and more people became involved.

She won another grant to improve interracial relationships in the school. With the Re:Learning grant, the building coordinator was appointed and given released time from teaching to organize a building committee of faculty, parents, students, the associate principal, and a school board member. In one report he noted that the school administration gave teachers responsibility and authority to decide the directions for change. Faculty decided to focus on the Principles of "Student as Worker" and "Teacher as Coach," which entailed changing their relationships with students and teaching practices. They reexamined the curriculum to develop clear, common goals for all students, and established advisories. Twenty-five students volunteered for a student leadership group.

What the School Accomplished. All told, school leaders at Valley Vista employed CES to fulfill their intentions for reform for 10 years. Most of the changes they made were substantive, and have already been mentioned. A site visit by a CES consultant praised the school for its tone of decency and personalization, enthusiastic and collaborative faculty, and focus on classrooms and students. The school's social context in a metropolitan area with other CES schools, as well as foundation funding, seemed advantageous. Nevertheless, Valley Vista's commitment to CES waned. Some faculty continued to resist block scheduling and teaming. A new assistant superintendent seemed intent on "micromanaging" the school, according to Nebbits. The district in general pulled back from its enthusiasm about restructuring. Valley Vista remained in CES after the nearby regional center closed, but dropped out in 2000. Eventually, the long-time supportive principal retired, Nebbits went to another state, and some teachers involved with CES retired or left. Many schools in this area, which was once known for its exemplary CES schools, have also withdrawn, which means that there is no longer a supportive local network. School leaders face a very different external context. The state has increased pressure on schools to respond to state standards and testing, with lack of improvement linked to serious consequences for school accreditation. The media in Valley Vista's metro area intensify this pressure through publication of reports comparing school districts and schools. Without a state, regional, or local support network, many leaders in this area no longer seem to view CES as a viable approach to improving their "standing" in this competitive climate.

Rolling Hills High School

In the late 1980s, rapid growth in the population of the midsized city in which Rolling Hills is located brought about a change in the student population of this large (more than 1,200 students) school. As the district expanded and built new high schools in suburban developments, the students remaining at Rolling Hills were less affluent and less academically successful. The school district had a history of conservative, centralized governance and administration, but new district leaders decided to experiment with site-based management (SBM), beginning with a few pilot schools. A group of teachers at Rolling Hills approached the principal about becoming an SBM pilot school, and he readily agreed. This move opened the door for CES.

School Leaders' Intentions for Reform. The male principal, a veteran teacher and former assistant principal in the school, was in the second year of his principalship. He wanted to afford more equal opportunities to students and to improve their performance. His process intentions were to welcome and involve all stakeholders (teachers, students, parents, community members, and higher education partners); to step back and allow others to lead, providing them with support; and to give students more responsibility and power. Echoing the words of Andy Hargreaves (1991), he argued that the process should seem "natural," not "contrived." The teacher leader in our study described him as a "risk taker" rather than a "building manager." He surrounded himself with good teachers, and then said to them, "do what you need to do, bring me ideas, I'm a resource for you, I'm going to support what you feel like you have the rationale for—which is pretty unique."

The female teacher leader in our study, Pat Burris, arrived at the school in 1989 after working in another district where she had been a math teacher, curriculum coordinator, and NCA team member. She had an understanding of school reform processes and experiences with SBM. She described herself as caring, student-centered, and having a "passion" for teaching. As a newcomer, at first she "stayed quiet" and kept her impressions of the school to herself. She saw her new colleagues as fine teachers for the most part, but isolated, traditional, formal, and cliquish. Walking down the halls, she said, she observed them next to their overhead projectors lecturing to bored silent students sitting in assigned seats. They were also "strict, [with] long lists of rules, 'don'ts' on the door as you walk in." She especially hoped to improve the teaching of math, to respond to students' different rates and styles of learning, to get students to "like learning," and to boost very low enrollment in advanced math courses. Her initial strategy was to "earn respect" from colleagues by succeeding with the "low groups" of students she was assigned. Soon students were requesting her classes, and colleagues were asking for advice. She won a state grant for technology implementation. Gradually, "the things I had done in the past began to come out." The principal appointed her to the school leadership team, a group of teachers/department chairs "who were willing to donate time . . . to attend meetings, and do the extra as far as involving parents and looking at different reform movements and grant writing." When she reached this point in her narrative, her discourse changed to refer to "we," reflecting her emphasis on teachers' collective leadership. She resolved that "everything we had to do should revolve around . . . getting kids to be better students."

Why CES? When Rolling Hills became an SBM school, Burris said, the district gave the leadership team "the leeway of deciding our own fate and enabling teachers, to empower them to make changes. . . ." They studied various restructuring models, but CES was in the air locally. An influential teacher was learning about CES through her graduate studies at the nearby university, and a national CES figure had spoken at a local meeting. The deputy superintendent knew that the state was offering Re:Learning targeted incentive grants, and the Rolling Hills team was primed with the knowledge they needed to write an application. They also had the support of the principal, which was essential to negotiate district approval, because the district still controlled which schools could apply. Once they had approval, the team wrote a successful grant application.

Leadership Practices. As Burris recalls, when a team from Rolling Hills attended their first state CES conference, they entreated a National Faculty member to tell them

> How do you do this? And I can remember how naïve we were at the time and she kept saying, "It's up to you to decide because this is your local decision to make." And she never would answer us on how to do this prescriptive method of step one, step two, step three . . . we felt more confused when we left, but it all made sense two years later.

Because "there were no models for becoming CES coalition leaders within the building," the team had to play it by ear. The first question they asked themselves was, "Are we satisfied with what we're getting?" After looking at the evidence of student work, grades, and attendance, as well as parent involvement, "we decided we weren't satisfied." Therefore, they had to ask, "What do we want our students to know and be able to do?" During the first year, the team mostly "stayed home" to read and study. The process was open to anyone who "wanted to participate and had ideas." They used their political skills to muster other teachers' support, winning over a majority in the first year. In addition to the leadership team, the school created a site council of 28 members including students, parents, community, business leaders, and higher educators, who could help the school win approval for innovations from the still-powerful central administration.

The three keys to the process were time, communication, and shared leadership. The site council held "roundtables" once a month in the cafeteria to discuss important issues and get feedback. Faculty meetings were transformed into in-service sessions with mandatory attendance and no interruptions, at which the faculty shared what their departments were doing and constructed a vision for the school as a whole. "The biggest thing that I'd say about leadership," Pat Burris said, "You're not gonna move anything until you listen to others . . . a major part of our job is listening, not talking." The department chairs had a released hour for discussion and planning, and kept in touch with other teachers via a newsletter and e-mail network:

> The more you can put in writing to the teachers and keep them informed, the more likely that they're gonna support what you really are going for in all ways. . . . They want to be part of it, they really do, if they feel that there's something out there that's gonna make life easier for them.

"The main thing," Burris said, "was that we were able to divide up the work," with different teachers taking the lead on different projects or processes and trying to be realistic about what they could take on, and for how long. A core group joined the state faculty network and received training on facilitation and coaching. Because of district policy, no teacher received extended duty pay for participation. Burris had released time during a period when she served as CES building coordinator, but she said she would have preferred extended duty pay, because other teachers question when a teacher has fewer students to teach.

The principal somewhat compartmentalized his activities from those of the leadership team. While they focused on improving curriculum and instruction, he focused on student leadership and school climate, reducing the emphasis on rigid rules. Because he could not pay teachers for their efforts, he rewarded those who "made things happen" by giving them public recognition, responsibilities they wanted, or professional development opportunities. He spoke with resistant teachers, valuing their critical questions but asking them not to block change. Some responded to his pressure by leaving the school. He worked on other reforms in tandem with CES: a program for at-risk students, in-school suspension, and revised class scheduling. Similar to Green Fields, Rolling Hills won a competitive grant to participate in the state's restructuring model, and this brought in more funds to support teacher development.

What the School Accomplished. Both the principal and teacher leader felt that their intentions for CES membership were fulfilled. Burris, who retired in 2000, said that in the last 4 to 5 years of the school's 12-year CES process,

> it was absolutely marvelous . . . teachers were constantly coming to you, and they were looking for grant opportunities to promote what they would really like to do . . . we broke all the molds in [district] and asked for waivers to put integrative units together and put team teaching together, and . . . freshman teams, and we were the only ones in the city to do that.

She claimed that "the teachers were very united in the last four years." The school had block scheduling, with time for collaborative teacher planning; professional development on teaching methods such as Socratic seminars; and a better school climate. The faculty reached consensus on a set of proficiencies desired for all Rolling Hills graduates, coordinated with new state performance standards. Pat Burris reflected that

> it was a whole lot more outcomes-based, with the students setting the activities and planning backward . . . to take a unit and work and plan it backwards instead of just going page by page. More and more of us gave up the textbook as our primary resource. . . . We did a whole lot more performance assessment, multiple tasking, oral conversations with students, and so we began to assess them in many ways, and that's what we wanted. The kids began to buy into their own educations as soon as we did that. The teachers who could not do that, or for some reason would not do that, eventually left Rolling Hills, and they weren't comfortable. Students put a lot of pressure on the teachers.

However, several factors curtailed CES's progress at Rolling Hills. The most significant was high faculty turnover. Many veterans retired, and orienting new teachers required a great deal of the principals' and teacher leaders' time. A change in the district administration, as well as election of a more conservative school board, meant less support for school-level innovation. School leaders had to go "across town" to the district office to get many changes approved, and the "lawyers" would say what they could or could not do, "so those were the things that hurt us." Burris noted that incoming students seemed less motivated and continued to present challenges. She estimated that while about 75% of the students benefited from reform, 25% were still left out. Finally, in an increasingly test-driven political climate, CES advocates could not substantiate a consistent connection between the changes they had made and improved standardized test scores. After 12 years and many accomplishments, the school withdrew from CES. From what she had heard, Burris said, "there is very little CES allowed."

DISCUSSION

In this section we return to themes developed in the introductory sections of the chapter to interpret the three cases and to draw broader implications for leadership and school reform.

Transformation of Intentions: Uncertainty and Ambiguity

In each of these schools, leaders transformed CES's intentions as well as their own into a unique mix of structural and cultural changes.

According to CES, that is how the process should work—each school will interpret the Common Principles somewhat differently depending on the local context and the unpredictable outcomes of a democratic, inclusive process. The leaders in these cases said that they were particularly attracted to this feature of CES, but it also posed a challenge. If there is one "requirement" for CES leadership, it is the ability to cope with uncertainty, ambiguity, and one's lack of control over other people. State leaders in our study seemed especially uncomfortable with this aspect of CES, in comparison with other models or with state initiatives.

However, there are similarities both in the starting places of these schools and their change trajectories. These schools all began as places that Horace (Sizer, 1984) would recognize: too many isolated, discouraged teachers; fragmented curricula; an impersonal climate that alienated students and did not elicit their best work. After a long process involving studying, visiting other schools, and countless meetings to build consensus, all three schools focused on block scheduling, teacher teaming, curriculum reform, professional development, and school climate. Block scheduling is a structural change that transforms two key cultural norms of high schools—disciplinary fragmentation and teacher isolation. It requires collaborative decision-making and coordination within the school, as well as involvement of students and parents.

Distributed Leadership: "Inefficiency," Time, and Learning

In the theoretical framework we contrasted two kinds of leadership in U.S. schools: technical-bureaucratic and distributed. CES holds little attraction for leaders firmly entrenched in the first camp. We know of cases in which top-down principals have attempted to "force" CES on a school, always with negative results. Our short case studies cannot begin to represent the very long *time* required first to gain consensus on CES and then to translate the Common Principles into action. This could be perceived as "inefficient" leadership, but in the long run the accomplishments can be impressive. At a session on leadership at the state CES conference in spring 2001, a principal noted that

> I think a key to the beliefs underlying CES . . . is this idea of building leadership capacity within our building and establishing a philosophy of shared leadership throughout the building, with the leadership coming from students, staff, parents, moving across the board. And what we found number one was, a slow process. Because a lot of times . . . a lot of people aren't used to being in that capacity and aren't real willing to accept some of the responsibility that goes along with that. The thing that had to be established first is a real strong element of trust.

This principal "demoted" himself to being a "member" of major school committees, and turned the leadership over to teacher leaders,

> and that was probably the biggest step, because CES became such a major part of the school, the staff basically see it being led by themselves. They see that as a grassroots effort. . . . All of a sudden you've got a group of teachers who are excited about it, and it looks like it totally came from the teachers even though in the background as principal you're kind of the rudder. They don't see you leading anything, but you have a lot of background things going on.

One reason CES takes time is that leaders do not simply "do" the kinds of things this principal described—they *learn* to do them. School leaders whose experience and professional education have reinforced a managerial perspective have to acquire new skills and understandings. In our case studies we see administrators learning to be flexible facilitators and resource providers who shared power with teacher leaders. They learned to be more indirect, and more patient about the time and effort required to gain the voluntary assent of individuals and consensus of the community, including students and parents. For example, the administrator at Valley Vista unilaterally developed a plan to reduce class sizes and then learned that department chairs would not accept it. Teacher leaders at Rolling Hills learned how to lead through demonstrating or modeling good practices, persuasion, listening, collaboration, and using rewards and incentives that they know other teachers would value. The teacher team at Green Fields came back from a Trek ready to implement changes immediately, but realized that they needed to learn how to convince their skeptical colleagues.

In these cases, we saw the same problems with staff turnover identified in previous studies of CES schools. Staff turnover upsets the interactional patterns in the school and entails a loss to the collective knowledge base built up through the learning process. As principals and teachers leave, and new ones arrive, arrangements must be renegotiated. If a district hires a "scientific manager" for a CES school, one can predict problems. One unsupportive principal undermined 12 years of change at Rolling Hills. However, the teachers at Green Fields maintained their commitment to CES despite a series of unsupportive principals. A teacher at the spring CES conference credited both teacher and parent leadership with sustaining distributed leadership at her school after a change in principals. The parent community "just wouldn't tolerate it" when a new principal wanted to limit their participation: "They just would not abide that kind of leadership style anymore. They felt they were being ignored." When teacher leaders leave, experienced staff must spend time orienting beginning teachers who may have been prepared by their teacher education to work within a traditional school structure. A beginning math teacher, for example, could never "replace" the hard-won leadership skills, experience, and contextual knowledge of Burris. Her retirement, as much as the principal's departure, was a serious blow to the school.

Changing External Context

An added source of instability in these cases was the state's dismantling of the Re:Learning structure that had supported the schools through their long change processes. CES had hoped that the state would act as a middle-level sponsor and facilitator of school restructuring, so that the organization could grow in breadth but still develop the depth characteristic of the schools in the original core group. State leaders in our study tended to favor more "structured" or tightly coupled reform models, especially after the adoption of state standards, tests, and tougher accreditation measures. Green Fields demonstrated that a long-time CES school in a relatively low-funded district could more than measure up to new state requirements, but the state nevertheless expressed little interest in investing in CES. Affiliation with a national network is insufficient to support the kinds of complex activities these schools undertook. CSRD funding is attracting a number of new schools to CES, and is helping the remaining regional center survive. But what will happen when that funding ends? CES must continue to struggle with the scaling up issue and the creation of networks of schools that can support one another. For example, at a recent Fall Forum, one administrator talked about an "essential district" in which all schools are engaged in restructuring.

PRACTICAL AND POLICY IMPLICATIONS

Our study represents only a sample of schools in one state, and we would not presume to draw conclusions about all CES schools. We recommend comparative studies of CES schools in other states. However, there are some broader practical and policy implications of our work.

School Restructuring as Leadership Development

The case studies suggest that one can define CES as a leadership development process, as well as a school reform "model." As the leaders we featured in the cases have moved to other positions or schools, the skills and knowledge they gained through CES involvement are being further "distributed." CES's influence thus is much larger than the raw number of CES member schools. It would be important to study other school reform models from this perspective. What do participants learn from their participation? Are state or federal leaders considering this as a valued "outcome" of restructuring?

Restructuring Large Schools

Two of the schools in our study were large, and size presented a restructuring challenge. CES is currently emphasizing the importance of creating small schools (Clinchy, 2000). For example, the theme of the 2001 Fall Forum was "Schooling on a Human Scale." Distributed leadership may be better suited to a small, face-to-face community than a large bureaucracy. Charter schools or new schools might also be better homes for CES. It is interesting that Green Fields, the smallest of the three schools in the chapter, was a new school of sorts, created through the merger of two other schools. It is also the only one to maintain CES membership, although the proximity of the remaining regional center probably also contributes to this.

Principal and Teacher Preparation

The time-consuming unlearning and relearning school staff must undertake to implement CES in a very traditional school suggests the need for changes in the preparation of principals and teachers. When a principal or teacher leaves, the school loses its costly investment in their knowledge about how to exercise distributed leadership. Do education administration programs prepare principals to exercise distributed leadership that is antibureaucratic and procommunity? Are preservice teachers prepared to work collaboratively on whole school change?

Some Unanswered Questions

Our study is ongoing, and this first phase has generated the following questions for further study:

- There is a flow and flux in CES school participation. New ones enter as old ones drop out. But after curtailing involvement, what happens? Do the structural changes, such as block scheduling, remain, and with what effects? Do teachers continue collaborating and practicing the principles? Does distributed leadership continue? Another aspect of the flow and flux is that leaders leaving one school may stimulate or become part of the process at another school. It is of interest to know how often this is the case and how past experience comes into play in the new setting.
- We have heard from the literature and those in the field that the principal is essential to the project. We know from schools that failed to move toward CES membership that teacher leaders placed the onus on the principal. But is that because the principal did not symbolically provide legitimacy for the reform, failed to provide resources to facilitate it, or perhaps did not help respond to resistors? How and in what ways the principal affects the process remains to be answered.

- As an aspect of distributed leadership, CES has placed a unique and important emphasis on student leadership and participation in reform. Although there are writings about students in CES schools, it would be interesting to know the consequences of their participation in student leadership later in their lives. Similarly, does inclusion of parents in decision-making in CES schools encourage parent activism?
- Our experience is that pressure from state authorities through standards and testing is constraining continuing participation or initial interest in CES from local schools. Can leaders construct ways to make state reforms and CES compatible, or must they mediate the contradictions between them? What is the effect of either strategy on use of CES principles?
- Finally, the amount of resources through CSRD grants is substantially more than through Re:Learning, although the schools that are eligible are much more restricted. CES has also focused the "model" for CSRD on five "non-negotiable principles": Principles 1 (use minds well), 4 (personalization), 7 (school tone and family involvement), and 10 (democracy and equity) rather than the full set of ten (see Table 10.1). A major research question is, how do the available resources and the more focused model affect leadership practices and the restructuring process?

CONCLUSION

As we write this, the CES regional center is providing professional development services and coaching to some schools using CSRD grants to explore CES. In the next year they will decide whether to continue involvement once the funding ends. There is also the question for the center about the stability of CSRD funding and whether new schools will choose to explore the model. Of course, another issue is whether the process so far has produced improved student learning. There is preliminary information that some CES/CSRD schools in other regions have shown improvement in student achievement, which may encourage leaders to pursue CES involvement. CES is in the process of developing a three-year study to examine the question of student learning, looking at outcomes of both standardized and authentic assessments. CES is ambivalent about conclusions based solely on standardized tests, and the study will include outcomes of alternative or "uncommon" kinds of assessment that "powerfully demonstrate students' knowledge, ability to reason, and capacity to solve problems" (Coalition of Essential Schools, 2001, p. 1).

CES held its 2001 Fall Forum, providing both practical information and morale boosts to enthusiastic participants. Through its emphasis on small schools, charter schools, and expanding networks, the CES national organization remains positive about involving school leaders, broadly defined, in building a coalition of schools that demonstrate the possibilities of engaged, inclusive schooling in a democratic society.

REFERENCES

Clinchy, E. (2000). *Creating new schools: How small schools are changing American education.* New York: Teachers College Press.

Coalition of Essential Schools. (n.d.). Retrieved June. 21, 2002, from http://www.essentialschools.org.

Coalition of Essential Schools. (1995). *Looking to the future: From conversation to demonstration* [Report of the CES Futures Committee]. Providence, RI: Coalition of Essential Schools.

Coalition of Essential Schools. (2000). *The CES school benchmarks.* Providence, RI: CES National.

Coalition of Essential Schools. (2001). *Request for proposals for a study of CES schools.* Unpublished document. Oakland, CA: CES National.

Cushman, K. (1998). *Leadership in essential schools.* The collected Horace: Theory and practice in Essential Schools, Vol. 4. Providence, RI: Coalition of Essential Schools.

Gronn, P. (2000). Distributed properties: A new architecture for leadership. *Educational Management and Administration, 28*(3), 317–338.

Hall, P. M. (1995). The consequences of qualitative analysis for sociological theory: Beyond the micro level. *Sociological Quarterly, 35*(2), 397–423

Hall, P. M., & McGinty, P. J. (1997). Policy as the transformation of intentions: Producing program from statute. *The Sociological Quarterly, 38*(3), 439–467.

Hargreaves, A. (1991). Contrived collegiality: The micropolitics of teacher collaboration. In J. Blase (Ed.), *The politics of life in schools* (pp. 46–72). Newbury Park, CA: Corwin Press.

McDonald, J., Hatch, T., Kirby, E., Ames, N., Haynes, N., & Joyner, E. (1999). The Coalition of Essential Schools in its second decade. In J. McDonald, T. Hatch, E. Kirby, N. Ames, N. Haynes, & E. Joyner (Eds.), *School reform behind the scenes: How ATLAS is shaping the future of education* (pp. 45–66). New York: Teachers College Press.

McDonald, J. P. (1996). *Redesigning school: Lessons for the 21st Century.* San Francisco: Jossey-Bass.

Muncey, D. E., & McQuillan, P. J. (1996). *Reform and resistance in school and classrooms: An ethnographic view of the Coalition of Essential Schools.* New Haven, CT: Yale University Press.

Neuman, M., & Simmons, W. (2000). Leadership for student learning. *Phi Delta Kappan, 82*(1), 9–12.

Sizer, T. R. (1984). *Horace's compromise: The dilemma of the American high school.* Boston: Houghton Mifflin.

Sizer, T. R. (1992). *Horace's school: Redesigning the American high school.* Boston: Houghton Mifflin.

Sizer, T. R. (1996). *Horace's hope: What works for the American high school.* Boston: Houghton Mifflin.

Spillane, J. P., Halverson, R., & Diamond, J. B. (2001). Investigating school leadership practice: A distributed perspective. *Educational Researcher, 30*(3), 23–28.

Wagner, T. (1994). *How schools change: Lessons from three communities revisited* (2nd ed.). New York: Routledge Falmer.

Wasley, P. A. (1994). *Stirring the chalkdust: Tales of teachers changing classroom practice.* New York: Teachers College Press.

NOTE

1. Re:Learning States and National Faculty are official CES terms. They are usually capitalized in CES literature.

CHAPTER ELEVEN

The Comer School Development Process

Developing Leadership in Urban Schools

CHARLES M. PAYNE AND JOHN B. DIAMOND

Seems a stranger strolled into an urban school one day and asked if he could address the teachers. When they were gathered, he held up a big, shiny pot of gold and announced that it belonged to the school, he had brought it as a gift. The teachers, especially the veteran teachers, immediately started firing hostile questions at him. How come he was being so nice to them? And who was going to divide up the gold? Did the union approve of bringing gold into schools? Besides, some of them had heard he had already given a pot of gold to the school down the street. Was this pot of gold as large as the pot of gold he gave the school down the street? Because if not, they didn't want it. They didn't need any second-rate pot of gold, thank you very much. One stern matron rose to her feet, shaking a finger at the befuddled stranger, to testify that she had been teaching for thirty-five years and if you needed gold to teach she sure would have figured it out before now and anyhow, she knew the students and parents in this neighborhood, which was more than she could say for the stranger, and they just weren't the kind of parents and kids who could appreciate gold. Maybe gold made a difference in other neighborhoods but it wasn't going to do a bit of good here.[1]

The pot of gold story[2] reflects an aspect of life in inner-city schools that is well-known but underappreciated. In the worst inner-city schools, the social infrastructure has been so damaged by mutual suspicion, low expectations, factionalization of staff, and general pessimism as to make most school reform efforts irrelevant. Some of the problem is captured by the phrase "micropolitics of the school" (Ball, 1987), but that phrase does not clearly suggest the seemingly irrational relationships that characterize many urban schools. People who have been involved in school change efforts recognize the pot of gold scenario, with its predisposition to suspicion, its low expectations of students and parents, and its rejection of anything that comes from the world outside. It is a pattern that means, in its strongest form, that schools cannot build on whatever real strengths they have, cannot make use of resources—including financial resources and technical expertise—even if somehow they could be provided. It is a pattern in which the irrational component of behavior can be sufficiently large as to blunt (but not neutralize) the effectiveness of either positive or negative sanctions.

What does it mean to exert leadership in a demoralized social context? "Leadership" has become a major buzzword in discussions about improving urban schools, the focus of conferences and special journal issues. The Dewitt-Wallace Foundation has established a major national initiative to improve school leadership. This focus on leadership is an altogether healthy development but, as with previous hot topics in urban school reform, too much of the discussion still proceeds in a vacuum, discussing leadership without attention to the specific context in which urban school leaders must operate.

We might expect that James Comer's School Development Process would have something to teach us about how leadership works in these contexts. In recent years, parts of the charter school movement and the small schools movement as a whole have called attention to the salience of human relationships in urban school reform, but the Comer program has been making that point for more than 30 years. At the same time, the program has always been self-conscious about the need to support leadership, as reflected in the title of Comer's first book on the subject, *School Power* (1980). In fact, in the early phases of implementation, Comer facilitators could be thought as being primarily leadership consultants with a human relationships emphasis.

First established in New Haven in 1968, the Comer process—formally, the School Development Process—tries to change schools by improving working relationships among school staff. Comer believes that children in inner-city schools too often come to school without the social and moral development necessary for academic success, that too many school staff members do not have enough knowledge of child development to help them, and that relationships between poor parents and educators are often so dysfunctional that they are unable to collectively focus on the problems of children. Thus, the program tries to improve educators' understanding of child development while fostering healthier relations within schools and between schools and homes. There are nine basic tools for doing this—three teams, three guiding principles, and three ongoing operations. The planning and management team contains representatives of all adult stakeholders in the school and is responsible for the overall development of school policy. The parent team tries to increase the participation of parents in school social activities, in volunteer activity, and in school governance—all aimed at giving them a greater sense of ownership in what happens at school. The Student and Staff Support Team (formerly the Mental Health Team) addresses problems of individual students and teachers as well as addressing broader issues of social climate—discipline problems, morale problems, problems with teacher-parent relationships, or teacher-teacher relationships.

The teams are intended to work within three general guidelines. The most distinctive may be the "no-fault" policy, which means that discussions are to focus on problem-solving, not fixing blame. The second is collaboration, meaning that as many stakeholders as possible will be involved in making and implementing decisions but with the common understanding that the principal cannot be hamstrung. The last guideline calls for consensus decision-making, intended to keep staff from taking polarized positions on issues. The Comer program is important in itself but it is also important that its components reflect some of the strategies that have been most popular in school reform efforts over at least the past decade—shared decision-making, greater parent/community involvement, more collaboration among stakeholders, and more sharply focused services to individual students.

Of the ongoing operations in which teams will be engaging, three are so important that Comer separates them out: the development of a comprehensive plan for the social and academic rejuvenation of the school; staff development activities consistent with the school plan; and continuous assessment and modification of the plan's implementation. Comer has warned against equating the program with its component parts. What is important about the program is building community. "In every interaction you are either building community or breaking community. The mechanisms . . . are secondary" (Comer, Haynes, Joyner, & Ben-Avie, 1996, p. 148).

Over a 10-year period, the initial New Haven implementation was credited with making substantial improvements in two schools (Comer, 1980). Since then, the program has spread widely, particularly within the past 10 years. By 1990, at least 100 schools around the country were trying to implement Comer programs. By the year 2000, the number was nearer to 700. Successful sites claim improvements in test scores, suspension rates, student self-concept, parent participation, and the attendance of both students and teachers (Comer, 1989; Comer, Haynes, Joyner, & Ben-Avie, 1996; Haynes & Comer, 1993).

The Chicago Comer project has been among the more successful sites. In their quantitative evaluation of 10 of the Chicago schools over a four-year period, Cook and associates found improvements in social and academic climate. As compared to students in randomly assigned control schools, students in the Comer schools did about three percentile points better in both reading and math while also reporting lower levels of negative acting out behavior (Cook, Murphy, & Hunt, 2000). The magnitude of the gains may not have been large, but programs that demonstrate simultaneous improvement on academic and behavioral measures are not common. These results were achieved despite the fact that the program was not fully implemented.

This chapter is concerned with the Chicago Comer project, with what can be learned from it about the social demoralization of schools and about how leadership can function in such schools. It grows out of eight years of ethnographic research on the Chicago implementation of Comer School Development Process (SDP) between 1991 and 1999. During that time, Charles Payne led a team of ethnographers who watched 16 Chicago elementary schools adopt the program, most of them extremely disadvantaged schools. John Diamond was a member of the team. In 1991, fully 57% of the students attending these 16 schools had reading scores in the nation's bottom quartile, while only 14% were reading at grade level (Chicago Public Schools Database). The ethnographic team gathered data by direct observation at Comer team meetings, at facilitators' meetings, schoolwide retreats, training sessions in New Haven and Chicago, and through interviews, formal and informal, with facilitators, principals, parents, and school staff. The chapter draws in particular on data from the 11 schools that were still in the program in 1999 (which in 1991 had 54% of their students reading in the bottom quartile nationally and 15% reading at grade level).

The Chicago Comer implementation was been distinctive in a number of respects. The implementation there is led by a social work agency, not the local board of education. It is what might be called a moderate facilitation model in the sense that for most of the project's life schools have had two days a week of a facilitator's time, more than some Comer sites, less than others. The Chicago context is also distinctive. Because of Illinois's 1988 law decentralizing schools, Chicago during the 1990s was the site of aggressive experimentation with educational models. One of the things that has meant is that Chicago principals have had more financial resources under their direct control than is typical in urban areas, about $1,000,000 per inner-city elementary school by the end of the decade. It also meant that principals were under considerable pressure to look at new programs, making it possible for programs such as Comer's to go into schools that would have been closed to outsiders a few years earlier.

Drawing on the Chicago Comer experience, the first part of this chapter will look in some detail at one Chicago school and at how a confused, distrustful social climate there undermined the leadership's efforts at school improvement. The second part will draw on the experience of other Chicago Comer schools to see what can be learned from them about how to develop leadership that can function in dysfunctional environments.

WOODBINE SCHOOL: LEADERSHIP IN THE ABSENCE OF TRUST

Among the Chicago Comer schools, Woodbine is very much in the middle of the pack in most aspects. Serving an overwhelmingly low-income, Black and Hispanic population, it has an engaged, energetic principal, who is capable of accepting some criticism—an important issue for a principal involved with Comer. While many Chicago schools are virtually empty of staff soon after the afternoon bell, Woodbine has several teachers who regularly come early and stay late, suggesting a staff that has higher expectations for their students than is normal in inner-city Chicago. Although Woodbine's student population is low-income and at least two well-known street gangs operate in the area, it does not serve one of Chicago's housing projects with all the additional social problems that entails.

The Comer implementation has gone well in some respects. Woodbine is not a school where Comer is one program among many. At Woodbine, Comer has a visible and central role to play in the school. The Comer teams function well—despite a long history of tensions affecting the leadership team, which will be discussed momentarily, and at times some of the teams have been exemplary. One of the consequences of this teamwork is that delivery of individual social services to children is at a much higher level than before the program began. The principal-facilitator relationship might be described as stormy but strong. If the facilitator is persistent, she can make herself heard, but the principal, Mrs. Smith, has a strong predisposition to make the most important decisions on her own. In fact, Mrs. Smith brought in the Comer program with only minimal consultation with her staff, some of whom never let anyone forget that this so-called collaborative program got started in a noncollaborative way.

As that example suggests, Woodbine is a school where the staff has significant problems trusting one another, some of which start with problems on the leadership team and emanate out to complicate relationships throughout the building. Mrs. Smith is very concerned with test scores but, like most Chicago principals, is more of a manager than an instructional leader. Her infrequent classroom observations seem geared toward identifying the weaker teachers so that she can weed them out, not to being able to work with them on their weaknesses. On the other hand, she has hired some assistant principals who are more respected by staff for their knowledge of instruction, something not all principals are secure enough to do.

The principal's operating style, though, makes it difficult for her to get the best out of her staff. She is described as impetuous, much quicker to reprimand—often in public—than to praise. She is not very patient with the frequent criticisms of her insensitivity to staff; she hires people because she hopes they are professional enough to do their jobs without being stroked every few minutes. Despite the fact that the school is committed to shared decision-making, Mrs. Smith has difficulty making her staff, even the senior staff, feel that they have a real voice. She vacillates between asking for collaboration and consensus one day and expecting staff to respect her decision-making prerogatives the next.

The principal's vacillation about decision-making keeps senior staff constantly off balance. Is this a day when it is okay to disagree with the boss or not? A wrong guess and a staff member can wind up in big trouble. At one point, the principal decided that she wanted to reshuffle job assignments of the members of the leadership team (the assistant principals, the counselor, the social worker, and the curriculum resource specialist) in ways that, from her viewpoint, would allow for more effective curriculum supervision and more support for teachers on disciplinary matters. From the viewpoint of almost everybody else, it looked as if the reassignments failed to take advantage of the particular strengths and weaknesses of team members. Mrs. Smith originally presented the decision as a done deal. When she saw how clearly shocked her staff was at not being consulted sooner, she claimed she was only making suggestions, after all. However, she had presented the realignment so forcefully, that no one really believed that it was open for discussion. Few objections were voiced until she stepped out of the room, and the Comer facilitator pressed people for their reactions, which turned out to be almost entirely negative. Mrs. Smith was clearly annoyed to walk back in the room and find the issue still under discussion. According to the field notes, she "sighed and in a combative tone asked the group, 'What is the problem? Is there someone here who is unable to do what I have asked them to do?' " When Mrs. Johnson, one of the assistant principals, expressed her doubts about the new plan, Mrs. Smith repeatedly asked her if she was saying she could not accomplish what she had been asked to do. Mrs. Johnson repeatedly responded that she was "perfectly willing" to do her "very best," but she still had concerns. After going back and forth for a while, Mrs. Smith pushed her chair back from the table and said, angrily, "This is an administrative decision and I am the administrator. This is no longer up for discussion. As far as I am concerned, this meeting is adjourned." With that, she stormed out.

The observable fallout from this little brouhaha continued for months. In the short term, Mrs. Johnson was frightened, almost to tears at one point, that for voicing an honest opinion, she was going to get written up. Mrs. Smith was certainly in a mood to do that for awhile. She felt betrayed—that was her word—by her assistant. This was not the first time that Mrs. Smith thought that Mrs. Johnson had betrayed her by speaking out of turn, but it marked a turning point in their relationship. Mrs. Smith several times expressed skepticism about Mrs. Johnson's intentions, and Mrs. Johnson, who prided herself on being a hard worker, seemed to withdraw for a while. She did her job, but she was not always invested in it the way she had been. Perhaps it should not be surprising that the assistant principal's relationship with teachers sometimes replicated her relationship with her principal. Mrs. Johnson made several decisions that directly affected teachers without consulting them, and then she seemed surprised when teachers were upset or felt devalued.

It may seem that Mrs. Smith overreacted to a minor disagreement, but we have to appreciate the context within which she works. As with all Chicago principals, she is on a four-year contract, renewable at the pleasure of her Local School Council (LSC). For much of the period under discussion here, relationships between the principal and the LSC were markedly tense. The principal seemed to be right in her judgment that some members were out to confront her. At least two members seemed to automatically take the opposite side from her on any issue. There were periods, negotiated by the Comer facilitator, when the hostile LSC members tried to be less oppositional, but even during those truce periods the principal had a hard time believing they were sincere. She continued to interpret their behavior in the light of their previous behavior, perceiving attacks where probably nothing of the sort was intended. The principal was thus always on the defensive, confronted with a central administration that was becoming increasingly aggressive about insisting on test score improvement and an LSC that seemed to be waiting for her to slip up. The last thing she needed was senior staff openly disagreeing with policy. From the principal's point of view, that kind of betrayal is not merely personal, it jeopardizes her ability to continue to run and improve her school. A principal may firmly believe in collaborative, egalitarian ideals—Mrs. Smith brought the Comer program to Woodbine, after all—and yet bracket them off as not being applicable to particular situations. A principal cannot have everybody expressing their feelings on every single point in the middle of a battle. The principal felt, with some justice, that there had been plenty of issues on which she had gone out of her way to solicit and respond to staff input. She could not do it on every issue.

Her leadership staff would almost certainly have agreed with her on that. Still, they wanted to know, more clearly than the principal had communicated in the past, which issues were going to be principal's prerogative and which were open for input. Realistically, though, principals are themselves going through this reform process for the first time, and the political context in which they work is shifting all the time. They cannot always know in advance which issues can comfortably be thrown open for discussion.

However understandable, what is perceived as inconsistent behavior from principals can wreak havoc with their staffs. Soon after the blowup,

Mr. Ford, another assistant principal and perhaps the member of the leadership team least likely to disagree with the principal, seemed to become the fair-haired boy He seemed to have Mrs. Smith's confidence in a way the others did not, and he seemed to have access to information sooner than anybody else. Other members of the team resented what they saw as favoritism; in subsequent meetings when people disagreed with Mr. Ford, it was not always clear whether they were disagreeing substantively or just because he was the principal's favorite. At least one other member seemed to be always trying to protect Mr. Ford from any criticism. For several months, the atmosphere on the team was defensive and mutually suspicious, enough so that there were open discussions about distrust on the team and enough so that the simplest administrative tasks—supervising the lunchroom, devising a detention policy—became exercises in Byzantine intrigue, with each faction trying to discredit the other and each questioning the motives of the other.

In between squabbles over lunchroom duty, this group was supposed to be leading Woodbine school through a thorough revision of its curriculum. This was a project on which several Comer schools had embarked a year and a half earlier, intended to spur more professional collaboration among teachers, to align the material taught in one grade with that taught in contiguous grades while encouraging the use of more innovative teaching methods. It seemed to be largely an idea that the administration was pushing, but there was some degree of enthusiasm among staff at the beginning, which rather quickly got frittered away. The external consultant who was brought in got off to a rocky start; teachers initially thought he was talking down to them. From the very start, many, perhaps most, teachers were visibly uncomfortable with the idea of sharing what they were doing in the classroom. The reexamination of curriculum required dozens of meetings, after school and on weekends, and even the initially enthusiastic became resentful. Some teachers made earnest efforts to coordinate with teachers in other grades but many others didn't, and some of the latter involved cases of preexisting friction among teachers.

Other disagreements started off as curricular—including one between a proponent of whole language in the early grades and a proponent of phonics—but came to take on a personal caste as well, preventing any rational search for compromise. We suspect that when the administration failed to react forcefully to these problems, they sent a message to teachers about just how serious they were. In any case, most teachers seemed to find the whole process pretty abusive (but even so, it was clear that they learned a great deal about what their colleagues were doing; for all the problems, it was a new level of professional dialogue). The fruit of their mighty labor was a sizeable new curriculum handbook, completed just about when the long-festering leadership tensions were coming to a boil. The administrators acted as if the handbook were a great victory; teachers generally shrugged.

With or without a handbook, the school leadership was far too fractured to actually implement anything in the classroom. Assistant principal Johnson was probably the staff member with the most pertinent expertise, but the handbook project was assigned to one of the other assistant principals with whom Johnson was frequently at odds. Mrs. Johnson clearly recognized some problems while they were developing the handbook, but, given her tenuous relationship with the principal and some of her colleagues, she did not feel comfortable about raising issues too forcefully. Whenever she did raise issues, her questions were interpreted as personal attacks, and the other assistant principal countered with a series of optimistic reports that glossed over reality. Eventually, Mrs. Johnson was given more direct responsibility for the project, but the teachers' attitudes were pretty well-hardened by that time. They did not want to hear the phrase "curriculum revision." The very idea of visiting someone else's classrooms was still commonly referred to as "spying." Eight or nine months after the handbook was produced, it appeared that not many teachers could have found a copy of it, much less were they teaching from it. With reasonable leadership, the process might have had a chance of succeeding; other schools got a good deal more out of the process. At Woodbine, the fragile social situation made it impossible for the school to use expertise it actually had on staff.

Curricular revision is one of the most complicated tasks any school can undertake. Naturally, it requires building-level leadership. It is perhaps even more instructive that when Woodbine attempted more modest initiatives, they too frequently floundered on the social infrastructure.

Consider a teacher-initiated attempt to address discipline problems, which grew out of discussions on the Student and Staff Support Team (SSST). Teachers had long complained that the principal's office did not do enough to help them with misbehaving students. Largely at the urging of Mr. Steele, a White fifth-grade teacher, the middle-grade teachers initiated their own discipline policy. Each transgression earned students a certain number of points and as points added up, so did sanctions—loss of in-class privileges, detention, calls to parents, and so on. Maybe it was not the most creative response, but it worked. As long as all teachers were doing it, and kids faced the same rules and punishments in every classroom, classrooms and corridors were noticeably more quiet and referrals to the principal's office were reduced. Most of the changes occurred rapidly, but even the most chronic offenders seemed to improve after a couple of marking periods.

So here was a case where teachers had collectively identified a problem of vital importance to them, collaborated, and had come up with a way to substantially alleviate the problem, which is all perfectly consistent with the SDP model. Naturally, it did not last. It is hard to say exactly when things started falling apart, but it was clear that by the end of the first year, there was less consistency of effort. Mr. Steele, the person most visibly associated with the project, lost some leverage after getting involved in a conflict with the administration that took on a personal tone—such as Steele referring to the main office as "the lunatics." At least one teacher decided to stop using the point system. By the beginning of the next year, there were two nonconformists, one of whom went so far as to complain to the students about the teachers who were enforcing the rules. Her colleagues thought she was trying to win a popularity contest with the kids. Some thought was given to asking the administration to intercede to get everyone back following the same discipline policy, but the teachers decided that there was no purpose in that. Their thinking may have been affected by the fact that one of the nonconformists was widely perceived to be among the principal's pets. The program just kind of withered away, as teachers gradually tired of beating their heads against the wall. Midway through the second year, only a few classrooms were even trying.

We cannot be entirely certain what was happening at the level of individual teacher motivation, but outwardly we seem to have an inability to sustain minimally cooperative relationships, even when all involved seemed to have been profiting from them, an apparent absence of professional respect and of confidence in the ability of the administration to behave impartially. Teachers can sometimes craft a small victory but holding on to it takes more social capital than they have.

It would be an error to think of these problems as specific to the individuals involved. If only this particular teacher did not get into a dispute with this particular principal, maybe things would have worked out. In fact, the likelihood is that if that had not happened, something else would have. In the inner city, hostility can become structural. Put underprepared people in a highly stressful, underresourced, stigmatized environment where no one seems to be in control, where class and racial tensions are ever present, and you create an environment where dysfunctional relationships become as much a part of the social landscape as graffiti.[3] At Woodbine, that means that even with a staff that decidedly has not given up, they still do not have the social and organizational capital that will allow them to keep even simple innovations in place, even when the staff have ownership over the innovations.

With a variation here or there, what we saw at Woodbine—a distrust and a lack of confidence in one's colleagues that undermines reform efforts—has been acted out across the city. One study from the Consortium on Chicago School Research used a survey of teachers at 210 schools in an attempt to identify those characteristics shared by schools that are getting better. When the 30 highest-rated schools were compared to the 30 worst, a 13-item battery of questions about quality of relationships proved to be one of the best separators. Teachers almost unanimously agreed that relationships with their colleagues were cordial but that did not mean there was much respect or trust among them. Forty percent of teachers disagreed with the statement, "Teachers in this school trust each other." How teachers in a given school felt about that correlated very well with whether the school was improving or stagnating.

Social trust is a highly significant factor. In fact, it may well be that social trust is the key factor associated with improving schools. Teachers in the top 30 schools generally sense a great deal of respect from other teachers, indicating that they respect other teachers who take the lead in school improvement efforts and feel comfortable expressing their worries and concerns with colleagues. In contrast, in the bottom 30 schools, teachers explicitly state that they do not trust each other. They believe that only half of the teachers in the school really care about each other and they perceive limited respect from their colleagues (Sebring, Bryk, & Easton, 1995, p. 61).

In a very important update (Bryk & Schneider, in press) to this work, the Consortium has determined that if a low-achieving elementary school had relatively strong levels of social trust in 1994, it had a one in two chance of being among the city's most strongly improving schools by 1997. Schools with weak levels of trust in 1994 stood only one chance in seven of being among the improving schools in 1997. The strong relationships between trust levels and school outcomes hold even when several aspects of school context and staff composition student body have been controlled.

During the past three decades, ethnographic work has detailed how social demoralization undermines schools (Leacock, 1969; Rogers, 1969; Rosenfeld, 1971; Gouldner, 1978; Anyon, 1995). A new body of work emerging from the Consortium changes the conversation by giving us compelling evidence about the size of the potential impact of social factors. Had policy makers and practitioners been as clear about this social demoralization as they should have been, we can envision a national discussion very different from the one we have had during the past decade. We could envision a discussion in which structural arrangements were not treated as reforms in themselves. Consider the way that in the late 1980s and early 1990s some people were clearly overselling the impact of reforming decision-making structures. In retrospect, it is clear that while there is a relationship between changing structures of power and improving education, it is not necessarily a direct or reliable one (Conley, 1991; Malen, Ogawa, & Kranz, 1992; Weiss, Cambone, & Wyeth, 1992; Weiss, 1993; Easton & Storey, 1994; Wohlstetter & Mohrman, 1994), and that part of the problem is that some of the constituencies to which authority is being formally extended, teachers and parents in particular, do not have the social capital, including the self-confidence, to take full advantage of the formal changes.

If we had been taking the demoralized state of schools more seriously, we might have had a different debate between proponents of constructivist, open-ended, inquiry-based pedagogy and those of traditional, skills-centered, teacher-driven pedagogy (Delpit, 1988; Gibboney, 1994). Much of that debate has being waged in the abstract. Which way is better? That is a poor question. A better question would be, in demoralized social environments, what is required to implement either model well?

We might also envision a discussion in which we were far more cautious about the pace and scale of change. The mammoth attempt of the National Science Foundation to reform math and science teaching in this country during the 1990s is one case where we might wonder whether a more modest pace of change would have been better suited to the more troubled schools. Locally, it is sometimes well-meaning foundations pushing the pace. Comer wanted to start off in Chicago with just two schools. Local foundations in the city wanted him to start with 16. The compromise reached was that the program started with four schools the first year and added four more the second year, which in retrospect was not an advisable pace. They were moving into new schools before they had a handle on what was going on in their old ones.

Ironically, there are reasons to wonder if even the national Comer project is not growing too rapidly. As we noted earlier, between 1990 and 2000, the program ballooned from about 100 schools to around 700. The very pace of growth suggests questions about whether the small national staff can adequately monitor the degree to which individual projects continue to focus on relationships. In the absence of some such monitoring, growth pressures could easily undermine part of what has made the program distinctive over the years—its relentless insistence on the centrality of social trust and mutual confidence in the change process.

Comer has always seen issues of relationships as intertwined with those of leadership. "The paralysis of power," he wrote, "was the most pervasive and troublesome problem we had to address" (Comer, 1980, p. 18). When the SDP process is well implemented, it rebuilds the social and organizational infrastructure through which leadership can operate. In Chicago, addressing leadership issues, directly or indirectly, accounted for the bulk of facilitators' time in the early years of implementation. When the work takes, it seems to affect leadership in at least three ways: it creates a larger leadership pool, it changes the operating style of leadership, and it changes a school's receptivity to leadership.[4]

SDP AS A LEADERSHIP MODEL: DEVELOPING MULTIPLE LEADERSHIP

The complexity of the problems in inner-city schools should make us skeptical of the notion that any one person can provide all the leadership required for deep and lasting change. In the case of SDP, of course, the addition of a facilitator changes the amount of available leadership right away—one more person to see that things do not fall through the cracks, to lend a hand in crisis situations, to keep everybody else focused; one person who is supposed to think strategically in a situation where other leaders are often too busy to think past the crisis of the moment. In effect, schools are adding a high-caliber, part-time assistant principal, one whose "presence, involvement and constant persistence," to use the words of one teacher, can eventually draw out the best in other staff. Getting to the point where facilitators can make their contribution is far from automatic, however. Principals—despite the fact that they asked for the program—often experience the presence of a facilitator as an incursion on principal prerogatives. A number of principals now say they would have fired their facilitator outright had they been able to. (Chicago facilitators are employed by Youth Guidance, a social work agency.) Assistant principals are very likely to feel threatened by what looks like competition. Teachers juggling 30 children all day may resent having another professional in the building who makes no immediate, visible contribution to improve the work lives of teachers. Understaffed principals may try to throw the facilitator at pressing needs—disciplinarian, hall monitor, bus monitor, social worker—rather than letting him or her facilitate. Feeling a need to prove themselves to skeptical audiences, facilitators may slide into doing the Comer program themselves rather than taking the necessarily slower road of developing the capacity of each building to do it. (Make all phone calls for the parent meeting, type flyers, mail flyers, arrange the room, remind some teachers to come, prepare the agenda, type it, prep the parent leaders before the meeting, debrief them after, clean up, listen to gripes about how things should have been done differently.)

Nevertheless, in most schools facilitators were able to work through the period of rejection and carve out a very central role for themselves. They did this in part through an arduous process of relationship-building. The same question about expansion that hangs over the national Comer project hangs over the Chicago project. As the program expands, spreading facilitators over more and more schools—Chicago is now up to 21 schools with barely more facilitator-time than when it had 12—it is not clear that there is still time for the intense relationship work that characterized the earlier implementations.

At the beginning of the process, most Comer principals were working inhuman hours. When asked why they did not delegate more, the nearly universal answer was that they had tried that but their staffs had repeatedly let them down. Some principals originally saw the Comer process as a parent involvement process and bought into it largely for that reason. In the event, what most of them found was that the process gave them a carefully articulated structure for identifying and in the grooming leadership. This has been one of the most widespread impacts and in the long term it may prove to be the single most important program impact. In eight, arguably nine, of the first 11 schools, there are significantly more people regularly taking on leadership roles and getting more support from colleagues and their principals than was the case when they came into the program. In several schools, before the SDP, there was no meeting at which a significant part of the professional staff interacted regularly, not even staff meetings.

Principals delegated only to the "faithful few," a pattern that generated resentment among other staff, who understood that they were being judged and found wanting. The Comer teams and the constituency group structure gave some teachers a chance to show what they could do if given a chance and it has made a difference in the way principals operate:

> Mr. Hudson used to hate to see me coming [because I asked him to do so many things]. Now, it's gone completely over to the other side. He will never admit it but I think he feels pushed aside by the Young Turks doing all the things he and I used to have to do by ourselves.

> What's ironic is that some of the people who were very vocal and negative about the (Comer) process when it started are the same ones who are providing all the instructional leadership now. I don't have to know every little detail about what is or is not happening in everybody's classroom. All I need to know is that they know.

> Last year, Mrs. Seagraves organized the 8th grade graduation and it didn't come off the way it was supposed to; the kids were running her. She doesn't know it yet, but she's going to get it again this year. . . . There was a time I would have just crossed her off my list and moved on.

As the last comment suggests, some principals—it is not clear how many—are thinking strategically about how to groom leadership. This kind of intentionality about the leadership development process is something the program might want to put a great deal more emphasis on in the future. Getting principals to define their roles more explicitly around leadership development might be one way to get the principals themselves to internalize the Comer principles more rapidly.

PROTECTING THE POWERLESS

In these 11 schools, it was actually parent leadership that normally took off first, partly because there was so little of it to begin with, partly because parent teams were the constituency least resistant to facilitators at first. As parents organized themselves together, they enriched the after-school offerings of their schools, improved security, helped control the mayhem in the halls and play areas, and, ironically, frequently increased tension between themselves and the schools' professional staff. When principals and teachers ask for more parental participation, they do not mean organized, assertive parents, one of the things suggesting that school climates were not changing as broadly as one would wish. Some schools made a practice of having teachers attend parent meetings, which usually seemed to reduce frictions.

Just as facilitators have to fight for the space to do their jobs as facilitators, they have to fight for the right of other people to lead. Principals in high-stress schools tend to squash potential leadership in order to maintain control. Facilitators become privy to the school's hidden transcript, all the things people would like to say but do not, given power imbalances. In a variety of ways, facilitators make the hidden transcript a part of the public discourse, literally giving voice to the voiceless. In the most dramatic cases, things come down to an open confrontation between facilitator and principal in a School Planning and Management Team (SPMT) meeting. As facilitators continually take on the role of protector of the weaker party—insisting that teachers listen respectfully to parents, that principals acknowledge the right of teachers to professional disagreement, that everybody treat nonprofessional staff as partners in the enterprise—even teachers who do not like the program itself come to think of having the facilitator in the building as an advantage. People begin coming to the facilitator asking him or her to see that sensitive points get raised in meetings. It typically takes longer for principals to fully appreciate that a more open process operates to their long-term advantage, but it happened in most schools to some degree.

The significance of the buffering role played by facilitators is illustrated by what happened when Youth Guidance (YG) had to reduce facilitator time in some buildings. Under the terms of their funding, YG was expected to expand the program at a certain rate. In order to do that, they decided that, beginning with the 1993–1994 school year, facilitators would have their time in the first eight schools reduced to a day or a day and a half a week. Primary responsibility for the integrity of the Comer process in the first eight schools was shifted to in-house facilitators, regular members of the school staff. Despite the fact that most of the in-house facilitators were respected members of the staff, the process did not work, with the arguable exception of one school. There were three widespread complaints about in-house facilitators—they were not perceived as neutral parties in factional warfare, they were not seen as having the conflict mediation skills the YG facilitators had, and teachers did not think that in-house facilitators could protect them from the principal. Teachers felt betrayed and exposed. The process had encouraged them to be more open, to be more aggressive in expressing their feelings, and now they were being left to take the resultant heat by themselves. In their forthcoming study, Byrk and Schneider argue that reducing the vulnerability of staff is one of the most important ways to increase trust levels. When they were in position to act as buffer between principals and staff, Comer facilitators were doing exactly that.

CHANGING LEADERSHIP STYLE

The SDP process dictates a certain style of leadership—collaborative, non-blaming, and power-sharing. Over the course of the study, perhaps nine of the 11 principals made significant moves in that direction. In two schools, even more information-sharing, which seemed to be the lowest level of change, did not seem to take place on a reliable basis. Some schools came into the program with autocratic but respected principals and were essentially well organized, but all substantive decisions were made by a handful of people. The task of the program in these schools was to get leadership to become more inclusive, less reactive/punitive, and more developmental in its approach to staff. Principals at these schools were still autocratic in some respects, but they had greatly increased the areas in which they were willing to accept input from and leadership in others. They were also much more willing to accept critical thinking from their staff, which greatly improved the capacity of these schools to do self-assessment, a large step in the direction of developing a genuinely professional culture. The result was that a lot more got done in these schools. These were the schools that took off first and that have consistently posted the greatest academic and social gains by almost every measure. It should not be surprising that the program seemed to do best when there were already some leadership resources to build on.

Most of the other schools had significant organizational problems. Leadership was autocratic or laissez-faire or a shifting combination of the two, but whatever the leadership style, principals and staff were seldom working together. Principals were not very respected or, if they were, they were stalemated by factions or by strong negative norms among the staff. In these schools, it was necessary to get principals to become more organized and inclusive, but also to help them negotiate open resistance and maintain a focus on the school's larger vision rather than just responding to the crisis of the day.

No matter where they started, it normally took principals considerable time to get comfortable with the Comer leadership style. Even in some of the stronger schools, principals were still struggling with the Comer style, even in cases where principals were talking the language of inclusive leadership before the program began. Experiences varied greatly, but generally it took most principals up to two years to "walk the walk," to use a phrase much used by facilitators. What happens in the meantime, as we have seen at Woodbine, is that principals find various ways to hold on to power—such as not holding SPMT meetings as scheduled, dominating the discussion when they are held, and making sure the right people are on key committees and so forth.

We suggested in the discussion of Mrs. Smith that it may be particularly difficult for people in high-stress, low-resource environments to abandon the only source of stability they know, centralized power in this case. There is more to it than that, though. Comer was an early advocate of facilitative, inclusive leadership, but in recent decades it has become a kind of orthodoxy, the main model of leadership-advocated principal leadership programs and researchers. Here again, the model is usually offered without any consideration of the particular realities of urban schools. Principals have to know that simply sharing power means over the short term that they will still have a lot of distrustful and angry teachers, but now those people are going to have power. They have to know that they have some staff who have essentially given up and nothing will move them except the fear of sanctions from above. Power sharing in such environments has to be a carefully negotiated process, one in which principals often cannot possibly know what to expect until it happens, so they err on one side today and the other tomorrow.

What the Chicago principals have done is create something that might be called domain autocracy (or domain democracy, if you will). They have developed broad-based processes for developing school improvement plans, often involving all professional staff. Most principals have ceded substantial authority over the school budget (a move that often impresses even the more skeptical teachers) and more than half have developed hiring practices that give faculty a large voice in shaping the staff. They have given teachers much more voice in curricular planning and in developing appropriate staff development plans. Nevertheless, they make it quite clear that they as principals retain certain prerogatives, often in any area that involves relations with the board of education or with parents or with respect to anything that touches on public relations. The most successful of them, as judged by academic progress, can be quite ruthless about putting pressure on teachers deemed low performing. They have opened up their schools considerably, but there is no doubt about who is in charge.

The process takes its toll on principals, but the Comer program also offers them a measure of support. Some of that support comes directly from the facilitator giving on-going encouragement, but some support comes from the more-or-less monthly principal meetings. These meetings received mixed reviews in the program's early years. Participating principals have always said that the meetings were valuable as one of the few avenues of collegial exchange open to them. This was especially the case a few years ago when city policies seemed to be changing almost weekly, and some principals had information about those changes that they could share with others. At the same time, though, there was originally a kind of competitiveness among principals that prevented them from talking honestly about some of the problems they were having and their own personal struggles. In recent years, principals have been much more open about those sorts of issues, and, for some of them, the meetings have come to function as a source of emotional support.

RECEPTIVITY TO LEADERSHIP

We ordinarily think of leadership as a characteristic of individuals, but organizational context can impede it or facilitate it, even when individuals are willing and capable. Consider one ethnographer's description of a year-end meeting at her school. The meeting, she writes,

> was one of the most productive, substantive discussions regarding curriculum and instruction that I had ever heard at the SPMT level. What was most striking about the discussion was not necessarily the content, but the level of engagement and the openness of the discussion. (The content itself was also interesting: How do we meet the needs of our high achieving students so that we don't lose them to other schools? Should we use a period of the day on Fridays to set up special programs, clubs, tutorials, accelerated classes, etc.?) There was some tension around whose needs were more important, i.e., "at-risk" students or high achieving students. This was not resolved, but people were willing to share openly. It appeared as though there was a decent level of trust among members. People were taking risks. Emotions were running high, but people appeared to be really listening to each other and respecting the contributions people, including parents, were making to the discussion. [The principal] was very much a part of the discussion, but she did not dominate (which is an improvement considering [the principal's] typical MO was dominate or disengage). . . . We did a time check around 4:30 p.m. and people decided they wanted to continue the discussion. They were truly engaged. Perhaps more importantly, there was a sense that what they were saying mattered—there was a sense of empowerment that I had only caught glimpses of in previous meetings. I don't know if this was a "last meeting of the year" phenomena or what, but it was a powerful meeting.

> In terms of Comer's impact in the building, I am convinced that this kind of discussion, with all stakeholders participating, could not have happened without using the process—over the years—to get to this level of functioning. I realize that the process is not linear and I am not sure how the SPMT began this year, but the fact that teachers, administrators, and parents were able to engage in meaningful discussions, openly and respectfully disagree, and debate about what was best for children with regard to curriculum and instruction, indicates a major accomplishment. . . . I was literally flashing back to all of the discussions, team building, relationship building, encouraging, coercing, tears, facilitating, and modeling that had taken place over FOUR YEARS to bring about this type of meeting.

At the same time the project is directly trying to stimulate more and better leadership, it is also working to create a climate that is more receptive to leadership irrespective of its source. In a climate characterized by engagement, openness, and respectful disagreement, leadership is more likely to have an impact. On the other hand, in the school described above, and in many others, we see these traits most clearly among people who have served on school teams, not among the general staff. Still, even that seems to be enough to increase organizational capacity.

And how did Woodbine do? The ethnographer quoted above was describing Woodbine. As she suspected, the process did slip back somewhat the following fall. However, many staff members at the school continued to feel that they could participate in discussions about the school's direction while tolerating, more or less, the right of others to disagree. After the curriculum alignment experience, the school lost some strong teachers, some of whom were clearly looking for a more supportive environment. It was, however, able to replace them with strong teachers, partly because Mrs. Smith increasingly handed the hiring function over to teachers.

That impressive curriculum handbook developed during Woodbine's alignment process may never be used, but veteran teachers still see the effort as a watershed in the school's professional development. It marked the first time Woodbine's teachers had a sustained dialogue about their work. The relationships formed in the process survived the curriculum handbook's eventual failure. Afterwards, there was more discussion and collaboration across grades and within grades, which led to some innovations in teaching reading, social studies, and science particularly. Mrs. Smith no longer tried to closely manage the professional conversation among teachers; that responsibility rested in the hands of various people, easily eight or nine of them, who were formal or informal leaders of various curricular components. Parents made a substantial contribution to reducing some of the disorderly behavior, and the SSST, with ample funding from Mrs. Smith, was able to coordinate a much more intensive delivery of social service support for the most troubled children and their families. The principal still occasionally reverted to her old authoritative style, but less frequently. As the school improved, she lost that sense of being besieged on all sides, which probably accounted for her slightly increased openness. Nevertheless, there were veteran teachers who said they could not forget the old manipulative, head-strong Mrs. Smith and expected her to reappear the moment there was a crisis. Problems of trust continued, then, but the school was stumbling forward nonetheless. The percentage of students meeting national norms in reading scores went from the midteens at the beginning of the decade to the mid-thirties at the end.

The story of Woodbine School, and the larger story of the development of leadership in the Chicago Comer project, then can be viewed either optimistically or pessimistically. The optimistic view is that leadership can create momentum even in environments that seem initially hopelessly and irrationally dysfunctional. A grimmer view is that the kind of support needed to enable leadership in our most troubled schools goes well beyond what is being discussed at the national level. Certainly, there is growing skepticism about principal leadership programs that pull principals out of their school environments, expose them to the gospel of facilitative leadership, and then send them back to the same troubled environments with no support. However, there seems to be little discussion about where principals can get the resources to do better. We continued doing "drive-by" professional development for teachers decades after we knew it was nearly worthless. Perhaps the cycle is beginning anew, with the development of a succession of glitzy leadership programs for urban principals that may be fine in some abstract sense but that do not give principals the kind of sustained, multifaceted support they need to work in the most challenged schools. The Chicago Comer experience suggests that if principals can get the right support, many of them can take the first step to turning a school around.

REFERENCES

Anyon, J. (1995). Race, social class and educational reform in an inner-city school. *Teachers College Record, 97,* 69–94.

Ball, S. J. (1987). *The micropolitics of the school: Towards a theory of school organization.* London: Methuen.

Bryk, A., Easton, J., Kerbow, D., Rollow, S., & Sebring, P. (1993). *A view from the elementary schools: The state of reform in Chicago.* Chicago: Consortium on Chicago School Research.

Bryk, A., & Schenider, B. (In Press). *Relational trust: A core resource for school improvement.* New York: Russell Sage.

Comer, J. (1980). *School power.* New York: Free Press.

Comer, J. (1989). Child development and education. *Journal of Negro Education, 58,* 125–139.

Comer, J., Haynes, N., Joyner, E., Ben-Avie, M. (Eds.). (1996). *Rallying the whole village: The Comer process for reforming education.* New York: Teachers College Press.

Conley, S. (1991). Review of research on teacher participation in school decision making. In G. Grant (Ed.), *Review of research in education* (pp. 225–266). Washington, DC: American Educational Research Association.

Cook, T. D., Murphy, R. F., & Hunt, H. D. (2000). Comer's school development program in Chicago: A theory-based evaluation. *American Educational Research Journal, 37,* 535–597.

Delpit, L. (1988). The silenced dialogue: power and pedagogy in educating other people's children. *Harvard Education Review, 58,* 280–298.

Easton, J., & Storey, S. (1994). The development of local school councils. *Education and Urban Society, 26,* 220–237.

Gibboney, R. (1994*). The stone trumpet: A story of practical school reform.* Albany: SUNY Press.

Gouldner, H. (1978). *Teachers' pets, troublemakers and nobodies.* Westport, CT: Greenwood.

Haynes, N., & Comer, J. (1993). The Yale school development program. *Urban Education, 28,* 166–199.

Leacock, E. (1969). *Teaching and learning in city schools.* New York: Basic Books.

Malen, B., Ogawa, R., & Kranz, J. (1992). What do we know about school-based management? A case study of the literature—A call for research. In

W. Clune & J. Witte (Eds.), *Choice and control in American education* (pp. 289–342). New York: Fulmer.

Rogers, D. (1969). *110 Livingston street: Publics and bureaucracies in the New York City school system.* New York: Vintage.

Rosenfeld, G. (1971). *Shut those thick lips: A study of slum school failure.* New York: Holt, Rinehart & Winston.

Sebring, P., Byrk, A., & Easton, J. (1995). *Charting reform: Chicago teachers take stock.* Chicago: Consortium on Chicago School Research.

SERVE. (1994). *Overcoming barriers to school reform in the Southeast.* Greensboro, NC: Southeastern Regional Vision for Education.

Weiss, C. (1993). Shared decision-making about what?: A comparison of schools with and without teacher participation. *Teachers College Record, 95,* 69–92.

Weiss, C., Cambone, J., & Wyeth, A. (1992). Trouble in paradise. *Educational Administration, 28,* 350–367.

Wohlstetter, P., & Mohrman, S. (1994) *School-based management: Promise and process,* New Brunswick, NJ: Consortium for Policy Research in Education.

NOTES

1. In order to protect their anonymity, I have changed some details about schools and their staffs.

2. I am grateful to Michelle Adler, Chicago Comer facilitator, for the title story. The research upon which this chapter is based has been supported by the John D. and Catherine T. MacArthur Foundation, the Joyce Foundation, and the Spencer Foundation.

3. What proportion of big city schools are characterized by weak social infrastructure? In Chicago, one Consortium study finds that after three full years of reform, 39% to 46% of the city's schools were characterized by a consolidation of power in the principal's hands and another 4% to 9% were seen as dominated by adversial politics (Bryk, Easton, Kerbow, Rollow, & Sebring, 1993). So we might say that 43% to 55 % of the schools have the kind of internal power structures likely to be associated with distrustful, suspicious relationships—trust being a luxury the powerless cannot easily afford. (Principal autocracy can be viewed as legitimate; it seems a safe bet that inner-city schools are more likely to see the illegitimate versions.) Another study finds 42% of Chicago teachers seeing themselves as having only limited or minimal influence in school affairs (Sebring, Bryk, & Easton, 1995). This is all very, indirect but guessing that at least a third of Chicago's schools have social infrastructures that will frustrate reform attempts is probably safe. While these problems may find particularly sharp expression in the cities, they exist in less urbanized areas as well. One study of the slow pace of school reform in the Southeast concluded that the major barriers included the instability of leadership, the start-and-stop nature of reforms, the inability to reach consensus on goals, under-investment in training, and a pervasive lack of trust, all breeding cynicism and a "them against us" mentality (SERVE, 1994).

4. From an ethnographic standpoint, we can make a much stronger case that these schools changed organizationally, particularly in terms of leadership, than that they changed in terms of social climate. We find clear evidence of some attitudinal changes, but in private, professional staff continue to express strong

negative attitudes toward parents and children in private settings. This is not exactly consonant with existing Comer theory; it may be, however, that Chicago schools were initially more troubled than some of the schools in which the Comer process worked in earlier years, sufficiently troubled that just some organizational development was enough to produce some of the positive outcomes that elsewhere are associated with change in the social climate. More, it may be that unless schools are at some threshold level of development as organizations, improvements in social climate can't take. At some point a symbiotic relationship develops.

PART V

Conclusion

CHAPTER TWELVE

Leadership Lessons From Comprehensive School Reform Designs

JOSEPH MURPHY AND AMANDA DATNOW

As expected, many factors influence the level of implementation of CSR models and the different analyses identified similar conditions leading to higher levels of implementation. District, principal, and teacher leadership ranked high on this list of factors. (Berends, Bodilly, & Kirby, chapter 6 this volume)

In this concluding chapter, we weave together a tapestry of leadership in comprehensive school reform (CSR) designs. We explore the contributions of principals, teachers, and personnel at the district office, paying particular attention to alignment and overlap. In addition, we comment on how this information is deepening our understanding of the larger body of leadership theory and practice. Throughout the review, we emphasize the relationship between leadership and school reform. In the second half of the chapter, we provide some final insights about what we learned in the CSR analysis, noting especially unexpected findings. While our attention is directed first to the work of colleagues in this volume, we also rely on our previous theoretical and empirical work in the areas of school improvement and educational leadership.

During the past 20-plus years, we have learned a good deal about leadership. On one side of the equation we have discovered—or relearned—that leadership is important. Leadership, especially by those in formal positions, has been linked to a nearly endless list of school process and outcomes: successful change (Fullan, 1991); school improvement (Leithwood, 2002); overall school effectiveness (Teddlie & Reynolds, 2000); effective elementary (Beck & Murphy, 1996) and effective secondary schools (Murphy, Beck, Crawford, Hodges, & McGaughy, 2001); effective urban education (Johnston, 2001); school climate (Brookover, Beady, Flood, Schweitzer, & Wisenbaker, 1979; Smith & Muth, 1985); effective administration and management of schools (see Cotton & Savard, 1980 for review); successful implementation of new school programs (Berends, Bodily, Kirby, chapter 6 this volume; Hall, Hord, Huling, Rutherford, & Stiegelbauer, 1985); higher staff trust, stability, motivation, and job satisfaction (Smith & Muth, 1985; Viadero, 2001); and the effectiveness of specific institutional subsystems such as school discipline (Lasley & Wayson, 1982); professional development (Elmore, 1996; Little, 1982); and targeted instructional programs such as bilingual programs (Carter & Maestas, 1982), magnet schools (Blank, 1986), mathematics and science programs (Spade, Van Fossen & Jones, 1985), and literacy programs (see Murphy, 2001 for review).

On the other side of the equation, our knowledge of leadership is deepening. We understand more about what it means to lead than we did at the end of the intensification era (see Murphy, 1988; 1990 for reviews) or the restructuring era (see Murphy, 1994 for a review).

The authors of this volume, and others who work in and study CSR, reaffirm the first point above over and over again: leadership is crucial. More importantly, however, they enrich our understanding of leadership. In this chapter, we begin by exploring their ideas about leadership at three levels: the principal, the teacher, and the superintendent (district office). We then turn our attention to the insights from our analysis.

PRINCIPAL LEADERSHIP

The likelihood of project success tends to rest with the principal. (Anderson & Shirley, 1995, p. 421)

Our study strongly indicates that principal leadership matters in promoting school development and it matters a lot. (Smylie, Wenzel, & Fendt, chapter 7 this volume)

In our analysis of longitudinal data for schools implementing NAS designs four years into scale-up, we found that principal leadership was the single most important predictor of teacher reported implementation level, both at the teacher level and the school level. (Berends, Bodilly, & Kirby, chapter 6 this volume)

As we documented above, almost all the literature on school reform, educational change, and school improvement exposes the "essential" (Hall & Placier, chapter 10 this volume) or "crucial" (Copland, chapter 8 this volume) role played by the school principal (Teddlie & Reynolds, 2000). Thus it is hardly surprising that research on CSR in general and the studies in this volume conclude that there is a linkage between principal leadership and successful reform implementation. What is noteworthy is the ways that these chapters deepen our understanding of the complex and nuanced construct of principal leadership. We provide some examples of that leadership in this section, focusing exclusively on those areas where principals are in a unique position to mediate success.

One of the most visible patterns in the mosaic provided by these chapters features the importance of the principal in bringing a reform design to the school, even when the initial impetus might come from the district (as was true in some Success for All (SFA) cases) or from teachers (as was true in the Coalition of Essentials of Schools (CES) case). At the most elementary level, principals are the gatekeepers for their schools' change efforts. They can either "open the door" (Hall & Placier, chapter 10 this volume) to reform initiatives or block their entry. And, as Berends and his colleagues (chapter 6 this volume) reveal, principals can "ensure a well-informed selection process" or prevent one from being engaged. Most tellingly, there is a strong connection between the proactive work of the principal and the acceptance of a reform among the staff. Where principals act as "catalysts for change" (Copland, chapter 8 this volume) and have a personal "commitment to the project" (Finnan & Meza, chapter 5 this volume), reform designs have a fighting chance to succeed. Absent these, no matter how fervently others may desire change, implementation of an innovation is problematic at best.

Once a reform design enters the school, the principal's actions are influential in determining the reception it receives and whether it flourishes or atrophies, or as Datnow and Castellano (chapter 9 this volume) chronicle, "the role of the principal as an active and ongoing supporter of reform is critical to the success of a schoolwide change effort"—he or she is "often at the heart of successful deployment activity" (Smylie, Wenzel, & Fendt, chapter 7 this volume). Principals furnish support in a tangible way by helping build the planks of an effective organization, foundations that are beyond the power of individual teachers to construct. A good part of this scaffolding work is "creating conditions that encourage change" (Finnan & Meza, chapter 5 this volume). The balance is helping staff succeed in their collective efforts. Underlying it all in successful reform endeavors is a platform of trust.

In these case studies, we saw that principals were uniquely positioned to address the issue of resources required to fuel school reform. And, as a number of the chapters in this volume revealed (e.g. Kilgore & Jones; Berends, Bodilly, & Kirby; Smylie, Wenzel, & Fendt), schools that were more effective in implementing reform blueprints had principals who were more productive in garnering such resources. It is also clear that because of their "roles" these principals held power to: (a) shape the process by which others constructed meaning around the reform initiatives; (b) mediate between the expectations of the reform designs and the demands of the system around the classroom, especially reform press from the state and the district (see also Portin et al., in press); and (c) buffer "their schools from external distractions and interference" (Smylie, Wenzel, & Fendt, chapter 7 this volume).

It is perhaps a bit paradoxical but, as these cases demonstrate, it is the principal who occupies the position to bring teacher leadership to life. Also noteworthy is the conclusion that the robustness and viability of distributed leadership is "dependent on the support and direction of the principal" (Kilgore & Jones, chapter 3 this volume). Equally important, we learn that successful reform implementation is linked to the capacity of the principal to create a dense leadership organization, or as Copland (chapter 8 this volume) captures it, "the distributed leadership functions across a school . . . can provide the capacity, coherence, and ownership needed to sustain deeper reform."

We unpack the concept and practice of leadership density or distributed leadership in the next section. Here the spotlight is on the role of the principal in bringing the idea to life. What the empirical stories in this volume help us discern is that principals in schools that are successfully implementing reform are building dense leadership organizations less through the restructuring-era strategy of delegating authority and more through practices that help forge "communities of professional practice" (Goldberg & Morrison, chapter 4 this volume). Principals work to "broaden and deepen leadership" (Copland, chapter 8 this volume) by: (a) refining their own collaborative skills; (b) developing "leadership capacity" (Smylie, Wenzel, & Fendt, chapter 7 this volume) in teachers; (c) marshaling resources to support the formation, growth, and functioning of a professional community; (d) instilling teachers with the confidence that enriches their own feelings of efficacy; and (e) carefully managing the "leadership work" (Smylie, Wenzel, & Fendt, chapter 7 this volume) of the community (see also Riehl, 2000).

Finally, principals in schools that were experiencing success in implementing CSR blueprints in these cases took advantage of the unique opportunities that they enjoyed to glue together their organizations. They appear to emphasize two dimensions of this sense shaping work: They exercise stewardship for the vision and they weave the threads of coherence throughout the school and the reform work. On the first front, "clear sense of purpose" (Goldberg & Morrison, chapter 4 this volume), they "bring a unified sense of vision to the school and staff" (Berends, Bodilly, & Kirby, chapter 6 this volume). They act aggressively to help their colleagues see the sense of the possibilities attached to reform. They also act as "keepers of the vision" (Datnow & Castellano, chapter 9 this volume). They protect the reform architecture from attack, both from those inside the school and from external forces.

On the second front, principals help glue together the organization by promoting coherence throughout the school—a variable, as we saw above, identified as critical to reform success as early as the first effective schools studies. For principals in the cases in this volume, nurturing coherence includes: (a) actively helping staff see linkages among activities and functions; (b) wiring together goals, budgets, curriculum, instruction, and staff development; (c) promoting staff stability; (d) carefully nesting the reform design into extant school systems; (e) damping down external stimuli and work demands that compete with core activities; (f) identifying and legitimizing the abandonment of requirements that run at cross purposes to reform goals; (g) linking teachers into a community of practice; (h) aligning the pursuit and use of resources with the reform blueprint; and (i) forging teacher leadership around core purposes.

TEACHER LEADERSHIP

> For schools to have leadership, they need leaders—not a single leader. (Donaldson, 2001, p. x)

> Viewing leadership as practices distributed among leaders, followers, and the situation is more compatible with changing culture than other ways of viewing leadership. (Finnan & Meza, chapter 5 this volume)

> Findings suggest that broad-based leadership structures are linked with a school culture that supports reform work. (Copland, chapter 8 this volume)

It is probably accurate to claim that the most significant contributions to the general body of leadership provided by the cases in this volume can be traced to their treatment of teacher leadership and their examination of distributed leadership. To begin with, these chapters help us see that more diverse, nontraditional leadership structures are associated with successful reform implementation—or more specifically, that "the strength and breadth of leadership distinguish[es] more highly developed and developing schools from nondeveloping ones" (Smylie, Wenzel, & Fendt, chapter 7 this volume) and that "without willing and able teachers who embrace reform and provide the necessary leadership, no reform can be enacted, no matter how effective it may be" (Berends, Bodilly, & Kirby, chapter 6 this volume). Second, and in considerably more detail than they explore implementation, chapter authors portray the range of alternative leadership structures that nest within the concept of leadership density and present some tentative insights about the strengths and weaknesses of some of the various forms of distributed leadership. It is this landscape-shaping work that occupies most of our attention in this section.

At the core of many of these chapters is a conception of "leadership less dependent on the actions of singular visionary individuals, but rather one that views leadership as a set of functions or qualities shared across a much broader segment of the community" (Copland, chapter 8 this volume). Across these chapters, there emerges a perspective on leadership that meshes nicely with the seminal contributions of Sergiovanni (1992a; 1992b) on "leadership density" and Spillane and his colleagues (n.d.; 2000) on "distributed leadership"—views that maintain that "school leadership practice is constituted in the dynamic interaction of multiple leaders (and followers) and their situation around particular leadership tasks" (Spillane, Halverson, & Diamond, n.d., p. 6).

On one dimension, these chapters represent a body of research that explores structures that decouple leadership from traditional leadership roles, for example, the principalship. The designs presented herein carry us away from individual, administratively anchored models of leadership, thereby spotlighting the roles played by other key actors, especially teachers. Interventions in this dimension cluster around three strategies, the first two of which continue to feature positions or roles within the new architecture of leadership functions or tasks.

First, these chapters reveal that leadership density can be promoted by distributing existing leadership tasks to others besides the school principal. For example, administratively anchored curriculum responsibilities can be partitioned out to curriculum leaders at each grade level. Second, leadership density can also be nurtured by establishing new leadership roles. For example, the SFA design and both of the Annenberg initiatives expand current roles by employing site-based facilitators or coordinators, an approach that has been linked to "growth in overall school leadership" (Smylie, Wenzel, & Fendt, chapter 7 this volume) and to more successful reform implementation. Finally, density can be advanced not through attempts to divide functions but by creating teams that collectively engage leadership assignments. This approach was highlighted in many of the chapters in this volume, for example the use of school-based leadership teams and task forces in SFA and Modern Red SchoolHouse.

On a deeper dimension, these narratives reflect efforts to "move past the idea of . . . leadership positions to more dynamic, organizational views of leadership" (Smylie, Conley, & Marks, in press). The portraits in these chapters are consistent with the scholarship of analysts who are currently constructing the knowledge base on distributed leadership. These researchers remind us that "leadership is not a quality with which individuals are imbued or a process that selected individuals conduct with followers" (Donaldson, 2001, p. 40). Rather, "leadership is a relational, not an individual phenomenon" (p. 7).

According to major analysts in this area such as Elmore (1999), "the functions of leadership flow from the expertise required for learning and teaching, not the formal dictates of the institution" (p. 38). While work in the earlier dimension carried us beyond administratively grounded leadership, the lines of work here move us beyond positional conceptions of leadership all together, whether situated with an individual manager or shared by teachers and school administrators. Leadership in this second dimension has less to do with one or more of the boxes on the organizational chart than it does with the dynamics about the boxes. It is less about "locating leadership functions" than it is about "creating networks or webs of leadership." It is less functional and more organic. It is what Spillane and his colleagues (2000) label a "person-plus" perspective on leadership. According to the scholars who are shaping this field, distributed leadership: (a) attends to leadership enacted by both role-based and informal leaders, (b) acknowledges the relational nature of leadership, (c) features the situation in which leadership actions unfold, (d) highlights the organizational quality of leadership, and (e) casts leadership as a collective as well as an individual endeavor (Donaldson, 2001; Elmore, 1999; Pounder, Ogawa, & Adams, 1995; Smylie, Conley, & Marks, 2002; Spillane, Diamond, & Jita, 2000; Spillane, Halverson, & Diamond, n.d.).

Across the chapters in this volume, we see how a functional, relational, organizational, and community conception of leadership is beginning to play out in CSR designs. Most consistently, the roots of this distributed conception of leadership are exposed in efforts to grow communities of professional practice.

DISTRICT LEADERSHIP

> Building supportive conditions at the district level is important to successful implementation and sustainability of whole school reform, particularly when moving from one school to many. (Datnow & Castellano, chapter 9 this volume)

> In short, district-level politics, policies, and practices—in terms of providing organizational, public, and instructional leadership— can promote or derail the effort to transform schools using CSR models. Schools look to district leadership, climate, and regulations to understand if it is worth investing the necessary time and effort to transform themselves. (Berends, Bodilly, & Kirby, chapter 6 this volume)

As we discuss in the final section, we began this review with the assumption that we would have something to say about leadership by actors in four venues outside the schoolhouse—parents (and members of the larger school community), district administrators, unions, and state policy makers. While one develops a sense that state action can facilitate or impede the attractiveness of CSR, and particular CSR designs, the state-level leadership narrative is not well-developed in these chapters. Neither is the theme of parent leadership. And almost no attention is devoted to the role of teacher unions in leading reform. Consequently, we direct our review to leadership at the district office, a leitmotif that is richly integrated into these accounts, and a condition often assorted with stories of successful implementation in the general reform literature (Fullan, 1991; Murphy & Hallinger, 1993).

District leadership seems particularly important in encouraging schools to explore CSR and to adopt reform designs. As analysts from nearly every quadrant of school improvement have observed, principals and teachers pay attention to what is important to the superintendent and other district leaders. When superintendents signal that whole-school reform is valued, they can increase the level of receptivity for change at the school site. When they provide the type of leadership that encourages school faculties to thoughtfully analyze reform designs and assess the match between school needs and reform architecture, they serve as especially effective gatekeepers of reform.

Stability of district leadership has been linked to successful school reform, especially for improvement models that need time to take root and flower. The accounts in these chapters add weight to this finding: stable leadership at the district office, both in terms of personnel and purpose, "is essential to creating supportive conditions for reform" (Datnow & Castellano, chapter 9 this volume). Or, as Berends and his colleagues at RAND (chapter 6 this volume) cast it, "even in districts that provided initial political leadership, the key [is] to sustain . . . commitment over time": "Without continuing support from the top . . . many [CSR] programs tend to wither away" (Viadaro, 2001, p. 25).

District leadership is generally broadcast in terms of providing active support for schools implementing CSR models, that is, building capacity at the school site. It is also, however, a bundle of more nuanced and less visible actions. One of the most critical of these is helping schools see how school-level change efforts nest within the district's goals and the state's reform agenda. Absent this fit, school personnel can easily develop a sense that they are swimming upstream, a sure marker on the path to weak implementation.

Districts also foster CSR by damping down policy noise and reducing reform complexity. Reform work at the school level is difficult enough in its own right. Districts that promote successful implementation are adept at helping schools stay focused on the reform agenda. They labor diligently to filter out distractions and to connect other change initiatives to the whole school reform blueprints. As a variety of the cases in this volume disclose, districts exercise leadership in a related vein by buffering schools from the complexities of turbulent policy environments, especially protecting reform efforts "during periods of transition or crisis" (Datnow & Stringfield, 2000, p. 195).

While the emphasis in the reform literature is often focused on requirements and expectations flowing from districts, the chapters in this volume reveal that leadership is also about providing considerable degrees of freedom to whole-school reform sites to undertake reform work. And as Berends and his colleagues (chapter 6 this volume) in particular help us see, providing autonomy often requires district leaders to peel back confining regulations.

An especially cogent message in these cases is that instability in formal leadership at the school level, especially in the principalship, generally "foretells the demise" (Kilgore & Jones, chapter 3 this volume) of CSR initiatives. These studies consistently conclude that "of all the challenges involved in reform work, schools point to leadership turnover as the most disturbing factor in the support and encouragement of reform" (Copland, chapter 8 this volume). They also divulge something important about district leadership. Where school leadership stability is not on the district radar screen, district leaders are as likely to hinder school improvement efforts as they are to enhance them.

District leaders are also uniquely positioned to provide support to schools engaged in CSR. This support takes a variety of forms in the studies in this volume, and, regardless of form, is consistently linked to successful program implementation. One cluster of activities can be thought of as "direct assistance." Included here are activities such as providing financial resources; insuring budgeting autonomy, including the freedom to reallocate "existing funding streams to support whole school reform" (Berends, Bodilly, & Kirby, chapter 6 this volume); establishing pools of technical assistance, including a pipeline to district resources and linkages to design team staff; and negotiating helpful contracts for design team services. A second cluster of activities enhances local capacity-building strategies, such as supporting the development of communities of practice at the school level and "fostering lateral exchanges across schools" (Datnow & Castellano, chapter 9 this volume).

INSIGHTS AND SUGGESTIONS

In this concluding section, we reflect on some of the insights we culled from these cases of CSR. Based on our analysis, we also offer some suggestions for further exploration and raise some questions that we believe, if addressed, would enrich the literature on leadership in CSR. We point out a few paradoxes with which these cases confront us. We also proffer a couple of caveats.

Insights

On one front, we observe that CSR research is strengthening many of the conclusions about leadership gleaned from the larger body of work on educational reform and school improvement. Here, most centrally, we would situate the conclusion about the importance of leadership in the school reform equation. Also, there is considerable reinforcement of the central role that formal leaders such as principals and superintendents play in ensuring successful design implementation. Finally, the evidence of the importance of teacher leadership confirms early findings on the significance of leadership density in comprehensive school improvement efforts.

From another vantage point, we discern that CSR research is extending our understanding of leadership. The most significant contributions here enrich our knowledge of teacher leadership, both in terms of adding robustness to and revealing the nuances of distributed leadership in action. Equally important, the researchers and the cases in this volume furnish new information about how principals work to make distributed leadership a reality. CSR analysts move us well beyond earlier notions of teacher leadership (see Smylie, Conley, & Marks, 2002) and the role of the principal as delegator of authority. In addition, the portraits of principals herein provide much needed detail about the functions site-based leaders perform in shaping schools to support the implementation of CSR models.

Still from a third perspective, we conclude that the studies chronicled in this volume are building new planks into the leadership edifice, with most of these additions crafted from the raw material supplied by the "systems" perspective that these CSR designs bring to the reform table. For example, the importance of principal stability is thoroughly documented in these cases. So too is the corollary, that is, the crucial role that superintendents perform in ensuring stable leadership at the school level—of both principals and site-based change agents such as project facilitators, coordinators, and lead teachers.

Finally, we have also learned that while a number of the CSR models define the role of school leaders in similar ways, as noted above, in some cases, different reform initiatives ask for different skills from school leaders. For example, Datnow and Castellano (chapter 9 this volume) found that the highly specified SFA model demanded management and monitoring skills from principals and teacher leaders. On the contrary, Hall and Placier (chapter 10 this volume) who studied leadership implications of the CES, a principle-driven reform model, concluded that, "if there is one 'requirement' for CES leadership, it is the ability to cope with uncertainty, ambiguity and one's lack of control over other people." Not all reform models are alike, and as a result, they have different implications for leaders. Some models are no doubt a better "fit" for some principals than others.

Suggestions

At the same time, we believe that some additions to the CSR storyline about leadership would be helpful. To begin with, as Datnow and Castellano (chapter 9 this volume) remind us, the leadership-reform pathway flows in both directions. While the spotlight herein was quite correctly focused on the role of leaders in molding reform, we maintain that the profession would be advantaged if we had a better sense of how whole school reforms shape the role of school leaders, especially principals. For example, we know that effective principals scaffold their actions much more frequently on powerful conceptions of learning, teaching, and school improvement than is the norm in school administration. Do CSR designs encourage principals to become more educationally focused? Or do they, as did earlier restructuring reforms, pull them away from the core technology and from learner-centered leadership? And what do we know about variability across reform blueprints in regards to this question?

After completing our analysis of these cases, it is clear that at the micro level more explicit attention might be devoted to exploring how CSR models influence leadership of organizational routines such as budgeting, professional development, hiring staff, and so forth. At the macro level, refocusing the spotlight on the question of how CSR is reshaping school reform writ large would be instructive. So too would be the reverse question of how the larger reform movement is interacting with CSR. Some attention to the interface of major reform streams, for example, those that feature direct citizen control as the reform engine (i.e. charter schools) and CSR, would be useful also.

Based on our earlier work in school reform, we entered our review with a framework and with coding strategies to explore the nature of community (especially parent)-based leadership in these CSR designs. As we moved into our analysis, it became clear that we would be unable to say much about leadership from parents or other interested actors in the school community, as only a couple of the chapters speak to this issue (e.g., Payne & Diamond, chapter 11 this volume) and the discussion is brief. Given the democratic and participatory foundations of much of the CSR movement, as well as the infusion of some market ideology, we were surprised by this state of affairs. While we can speculate on the reasons for this situation, the real assignment is to reexplore the work from which these chapters were drawn to see if this absence of attention to community leadership is an oversight (or more likely a consequence of the directives we furnished) or an accurate reflection of the state of parental leadership in CSR blueprints or actual implementation.

We were also left with a desire to know more about the role of three other sets of actors—students in the schools, union leaders at the school and district, and policy actors at the state level. Some of the chapters make clear that the role of these leaders could be important to our understanding of CSR. On the issue of students, Hall and Placier (chapter 10 this volume) mention student leadership as something that the CES seeks to cultivate. However, we learn little about student leadership from the chapters in this volume, which is perhaps not surprising given the dearth of research on the role of students in school reform more generally (Corbett & Wilson, 1995) and CSR in particular.

On the issue of the state, one chapter (Goldberg & Morrison, chapter 4 this volume) discusses state accountability systems and their influence on school reform and leadership, and another (Hall & Placier, chapter 10 this volume) explores the role of the state as a leader in school reform in a bit more depth. However, we need to know much more about the state's role as a facilitator or constrainer of CSR efforts. The advent of the Comprehensive School Reform Demonstration Program, in which states are charged with disbursing funds and providing support to schools adopting CSR models, provides a new opportunity for research on the state role as a leader in reform.

None of the chapters in this volume address union leadership in CSR. Yet we know that the National Education Association and the American Federation of Teachers, in particular, have been influential in the CSR movement at both the national and state levels. There are brief accounts elsewhere of local union leadership advancing or resisting CSR models. However, here, as is the case in much of the school reform literature, analysis of the leadership role of unions is conspicuous in its absence.

Moreover, we were actually amazed by the near absence of attention to the leadership provided by CSR design team staff in the school reform process. Other than a few references to the provision of some staff development, very little is reported in these chapters about the direct and indirect activities that would connect the design teams to program implementation, or lack thereof, or school success, or absence thereof. We believe that this is another theme that should receive additional consideration in future work on CSR, as it is clear that several of the reform design teams are providing leadership at the national, state, and local levels.

Further knowledge is also needed on the various leadership opportunities that are offered by the CSR movement. For example, Hall and Placier (chapter 10 this volume) discuss the possibility of leaders from CES schools bringing CES principles to new schools in which they are later appointed. They may also bring reform ideas and advocacy if they move into positions in the district office. But there is evidence to suggest that there is yet a third leadership path at work. That is, some leaders might leave the school system altogether and join the design team as trainers or mentors, helping to spread the reform ideas across a region or even in schools across the nation. Alternately, in some cases, principals stay in their schools and work on their own time as paid consultants for the design team, helping to train and mentor principals in new schools. Over time, we would expect to learn more about the alternative leadership opportunities that result from CSR, as it seems possible that they offer new leadership roles inside and outside school systems, as well as vehicles for reform ideas to spread.

Finally, we believe that more investigation is needed on how race, class, and gender influence the dynamics of leadership and comprehensive reform. Payne and Diamond's chapter (chapter 11 this volume) pointed to race and class as systemic issues that affect social relationships among individuals in schools, and Hall and Placier (chapter 10 this volume) noted that the leaders in their study were women, but neither chapter includes a thorough analysis of these issues. How gender, race, and class influence the roles and relationships of leaders in the CSR process has yet to be fully explored, and we believe that this is an area that merits further attention, particularly given the large number of urban schools involved in CSR.

CAUTIONS

As with all reform work, cautions, caveats, and context issues abound. And to be sure, CSR has a specific portfolio of items to worry about that supplement the many warnings emanating from the general reform literature. It is not our intention to cover all that ground here. Rather, our focus is on some cautions at the nexus of leadership and whole-school reform.

Most importantly, we recommend that careful attention be devoted to the construct of distributed leadership that is woven into many CSR designs. While we have been arguing for some time that fixing leadership to hierarchical roles is not a wise idea (Murphy, Hallinger, Weil, & Mitman, 1983; Murphy, 1988)—in other words that leadership is a function or set of activities, not a position—it is important to remind ourselves that changing leadership structures provides no guarantee of successful program implementation. As we know from every other area of school reform and improvement from the classroom to the statehouse, changing organizational structures has not, does not, and never will predict organizational performance. In short, while there are quite legitimate reasons to distribute leadership that have little to do with enhanced organizational outcomes, if outcomes are of interest, as much attention needs to be devoted to the content or substance of distributed leadership work as to the form. Ill-focused leadership distributed densely is hardly a recipe for reform success.

As the design of this concluding chapter makes explicit, the authors in this volume do a remarkable job in helping us understand that for CSR to work, leadership across many levels is desirable. They also furnish considerable detail about how superintendents, principals, and teachers actualize leadership. And, at the school level, we are exposed to some ways that administrators and teachers can co-construct a working platform of leadership. Nonetheless, we are offered very little information about how leadership at multiple levels "comes together to create the coherent whole needed for meaningful school change" (Berends, Bodilly, & Kirby, chapter 6 this volume). In the same way that we need to be skeptical about the power of new structures alone to be the answer to better leadership in schools, so too we need to be cautious about the assumption that simply distributing leadership across levels will lead to more effective program implementation. What would be helpful is more information about the co-construction of leadership across organizational levels and among outside agents and school personnel.

REFERENCES

Anderson, L. W., & Shirley, J. R. (1995, August). High school principals and school reform: Lessons learned from a statewide study of project Re: Learning. *Educational Administration Quarterly, 31*(3), 405–423.

Beck, L. G., & Murphy, J. (1996). *The four imperatives of a successful school.* Thousand Oaks, CA: Corwin Press.

Blank, R. K. (1986, April). *Principal leadership in urban high schools: Analysis of variation in leadership characteristics.* Paper presented at the annual meeting of the American Educational Research Association, San Francisco.

Brookover, W., Beady, C., Flood, P., Schweitzer, J., & Wisenbaker, J. (1979). *School social systems and student achievement: Schools can make a difference.* New York: Praeger.

Carter, T. P., & Maestas, L. C. (1982). *Bilingual education that works: Effective schools for Spanish speaking children.* Report submitted to the California State Department of Education.

Corbett, D., & Wilson, B. (1995). Make a difference with, not for, students: A plea to researchers and reformers. *Educational Researcher, 24*(5), 12–17.

Cotton, K., & Savard, W. G. (1980, December). *The principal as instructional leader.* Paper presented for Alaska Department of Education, Office of Planning and Research. Audit and Evaluation Program, Northwest Education Laboratory, Portland, OR.

Datnow, A., & Stringfield, S. (2000). Working together for reliable school reform. *Journal of Education for Students Placed at Risk, 5*(1), 183–204.

Donaldson, G. A. (2001). *Cultivating leadership in schools. Connecting people, purpose, and practice.* New York: Teachers College Press.

Elmore, R. F. (1996, March). *Staff development and instructional improvement: Community District 2, New York City.* Paper prepared for the National Commission on Teaching and America's Future, New York.

Elmore, R. F. (1999, September). Leadership of large scale improvement in American education (draft). Paper prepared for the Albert Shanker Institute.

Fullan, M. G. (1991). *The new meaning of educational change* (2nd ed.). New York: Teachers College Press.

Hall, G. E., Hord, S. M., Hulling, L. L., Rutherford, W. L., & Stiegelbauer, S. M. (1983, April). *Leadership variables associated with successful school improvement.* Paper presented at the annual meeting of the American Educational Research Association, Montreal, Canada.

Johnston, R. C. (2001, May). Test scores up in urban districts report says. *Education Week, 20*(38), 3.

Lasley, T. J., & Wayson, W. W. (1982, December). Characteristics of schools with good discipline. *Educational Leadership, 40*(3), 28–31.

Leithwood, K. (2002). Organizational conditions to support teaching and learning. In W. D. Hawley & D. L. Rollie (Eds.), *The keys to effective schools: Educational reform as continuous improvement* (pp. 97–110). Thousand Oaks, CA: Corwin Press.

Little, J. W. (1982, Fall). Norms of collegiality and experimentation: Work place conditions of school success. *American Educational Research Journal, 19*(3). 325–340.

Murphy, J. (1988, Summer). Methodological, measurement, and conceptual problems in the study of administrator instructional leadership. *Educational Evaluation and Policy Analysis, 10*(2), 117–139.

Murphy, J. (1990). Principal instructional leadership. In L. S. Lotto & P. W. Thurston (Eds.), *Advances in educational administration: Changing perspectives on the school* (Vol. 1, pp. 163–200). Greenwich, CT: JAI Press.

Murphy, J. (1994). Transformational change and the evolving role of the principalship: Early empirical evidence. In J. Murphy & K. S. Louis (Eds.), *Reshaping the principalship; Insights from transformational reform efforts* (pp. 20–53). Thousand Oaks, CA; Corwin Press.

Murphy, J. (2001, October). *Leadership for literacy: Policy leverage points.* Keynote paper prepared for ETS/ECS National Forum on Leadership for Literacy. Washington, DC.

Murphy, J., Beck, L. G., Crawford, M., Hodges, A., & McGaughy, C. L. (2001). *The productive high school: Creating personalized academic communities.* Thousand Oaks, CA: Corwin Press.

Murphy, J., & Hallinger, P. (1993). Restructuring schools: Learning from ongoing efforts. In J. Murphy & P. Hallinger (Eds.), *Restructuring schools: Learning from changing efforts* (pp. 251–271). Thousand Oaks, CA: Corwin Press.

Murphy, J., Hallinger, P., Weil, M., & Mirman, A. (1993, Fall). Problems with research on educational leadership: Issues to be addressed. *Educational Evaluation and Policy Analysis, 5*(3), 297–305.

Portin, B., Beck, L., Knapp, M., & Murphy, J. (In Press). The school and self-reflective renewal: Taking stock and moving on. In B. Portin, L. Beck, M. Knapp, & J. Murphy (Eds.), *Self-reflective renewal in schools: Lessons from a national initiative.* Westport, CT: Greenwood.

Pounder, O. G., Ogawa, R. T., & Adams, E. A. (1995). Leadership as an organization-wide phenomenon: Its impact on school performance. *Educational Administration Quarterly, 31*(4), 564–588.

Reihl, C. J. (2000, Spring). The principal's role in creating inclusive schools for diverse students: A review of normative, empirical, and critical literature on the practice of educational administration. *Review of Educational Research, 70*(1), 63–81.

Sergiovanni, T. J. (1992a, February). On rethinking leadership: A conversation with Tom Sergiovanni. *Educational Leadership, 49*(5), 46–49.

Sergiovanni, T. J. (1992b, February). Why we should seek substitutes for leadership. *Educational Leadership, 49*(5), 41–45.

Smith, C. R., & Muth, R. (1985, April). *Instructional leadership and school effectiveness.* Paper presented at the annual meeting of the American Educational Research Association, Chicago.

Smylie, M. A., Conley, S. S., & Marks, H. (2002). Teacher leadership: Exploring new approaches for school improvement. In J. Murphy (Ed.), *The educational leadership challenge: Redefining leadership in the 20th century* (pp. 162–188). Chicago: University of Chicago Press.

Spade, J. Z., Van Fossen, B. E., & Jones, J. D. (1985, April). *Effective schools: Characteristics of schools which predict mathematics and science performance.* Paper presented at the annual meeting of the American Research Association, Chicago.

Spillane, J. P., Halverson, R., & Diamond, J. B. (n.d.) *Toward a theory of leadership practice: A distributed perspective.* Evanston, IL: Institute for Policy Research, Northwestern University.

Spillane, J. P., Diamond, J. B., & Jita, C. (2000, April). *Leading classroom instruction: A preliminary exploration of the distribution of leadership practice.* Paper presented at the annual meeting of the American Educational Research Association, New Orleans.

Teddlie, C. & Reynolds, D. (Eds.). (2000). *The international handbook of school effectiveness research.* London: Falmer.

Viadero, D. (2001, November 7). Whole-school projects show mixed results. *Education Week, 21*(10), 1, 24–25.

Index